My Cross-Country Checkup

ALSO BY WALTER STEWART

NON-FICTION

SHRUG: TRUDEAU IN POWER
DIVIDE AND CON: CANADIAN POLITICS IN ACTION
HARD TO SWALLOW
BUT NOT IN CANADA
AS THEY SEE US
STRIKE!
TOWERS OF GOLD, FEET OF CLAY: THE CANADIAN BANKS
TRUE BLUE: THE LOYALIST LEGEND
UNEASY LIES THE HEAD: CANADA'S CROWN CORPORATIONS
THE GOLDEN FLEECE
TOO BIG TO FAIL: OLYMPIA & YORK, THE STORY BEHIND THE HEADLINES
BELLY UP: THE SPOILS OF BANKRUPTCY
BANK HEIST
DISMANTLING THE STATE: DOWNSIZING TO DISASTER
M.J.: THE LIFE AND TIMES OF M.J. COLDWELL
CANADIAN NEWSPAPERS: THE INSIDE STORY (EDITOR)
TOMMY: THE LIFE AND TURBULENT TIMES OF T.C. DOUGLAS (FORTHCOMING)

FICTION

RIGHT CHURCH, WRONG PEW
HOLE IN ONE

My Cross-Country Checkup

ACROSS CANADA BY MINIVAN,
THROUGH SPACE AND TIME

Walter Stewart

Published in 2000 by Stoddart Publishing Co. Limited
34 Lesmill Road, Toronto, Canada M3B 2T6
180 Varick Street, 9th Floor, New York, New York 10014

Distributed in Canada by:
General Distribution Services Ltd.
325 Humber College Blvd., Toronto, Ontario M9W 7C3
Tel. (416) 213-1919   Fax (416) 213-1917
Email cservice@genpub.com

04 03 02 01 00 1 2 3 4 5

Canadian Cataloguing in Publication Data

Stewart, Walter, 1931–
My cross-country checkup: across Canada by minivan,
through space and time

ISBN 0-7737-3269-1

1. Stewart, Walter, 1931– — Journeys — Canada.
2. Canada — Description and travel. I. Title.

FC75.S74 2000   917.104'648   C00-931259-5
F1017.S74 2000

Jacket Design: Angel Guerra
Text Design: Tannice Goddard

THE CANADA COUNCIL   LE CONSEIL DES ARTS
FOR THE ARTS   DU CANADA
SINCE 1957   DEPUIS 1957

*We acknowledge for their financial support of our
publishing program the Canada Council, the Ontario Arts
Council, and the Government of Canada through the
Book Publishing Industry Development Program (BPIDP).*

Printed and bound in Canada

For David and Betty Milner:
Let's try again

Contents

Deep Thoughts

1. Canada will never run out of doughnuts.
2. Beware of old men in hats at the wheel.
3. Truckers are bloody rude.
4. Unisex washrooms at gas stations are not an improvement.
5. No matter how many campers you pass, another lurks ahead.
6. Everybody wants good highways; nobody wants highway construction.
7. Never eat in an empty restaurant; there is a reason.
8. Never eat in a restaurant named after a relative, viz., Grandma's Kitchen.
9. "Country Cookin'" means over-cooked in grease.
10. The weather is always better where you were than where you are, and worse still ahead.
11. Mobile phones, bought for emergencies, work well unless you have an emergency, when you won't get a peep out of them.
12. When your waitress asks you how everything was, she really doesn't want to know.

Best and Worst

Cheapest gas — Charlettown, PEI, and Vermillion, Alberta, 47.9 cents a litre.

Most expensive gas — 87.9 cents, Eagle Plains, NWT.

Best meal — Château Frontenac Hotel. Most expensive meal, ditto.

Best tourist information handbook — Newfoundland. Quebec handbooks are even better, but are broken down by region. It takes 28 of them to cover the province.

Worst tourist information handbook — New Brunswick. The book consists entirely of ads.

Best T-shirt — "I know I'm not perfect, but I come so close it scares me," Grand Falls, Newfoundland.

Best bumper sticker (on a camper) — Dad's Pad When Mom's Mad.

Runner-Up — Please Lord, Winning A Lottery Won't Spoil Me, Sault Ste. Marie, Ontario.

Best vanity licence plate (from California) — IOKHOWU

Runner-Up — EXQQSME

Best roadside sign — FREE ROCKS (near rockbound Peggy's Cove, Nova Scotia).

Best roadside attraction — Beringia Interpretive Centre, Whitehorse, Yukon.

Worst roadside ripoff — $7 to park near Montmorency Falls, Quebec.

Worst road for scenery — Highway 11, between Barrie and Washago, Ontario; a clamorous clutter.

Best road for scenery — The Dempster Highway.

Worst road for driving — The Dempster Highway.

Best road for driving — The Trans-Canada in Alberta.

My Cross-Country Checkup

Introduction
ON THE ROAD AGAIN

Suddenly, the land looms out of the mist, low-lying, rock-strewn, barren, backed by boulders and stunted trees, but land, at last. Harsh and forbidding, and apparently empty, it nevertheless looks more than welcoming to me. It has been a long voyage in our cramped, open sailing craft, across the storm-tossed seas from Greenland, and behind me a cry of joy goes up among the men.

"Is it Vinland?" asks Haldimur Haraldson.

"Looks more like Stone-land to me," says Bjarni Herjolfsson, moving up to stand beside me in the narrow bow while the waves bring us ever closer to the sloping shingle of beach. There is a small symphony of sounds as we glide shorewards and the men ship their oars — the single, sharp crack of the sail when Thornfinn Karlsefni lets go the sheet; the slap, slap of waves against the hull; the rumble-mutter of the surf-turned-gravel as it rolls against the shore.

"Look, there's a native!" Bjarni calls.

"Where?"

"Over there, by that tree."

Sure enough, I soon descry a skin-clad figure loping down a crude path to the water's edge.

"By Thor!" Bjarni exclaims. "I believe it's a woman!"

So it is, her shapely figure showing clearly as the skins that form her clothing fall away when she lifts her hands to call . . .

"Say, are you going to stand there all day gawking or get back in the van? We haven't checked into the motel yet."

So much for glamour, romance, and the glorious past. We are back in the present, standing on the roadside, next to the (closed) gate that leads to L'Anse aux Meadows (locally pronounced "Lansy Medders"), Newfoundland, where Norse traders landed, camped, and stayed for a while, five centuries before Christopher Columbus ever went before Queen Isabella with his unlikely story of an ocean route to the Indies. This is where we will begin our voyage of re-exploration, our trip through space and time. Setting out from the period and place where the first European explorers touched down, on the eastern tip of what would become Canada, in about 1000 A.D., we will work our way westward to Vancouver Island, then north along the Dempster Highway to Inuvik, near the top of the Mackenzie River, which is as close as you can come, by road, to the new territory of Nunavut, our nation's leap into the future. We will go, if you like, from ocean to ocean to ocean, over land, and from the eleventh century to the twenty-first.

My wife, Joan, and I have been down this road many times before in search of stories. This year, as the millennium closes in on us, we mean to accomplish two goals at once. One is to retrace much of the first trip we made across the nation, for a series of stories that appeared in the late, lamented *Star Weekly*, on the then just opened (but not yet finished) Trans-Canada Highway, in 1964 — more than a third of a century ago. The second is to take the nation's pulse, to check up on how things are going, have gone, since that first coast-to-coast ramble.

Work and pleasure have driven us across the country, usually by car, at least once every year since then, but we've always gone in pursuit of a singular story, election, upheaval, or happening — or else on one of those promotional book tours, officially known as the Flog, which are part of an author's punishment for writing things down. Now we will take the time to look at the land as a whole, to stop and report on the things that interest us, and on those that reflect where we have come from, where we are, where we seem to be heading as we broach the twenty-first century.

In 1964, we drove from St. John's, Newfoundland, to Victoria, British Columbia, with our two children, Craig, then seven, and Sandra, then six, one Scotch terrier, McNab, and one of the nation's outstanding photo-journalists, John de Visser. We travelled exclusively along the Trans-Canada Highway, the world's only national roadway that has two beginnings and no end. You start from Mile 0 on Water Street in downtown St. John's, Newfoundland, drive 7,714 kilometres, and finish up in Beacon Hill in downtown Victoria, where the sign reads — guess what? — Mile 0. Neither city wanted to be at the tail of the procession, so we made a road with two heads and no foot. Very Canadian, very sensible. The idea of that first trip, a generation ago, was to see how the opening of that new artery was affecting, would affect, the land through which it passed.

The answer was, all in all, that the TCH, as she is known to her friends, was a new national treasure. Although it brought some inevitable costs to a few areas of the country (for example, when Rogers Pass opened through the Rockies, communities along the Big Bend Highway, which got you around the stretch of mountains between Golden and Revelstoke, B.C., withered and died), for the most part, the new road was well worth the $1.4-billion price tag. (The federal government chipped in $825 million; the provinces put up the rest. In 1999 dollars, the cost was closer to $8 billion.)

We took thirty days to ramble across the TCH from ocean to ocean, and spent $1,298.49, or $43.28 a day, all in, including meals, gas, repairs, and hotels. Our average bill for accommodation came to $14.13 a night, considerably less than we will spend in taxes per night this time. The final *Star Weekly* article ended:

> *We concluded that, although it is the longest paved highway in the world, and boasts 500 bridges, 800 million tons of fill and 12 million tons of paving, there isn't enough of it. Only about one-tenth of its length is*

composed of four-lane highway and over the other nine-tenths, two lanes
are not enough to discharge its double duty as scenic link and business
artery. Agitation for another Trans-Canada is well advanced.

You will learn more of how the TCH looked shortly after it opened as we go along; for now, the thing to remember is that we will be driving along the old trail we first took in 1964, with some significant exceptions: we will start in L'Anse aux Meadows, rather than St. John's, and instead of finishing in Victoria, we will turn north and cross the Arctic Circle. We will also detour along the way, to look at stories, old and new, that will give us some idea of how the nation seems to be ticking over today, compared with 1964.

I have always subscribed to the notion that you can tell much about a nation by the heroes it chooses. And that is part of our mandate, too — to look both at the heroes we have selected over the centuries, from Madeleine de Verchères to Sir Wilfred Grenfell, from Crowfoot of Alberta to the Mad Trapper of Rat River, and at those we have chosen to bury in benign neglect, such as Marie La Tour and Molly Brant.

This time, we left Sturgeon Point, Ontario, on May 18, and arrived back there on July 21. With our wanderings, we travelled 24,816 kilometres. Our costs, including everything from car repairs and ferry fees to hotels and meals, averaged $240.69 per day; while our average on the first trip, $43.28, seems much lower, in fact in current dollars it would be $238.04 — just about the same.

She Drove Me to It

On that first trip, driving was a shared responsibility, although that made no sense. Hard to believe now, but in those days, driving was sort of a Guy Thing, and females were considered too emotional for such stern work, except to take the kiddies to dance lessons. When it became clear that Joan was a better, safer, more level-headed driver — and one who did not conk out at the wheel after the first two hours and nod off to sleep, a victim of the Lullaby of Roadway — a new arrangement was struck.

We are now divided into the Driver and the Author. The Driver undertakes not only to waft us from coast to coast, but also to correct the automotive habits of the entire populace as we go along. (Because of this arrangement, I once dedicated a book to "My wife, who drove me to it." Bad idea.) When you operate from the assumption that anyone ahead of you is an idiot and anyone who passes you a maniac, the possibilities for constructive criticism are endless, so the Driver keeps up a running commentary as we go.

The Author is responsible for Scribbling and Getting Lost. As in, "You've got nothing to do all day but look at a map, and now we're lost." Usually, that is because the Author fell asleep just about the time he should have been calling for a turn. From time to time, it strikes me that driving is a hard chore, and I offer to share. This provokes about the same response you would expect from the pilot if the guy who clears the ashtrays on an Air Canada 747 offered to take a turn at the controls.

Oh, yes, the Author is also responsible for Spotting, which is to say, murmuring, on a rising note, "Acopacopacopacop," in time to dodge the radar traps, since the Driver does not always remain within the legal limit, to put it kindly. On this trip, we will navigate our 24,816 kilometres without getting really seriously lost, and we'll never pick up a speeding ticket. I rest my case.

Our first trip was in a rented Ford, brand new, which wished, by the time we were finished, that it had never seen us. This one will be in a Chevrolet Venture minivan, which the Driver professes to hate because it can't catch a Jaguar, but which is roomy, comfortable, and will never give us a moment's unease.

Start your engines.

1

Newfoundland

FROM VIKINGS TO VOISEY'S BAY

I asked my wife, "Well, which province did you like best?"
The answer came back in a shot:
"Newfoundland."
"What? With the rocks and dust, and flat tires, and a sick dog?"
"Newfoundland."
Who could argue?

— STAR WEEKLY, APRIL 3, 1965

I am standing outside the gates of L'Anse aux Meadows World Heritage Site, on the tip of the Great Northern Peninsula, which sticks up along the west coast of Newfoundland. If you think of Newfoundland as shaped like a lobster's claw, then the peninsula is the long finger of that claw, and we are just inside the very tip, on the left-hand side. It is raining, a sullen, steady wet. Just behind the fence over the way stands a long, low, thatch-covered sod hut of the sort that stood here a thousand years or so ago. Beyond that, across a swell of grassy meadow, a shingle of rock and gravel runs down between forlorn-looking bushes to the glint of water. The Atlantic Ocean.

In the background I can hear the wind, the water, the low chug-chug of our minivan's idling engine, and from one of the bushes, a bird singing — either singing or cursing, it is hard to tell; this is not a great day for birds, unless of the duck variety. I am shivering, partly from excitement, because this is the beginning of a Grand Adventure, but mainly because even now, at the start of summer, there is a wind that apparently springs up somewhere around Baffin Island and, gathering speed and resentment as it comes, batters Newfoundland with constant, joyous rage. It will, while you stand there with your head full of romantic visions of Leif Ericsson and other heroic figures, pluck off your hat and blow it to Bermuda, leaving you bereft. The Driver is, very sensibly, sitting in the minivan, at the wheel, with the heater on, waiting for me to stop stomping up and down and declaiming, like Farley Mowat minus beard and kilt, and go back to the motel. We have come here in a rush, three days of furious driving from Sturgeon Point, Ontario, where we live, to this point, where our official travel begins.

"Leif Ericsson may have stood on this very spot," I say.

"Possibly on that very pavement," says the Driver, kindly. Actually, the famous Norse explorer probably never came near the place, but all I can remember of my high-school history is that Leif and the boys looked in at a place called Vinland, which was in either Newfoundland or possibly Labrador. Someplace like that. They called it Vinland because there were so many grapes growing there, which suggests either that the climate was very much warmer in those days, or that the boys had been into the grapes themselves. In *Westviking*, Farley Mowat wrote that Vinland was at the foot of Trinity Bay, hundreds of kilometres south and east of here. Never mind, it's the romantic idea that counts. I like the fact that nobody knows exactly when or where Canada got its start; it gives us an air of mystery and intrigue, and in the tribe of nations, where we are generally regarded as about as exciting as a cubic yard of gravel, we need all the mystery and intrigue we can get.

When you see L'Anse aux Meadows today, it all seems quite civilized, regulated, inevitable. There are full-scale replicas of the sod buildings the Norse traders put up — four dwellings, three workshops, and a smithy. The largest house had five rooms and an attached workshed, and probably served as home for five families. The place is, as it should be, wheelchair accessible — it is, after all, a UNESCO World Heritage Site — and we can make a shrewd guess that this was not the case when the Vikings first came calling. There are guides dressed in authentic costume, and they can tell you not only of the sort of life these early traders lived but also all about the discovery of this site through a series of excavations in the 1960s. The guides play the roles of the merchant adventurer, Bjorn; his wife, Thora; their slave, Astrid; and three crew members, Gunnar, Kol, and Harald. They look very handsome in their Viking getups, and they are very good at explaining how the artifacts unearthed here prove conclusively that, yes, this was a Viking encampment. The first, authenticated Viking encampment (so far) in North America.

What is harder for the guides to get across is just how chancy the whole thing was, and what an appropriate way to begin what would become Canada. For starters, it is not at all certain exactly when the Norse traders came, or when they left. Farley Mowat said it was "probably about 1003." But it may have been 999, or 1001, or some other year. And it is not as if the boys were sitting around the campfire over in Greenland one day and somebody said, "Let's go and find Canada. I understand they make good beer." The whole thing was a fluke. They were traders, entrepreneurs, and explorers, in that order. In 986, a man named Bjarni Herjolfsson was blown off course while sailing from Iceland to Greenland, and he wound up spotting some land where land was not known to be — might be people there, might be worth looking into. He went back and reported the sighting. A decade or so later, another trader, a relative of Eric the Red, according to Mowat, followed this lead with an expedition of four boats, establishing a camp here in hopes of going into the fishing and trading business.

This was not an empty country; the permanent dwellers were Beothuk First Nations people and the usual visitors were Dorset Inuit, who lived in the High Arctic and came here after whales. They were newcomers, too, shoving in where others had been before, and where they were not particularly wanted. The Beothuk and the Inuit did not get along, and none of them got along with the visiting Vikings. Diplomacy was not the strong suit of the Vikings; even when trading, they tended to hit first and ask questions afterwards. The long and the short of it is that there were not enough of them to hang on in the face of Native hostility, and they left, after a very few years, with windblown headgear and bitter memories. Stay away from that joint, they told each other, and it was hundreds of years before Europeans would return. Robert McGhee, an archaeologist, notes in his book *Canada Rediscovered* that the two necessary ingredients for a successful invasion of the New World turned out to be gunpowder and "Old World diseases" like smallpox. The Norse didn't have either.

Still, this is our place, our beginning, our false start, if you like, and thus is important to us. It also underlines the fact that Canada has always been a place where strangers blew in, sometimes left, more often stayed, and made a nation. When we read, a thousand years later, that unauthorized visitors from exotic climes have slipped over the fence of immigration department regulations and simply dumped themselves on our shores, we can hardly be surprised.

They are us — always have been, always will be.

When I have taken aboard enough of the spirit of the place — or to put it another way, when I am soaked to the skin and sore because I can't take any pictures in this murk — we drive back the thirty kilometres to St. Anthony, and (naturally) the Vinland Inn. St. Anthony is a pretty town, slung over the boulders along the shore, with bright, snug, highly painted houses standing out against the fairly frequent fog and gloom that nature provides.

The next morning, a sunny Saturday, we drive out to the lighthouse and watch the parade of icebergs sailing by the headland. They calved far to the north, between Greenland and Baffin Island; sloshed into the sea with a tremendous, unheard splash; and began the long float south, around the corner at Labrador, past St. Anthony, on their way to St. John's to melt. The current has put them all in a line, and with their swelling fronts they remind me of a parade of the Imperial Order Daughters of the Empire, solemn, stately, silent, and serene. At Goose Cove, a tiny fishing village just down the road, several icebergs have come rolling into the harbour and hit bottom, like so many beached whales. You can see the mist rising off them in the sunshine, can see their clumsy bottoms, so much larger than their tops, stuck along the shore, where they fasten themselves and die. *Sic transit gloria* ice.

Talk Sealing, and You Could
Get Laid Out Like a Whitecoat

St. Anthony is where the anti- and pro-sealing forces gather every spring, at calving time for both seals and icebergs. This is the closest major centre to the ice floes where the baby seals are born, and bopped on the head, and skinned. Before we ever left home, I had to undertake a solemn vow not to broach the subject in a bar, because that is a very easy way to get yourself laid out like one of the whitecoats, though possibly not skinned. The sealing vessels, which used to take off from St. John's and then pick up crews on the way north, now often start from here and are provisioned here.

This is also HQ for the anti-seal lobby, whose members fly out by helicopter from the airport here, with their furious video cameras, and stay in the motels. They return with images of bloodied fishermen wielding vicious-looking clubs over the heads of fuzzy whitecoats that look like children's plush toys. This spring, 275,000 animals were slain this way, bringing disgust to animal-rights groups and prosperity to the locals. To raise the subject of sealing at any time in town is a little like asking the patrons of a Dublin pub how they feel about King Billy, but I broach the subject gingerly, in a lineup in the grocery store, on the street, at a gas station.

The argument of the pro-sealing forces is that, first of all, those on the other side are all liars who fake the film footage that creates such a stir in Europe; and that, second, sealing is their livelihood, always has been — what else are they to do? — and that, third, the quotas put on the number of seals that can be slaughtered each year have allowed the herd to swell, to multiply, to become so numerous that the codfish stocks on which seals feed have been destroyed.

The argument of the anti-sealing forces is that, first of all, those on the other side are liars who fake the film footage that shows humane killing; and that, second, there are other, less brutal ways to make a living than one that deals death to animals and callousness to humans; and that, third, there is no need for seal pelts, so why should there be any quotas at all?

No one who has been through a packing plant, even a modern packing plant with the most up-to-date killing devices, will find much that is any worse with the process of seal slaughter. No one who has seen calves crippled and crammed into tiny, plastic cages to produce the most tender veal, or has wandered through a modern chicken operation, those concentration camps where the prisoners are lined up on caged nests, will think we are any meaner to the seals than we are to other creatures. We are the cruellest animal, always have been, and the distinction over whether the critters we massacre come from the wild or are raised in captivity seems unimportant to me. I cannot see the argument against sealing, provided — and it is a big proviso — we can get some agreement as to whether the present herd is too large, which is the official government position, or is in danger of extinction. Bear in mind that the people we ask to advise us on these matters are the same experts who have made all the bum guesses about cod stocks, and salmon stocks, and trout stocks, and you see the difficulty of trying to come to a rational decision about sealing.

The earliest accounts of the fish population off St. John's claimed that the schools of cod slowed down the sailing vessels because they jammed the waters so, and similar tales of endless plenty echoed down the years until just recently, when the Grand Banks crews began to complain that they were "fishing for water." Since then, there has been no agreement on what happened to the fish, or what did the damage, or how many are left. In the circumstances, a reluctance to trust official counts is understandable. One of the regional newspapers I run across at the motel carries a piece centred on the dire views of John Efford, fisheries and agriculture minister in the Newfoundland government. Efford is pro-sealing, and anti-seals, because he thinks they have destroyed the cod stocks that were the lifeblood of Newfoundland for centuries. "It's the last bit of fish we've got, and I'm worried about it. Now we're putting that at risk. . . . It's not only about seals and fish, it's about people. It's about our future."

Efford notes that there has been a moratorium on northern cod since 1992. "Now, seven years later, our stocks are even worse. . . . Yes, it's about seals because there are over six million harp seals alone, then there are grey seals and other seals, and yes, they do eat fish. . . . No, I'm not a scientist, but you need logic and common sense. If each seal ate only one fish a month for twelve months of the year, that would be 72 million seals."

You see the difficulty? Obviously, the Cabinet minister took the 6 million harp seals and gave them one cod apiece per month, which would be 72 million cod, not seals, and even the wildest guesses of the experts won't produce 72 million cod in the North Atlantic for his 6 million harp seals, if they exist, to feed on. Not all the fog hereabouts hovers over the sea; the seal issue will be with us for some time.

At the Vinland Inn, we don't talk of such matters; we eat baked salmon, canned peas, and mushy potatoes and hear quite a lot about Grace, a friend of one of the waitresses, who appears to have strayed from the paths of righteousness with "a fella from Upper Canada. Said he was gonna give her a ring, I don't think, and she fell for it. Now the kid's comin' and he's going, going, GONE!" The table gets a bitter wipe, and I get a glare. Men, they're all alike. I was already feeling guilty enough because I had, secreted in my luggage, perhaps the most enthralling book ever written about sealing, Cassie Brown and Harold Horwood's *Death on the Ice*, a harrowing account of the wickedness of a fella not from Upper Canada, but from St. John's, Abram Kean. I sneak upstairs to read it after dinner.

Death on the Ice

In the early part of this century, Kean, a stocky, bearded, vigorous sea captain, was the acknowledged leader of the Newfoundland sealing fleet, a man revered for his tough, no-nonsense approach to business. He lived in a mansion in St. John's, moved with all the best people, gave to the church. He made a fortune by keeping his crews in conditions of appalling cold, squalor, and hardship, for which they earned an average twenty-nine dollars a season. The work was dangerous because the floating, wheeling icefields frequently caught and crushed the ships that nosed around them looking for pups. On board, the men were fed mainly on hardtack; their clothes offered little protection on the windswept ice where the seals were killed and cleaned. As the ships' holds filled, even their crude bunks disappeared to make room for animals, and they flopped down at night atop the bloody, half-frozen pelts.

In March 1914, Kean was leading a group of ships out among the floes, just north of here, when all the weather signs pointed to the onset of a nasty storm. Men from one of the other ships, the *Newfoundland*, sought shelter on Kean's vessel. He took them aboard briefly and gave them a meal, then ordered them to go back, kill a bunch of 1,400 seals he had spotted, and work their way back to the *Newfoundland* — if they could find it. In the gathering storm, 132 men set off across the ragged, broken, heaving ice pack into the teeth of a bitter wind and swirling snow. For two days and nights, the men wandered over the floes, fell through the ice, huddled together to keep warm, and died. The conditions were appalling; one man froze his lips biting ice off his companions' eyelids. By the time they were picked up, on the third day, seventy-eight men had frozen to death and all the survivors were in serious condition, many of them crippled for life. The dead were stacked like cordwood, one on top of the other, to make it easier to pick them up.

Kean learned of the tragedy from two other ships that had come across the exhausted survivors and were on their way back to St. John's. He stopped long enough to pick up a few bodies, and then went back to the important business of sealing. It was only when his own crew threatened mutiny if he did not desist that he turned back to the home port. The scale of the disaster sparked a public inquiry, which unearthed a catalogue of ignorance, callousness, cupidity, and stupidity on the part of all the sealing masters and shipowners. There was some — not much, but some — concern over the fact that the ships were unable to communicate with each other, both because Keen had ordered all radio sets taken out to save money and because he had sent the men off without proper food, survival gear, or signalling equipment. Two commissioners said that Kean had made an "error of judgement" in putting the men back on the ice; the third said the whole affair was "an act of God." Kean's defence was that he did what he thought proper, and that he didn't mistreat his crews any more than anyone else did. His only mistake, he said, was one of compassion — in taking the men of the *Newfoundland* aboard to feed them. Otherwise, they might have found their own ship in good time.

No damages were forthcoming for the families of the dead sealers, or for the men who lost health, limbs, and livelihood through their ordeal. Indeed, the only damages ever paid came in the form of a hundred-dollar award for libel, paid to Captain Kean because a St. John's newspaper dared to criticize his actions in abandoning the sealers to their fate. Kean sailed and sealed for another twenty years, killed more than a million seals, and was awarded an OBE for his splendid slaughter.

Grenfell: A Man with a Mission

I dare not mention Abram Kean to any of the locals, but it is with a swinging step and head held high that I go, on Monday morning, to visit the Grenfell Museum, which celebrates a somewhat different hero from roughly the same time as Abram Kean.

Wilfred Thomason Grenfell was one of those extraordinary Victorian-era characters who took it upon themselves to set the world right — or at least, that part of it that they could reach. Born the second son of an impoverished school headmaster in Cheshire, on the west coast of England, Grenfell, a deeply religious man, trained to be a doctor. He was recruited to work as a physician for the Royal National Mission to Deep Sea Fishermen in 1888, when he was twenty-two. He went to sea in a tiny vessel called the *Thomas Gray*, and performed surgical miracles in tossing boats, through gales, snow, ice, and fog. He attracted the attention of a Leeds newspaper, which described him as "a lithe, muscular Christian with a pair of honest brown eyes and a breezy manner which is likely to be quite as powerful for good as one or two drugs in the British Pharmacopoeia," according to Ronald Rompkey's *Grenfell of Labrador*, which is on sale at the museum.

In 1892, the mission sent him to Newfoundland in a hospital ship to serve the fishing fleet there, and with prodigious energy — and utter scorn for any who stood in his way — he soon succeeded in establishing hospitals both ashore and afloat, including one in St. Anthony, then a tiny collection of huts. His first such project was at Battle Harbour, along the Labrador coast, where he opened a small hospital in 1893; he hired another doctor, at higher pay than his own, to run it. The next year, he founded the Grenfell Labrador Medical Mission, which he moved to St. Anthony in 1900. He performed prodigies among the men of the fishing fleets, whether Newfoundlanders or visitors, and then expanded to establish a co-operative lumber mill, an orphanage, a travelling library, and a school.

Grenfell was a gifted journalist, publicist, lecturer, dog-sledder, social activist, fund-raiser, and author, as well as a physician. (But he was a rotten sailor; although he held a master mariner's certificate, he paid little heed to charts, much less shoals, and often shipwrecked himself.) He achieved world fame when he nearly perished on an ice floe while on one of his sledding trips

— he survived by slaughtering his dog team and wrapping himself in their hides, which kept him from freezing until a search party found him. He later wrote a book called *Adrift on an Ice-pan,* which became an instant international best-seller and brought in large amounts of money. Not to Grenfell, though — he lived on a tiny salary and used everything else to keep the mission going.

He quarrelled with the Water Street merchants who ran Newfoundland, with the politicians — especially Sir Richard Squires, the premier, of whom more anon — and with the board of the mission back home in England. They wanted him to stop fooling around in Labrador, and stay home to run things in Europe.

Grenfell was aboard the *Mauretania,* on his way back from England after one of these disputes, when he met Anne Elizabeth Caldwell MacClanahan, a beautiful heiress from Chicago. Typically, Grenfell proposed to her without knowing her last name — he thought it was Stirling, because she was travelling with people named Stirling. When she taxed him with this, he replied gallantly that he didn't care what her last name was, only what it would become, and they were married on November 18, 1909. Anne was the perfect mate for Grenfell; tough-minded, able, a gifted writer who actually turned out many of his thirty-four books, she supported him when he battled with others, and battled with him herself when she thought he was getting too big for his britches.

He was knighted in 1927 but grew no mellower, and he spent much of his later life striving, in vain, to persuade rich Newfoundlanders that they ought to devote more of their wealth to social services, and ordinary Newfoundlanders that they ought to join Canada. He was a social reformer, a co-operative industrialist, an enthusiastic evangelist, an incurable egoist, and a grand man.

Grenfell, who suffered a number of heart attacks, worked almost literally until he dropped, in 1940 (his wife died in 1938). The International Grenfell Association, which he established in 1912 to tap into the rich American charitable markets, became one of the largest and most effective international charities in the world. It continued to serve Newfoundland and Labrador long after his death, and was not wound up until Newfoundland, when it became part of Canada, took over all the hospitals as a provincial care. The Grenfell Mission became a provincial regional health corporation, which was sold to the province for one dollar in 1981.

St. Anthony, quite rightly, celebrates this quarrelsome, agitating, fabulous figure with a series of museums, including one situated in his and Anne's home; the collection of buildings called the Grenfell Historic Properties is now run by the Grenfell Historical Society, which is not a charity, as you can tell by the prices in the gift shop.

In Newfoundland, Even the Moose Are Different

After visiting this, and loading ourselves up to the Plimsoll line with sou-venirs, noble thoughts, and baked salmon, we turn west to cross the arm of the Great Northern Peninsula, a flat, scrubby land of short trees and tall moose. Perhaps it is something in the air, but the Newfoundland moose, like other island residents, lack reticence. They wander out onto the highway, or stand along the verge, to gawk at us as we gawk at them. Moose, close up, are an even more unlikely animal than camels; there is so much leg that they look unbalanced, awkward, clumsy. They are anything but; rather, they are swift, sure-footed, and sometimes very aggressive. The roadside signs do not carry images of graceful animals leaping away, as in other provinces; instead, they feature a moose glowering at the wreck of a car that has dared to contest the right of way. We even pass a sign listing the fatality odds so far this year — six-teen moose and five people — which gives us pause. We see so many moose that I stop keeping track, and the Driver wants to know if there is a special collective noun for a whole bunch of the animals. "Yes," I say. "A service club of moose."

Some don't even deign to look up as we roll past; others will glance up from foraging, mutter to themselves — Oh, my God, more folks from the mainland, come to wreck things — and go back to work. We also pass a small herd of caribou, which very decently scamper off into the brush, showing proper respect, and a gaggle of wild sheep, we assume, which are even bolder than the moose. They clomp out onto the highway, six ewes and about a dozen lambs, dirty, scruffy, wool-matted, red-eyed critters that look as if they, at least the mommas, have been on a monumental toot and are suffering a hangover. One of the lambs decides it is lunch hour, right now, right here in the middle of the road, and the momma tries to get away a couple of times, then gives up and stands still to be milked on the white line. She has the decency to give us an apologetic glance — Kids, what can you do? — while we wait.

Soon after we turn south to run along the Strait of Belle Isle, between Newfoundland and Labrador, past Nameless Cove, Forester's Point, and Plum Point, we come across the first and only really horrible stretch of highway we will hit in Newfoundland, a twenty-two-kilometre nightmare of broken pavement, ragged rocks, heaving potholes; a bone-jarring, teeth-rattling, temper-blowing run of road that slows us to about ten kilometres an hour and transports us back to our very first visit to this province, in 1964, when we learned how horrible the roads could be, and how kind the people.

The Trail of '64

At that time, the only stretches of paved highway along the Trans-Canada were a hundred-kilometre bit from Channel-Port aux Basques, where you get off the ferry from Nova Scotia — to suck you in, you see, and make you think the cross-island trip will be fun — and another similar length at the other end, where the asphalt ended, happily, just about at the front gate to the then premier Joey Smallwood's farm. In between was about 500 kilometres of rock and ruin, with all those cheerful signs saying that the job would be done in '65. We lost our first tire near Deer Lake, on our second day in Newfoundland, and then lost our gas tank when a rock about the size of the planet Mercury met us in the middle of the road. We didn't know we'd been wounded until, when we pulled off the rocks onto a picnic site west of Gander, Joan announced, in the tone of pride she reserves for really bad news, "I smell gas."

"Nonsense," I said, which is what I always say on these occasions, but I went back to peer at the gasoline tank. Sure enough, there was a gaping wound in it, and a stream of fluid about as thick through as a pencil splattered the ground.

"What's the matter?" Joan called from the car.

"We seem to have a slight leak."

"How bad is it?"

"Oh, not too bad."

"We'd better get it fixed right after lunch."

"I have a feeling we'd better do it before lunch . . ."

"Well, if it's only a slight—"

"Or somebody may drop a match and blow us to kingdom come."

We got back into the car and set out in search of a service station. We hadn't seen one for two hours. There was an air of tension inside, which set seven-year-old Craig to chattering like a magpie and six-year-old Sandra to announcing that she thought she would have a little sleep now. By a miracle, we found a service station within a kilometre, pulled over to the pumps, and waited while a slim youth in coveralls chatted with a friend for about ten minutes in the office. Finally, Joan honked the horn. Coveralls got up, strolled over, and explained, "I'm talking to my friend. I'll be with you soon enough."

Joan bit her lip. Then we could hear, besides the low background chatter, the sound of our car's lifeblood dribbling out of the pierced fuel tank, soaking into the ground. We leapt out of the car as if the seats had been electrified, and that got Coveralls' attention.

"Bring her in," he said, pointing to a combination tool- and potato-shed with a dirt pit. He hopped down into the pit to survey the damage, re-appeared, shaped a piece of pine with a paring knife, covered it with a generous layer of Sunlight soap — "to seal 'er" — and dived back down below, where a series of thumps and clangs announced that he was driving the bung home. A few minutes later, we were on our way again, poorer by one dollar cash money but richer by the assurance that "she'll plim up." Plim up she did; the pine swelled and blocked the hole.

We escaped a shattered windshield, the usual fate of cars along this road, and met no further disaster until we passed Joey's farm and mounted the asphalt, when a rear tire blew out and sent us skidding to the shoulder. While we stood examining the smoking tire, the pine plug gave with a soft pop and gasoline began to stream out.

"It's going to explode," said Joan calmly.

"Nonsense," I replied.

This ritual satisfied, I herded the family down the road, just on the off chance that she was right, while I unloaded the trunk and unearthed the spare. While I was changing tires, McNab, our Scottie, licked some grass that had been sprayed with weed killer; as soon as we were under way once more, he began to be violently ill. We couldn't stop, because of the gasoline leak, so we just had to bear it. Our entry into St. John's on that occasion was not auspicious. We couldn't find a mechanic to fix our car or a vet to save our dog. It was the Saturday of a long weekend, and everybody was away fishing. We were standing outside the largest Ford agency in town, some of us wringing our hands, some cursing, some being quietly but pathetically ill, when Alec Udell appeared. This middle-aged man lived nearby and had dropped in to have his car washed. He read the gloom in our faces at a glance, and soon had the outline of our predicament. He marched us back into the car-agency office and accosted the manager.

"You can't leave these people here stranded," he shouted. "They've just driven all the way from Canada!"

An hour later, a mechanic had been torn from his fishing pole and put to work. Meanwhile, Udell drove us to a motel, which turned out to be badly crowded — booked for the night, in fact — but he bullied the manager there into giving us a room anyway. To underscore our need, I led in the family and treated the manager to an edited version of our plight — leaving out the dog until I learned whether the motel accepted pets. The manager clucked sympathetically and handed across a key.

"And that's not all," Sandra piped up. "The dog keeps getting sick all over the place."

I grabbed the key and fled.

Go Where the Dirt Is

That was then, this is now. The roads, with this appalling exception along the Strait of Belle Isle, range from adequate to fine all across the province. They are not interstates, to be sure, and we sometimes have to hang back and wait for a place to pass, but all in all the highways are more than acceptable, and seldom crowded. When you take a population smaller than Edmonton's and spread it over 405,720 square kilometres (a population density roughly comparable to that of the Sahara Desert), overcrowded highways are not a serious menace.

Along the verge we see, at frequent intervals, small gardens surrounded by homemade fences, with no houses anywhere in sight. This makes sense when we remember that most of the villages hereabouts are built along rocky headlands, where soil is scant or non-existent, so if you want to grow your own vegetables, you have to go where the dirt is. Many of the gardens are no larger than a living-room rug, scratched out of the roadside and guarded by a strand of wire and some plastic bags, which presumably flap in the wind and frighten away birds. Others are more formal affairs, fifteen to twenty square metres in size, with decent fences, straight rows. We pass one where there appear to be three generations of gardeners at work, from a bent old grandfather to a little boy of about three, wielding a spade as tall again as himself.

Another roadside attraction is something that looks like a lobster pot, but about three times the size, and can be found at the end of many driveways. At Davie's Cove, where we trade a purse of gold for a tank of gas (70.8 cents a litre), the Driver asks the old boy who runs the pump about "those round things."

"What round things?"

"You see them by the gates, about three feet long, barrel-shaped."

"Oh, dem. Dem's for the garbidge. Get dem from the tings dey puts the cable on."

"They look like huge spools of thread," says the Driver.

"That's it, that's it. Dey gets dem from the hydro boys, bashes the circles out to the end, puts boards across, and there you have a garbidge pen the animals can't get at, smooth as paint."

"Does the hydro company know about its generosity?"

He waves a scornful hand. "Dat'd be telling."

Soon after this, we whirl past the brooding vastness of Gros Morne National Park, another UNESCO World Heritage Site, described in the Newfoundland guidebook as "a hiker's dream, with a full spectrum of trail types and hiking challenges." Perhaps another time — our idea of a hiking challenge these days is an upstairs bathroom. Still, we appreciate a rolling vista of granite slabs, spruce-clad hills, tumbling brooks (the signs are bilingual —

Ruisseau Bottom is my favourite), and for a while, a bald eagle soaring on scornful wings above us. It is the frequent habit of the bald eagle to roll around the sky watching until an osprey catches a fish, and then to dive on the osprey, which is forced to abandon its prey to the bully of the skies. I think the bald eagle makes a perfect symbol for the Americans.

Just south of the park, near Deer Falls, we catch up to the Trans-Canada on its way from Port aux Basques, at the western tip of the island, to St. John's. Here, the road is broad and smooth, with paved shoulders — don't have them along most of the TCH in Ontario — gentle curves, and spacious views. We stop in Grand Falls-Windsor, the halfway point of the east-west route. This used to be two cities, but when they amalgamated a few years back, they kept both names, as modern couples often do. Here, at a first-rate motel named for nearby Mount Peyton, we learn about wild sheep and toutons. Our waitress, Joan, tells us those dissolute specimens we saw down the road were not wild at all.

"Lord, no, they belong to folks who just turn 'em out to fend for themselves."

"They must lose a few to cars," says the Driver.

"Oh, aye, cars. And other things." She rolls her eyes.

It is in return for this information that I venture to try the toutons, a popular and famous Newfoundland dish that is made by deep-frying bread dough and soaking the resulting slab — which looks like a sun-tanned hockey puck — with molasses. Some weaklings use corn or maple syrup, instead of genuine blackstrap molasses, just as some pronounce the dish "too-tons," instead of rhyming it with "bough-tons." My order consists of two of these crowding a large plate, and the waitress keeps coming back, again and again, anxiously affirming that I find them delicious, and don't I agree that they are wonderful? Nodding with a full mouth, I feel that I have to finish the whole molten mass to the last crumb, although I know that even a bottleful of Tums will not restore order to my innards this night. The Driver, after one tiny nibble, bows out. (Toutons are known as Damper Dogs when cooked right on the damper of a wood stove, which, possibly, makes them easier to digest.)

"Look at it this way," I say. "They're less lethal than cod tongues or seal flippers."

The Beothuk

The next morning, we go to visit the Mary March Museum downtown, a local bow of shame to the Beothuk. This group of aboriginals, probably related to the Algonquian peoples, once roamed Newfoundland, but by the time the Europeans spread out in the seventeenth century, the Beothuk were confined pretty well to the Exploits River valley, which runs through the heart of Grand Falls. They lived mainly on fish and caribou; dwelt in huts, wigwams, sometimes in log or even stone houses; and made a decision, quite early on, not to trade with the incoming Europeans, for fear the contact would distort their religion and way of life.

John Cabot spotted them on his first trip to Newfoundland in 1497, and he noted that they painted their bodies with red ochre as a protection against the local flies and mosquitoes. His description gave rise to the notion that North American Indians were "redskins." By the middle of the eighteenth century, when the English were pushing permanent settlement farther inland, while at the same time Micmac (now, properly, Mi'kmaq) tribesmen from Nova Scotia and Inuit from Labrador were increasingly invading their fishing grounds, the Beothuk were in bad shape. The official version, the one touted in a pamphlet handed out at the museum, is that "the Beothuks were forced to live on the inadequate resources of the interior. This proved impossible, and the last known Beothuk, Shawnandithit, died in 1829." In this account, the tribe was the victim not of genocide, as appears in "sensationalist accounts," but of history:

> Both the Micmacs and the Europeans were in competition with the Beothuks for the island's limited resources. Reduced in numbers, relatively poorly armed, and lacking in allies, it is perhaps not surprising that the Beothuks ultimately suffered the same fate as the earlier, prehistoric people who once lived in Newfoundland.

This version — hey, it happened because it happened — seems to me far too modest. It leaves out the fact that bounties were offered on Beothuk; that they were hunted down for sport and profit; and that, like all our Native peoples, they suffered appallingly from imported diseases, from superior weapons, from people who simply marched into their country and appropriated it. By one of those nice ironies, the academics have decided that it was the Beothuk who were thieves, because they pilfered things, especially nails and other bits of metal, from whites who grabbed their land. For this, the Beothuk were hunted down and slain as vermin, villains, and infidels who had dared to insult the most sacred of white gods, Property Rights.

In March 1819, on one of these punitive expeditions, a group of English soldiers came upon a Beothuk woman named Demasduwit at a place called Red Indian Lake, near here. She was unable to flee to safety because she had just given birth to a baby girl, and when her husband tried to free her, her captors shot him dead. Seems reasonable. Then they took Demasduwit back to St. John's, and her baby died on the way. Later that year, it occurred to someone in charge that marching into a Beothuk camp, killing people, and hauling off new mothers was perhaps not in accord with the highest canons of Christianity. A detail was told to take Demasduwit home again. She died of disease on the trail.

Now there is a museum that has a good deal of information about the Beothuk in it, and they call it Mary March, the name that was forced on Demasduwit during the eleven months she lived after her capture. She was taken in March, see, and Mary is a much better name than her own dumb thing, wouldn't you say? The young man who collects my two bucks to visit the museum is taken genuinely, completely, aback when I ask him whether he thinks we have learned one bloody thing if we cannot even give the woman back her own name in her own museum.

"Gee, you're really sore," he says in wonderment. Damn right.

Joey Was Remarkable, and a Rascal

Grand Falls-Windsor, once I get over my grumps, is a beautiful town, and we leave it reluctantly to drive to Gambo, which is where Joey Smallwood, the tiny giant of Newfoundland, was born. There is a rather strange statue of him right down by the tourist bureau as you come into town, a superbly rendered more-than-life-size Joey growing up out of a lump of rock. The bronze rises right up out of the bedrock of Newfoundland, symbolizing Joey as an offshoot of the provincial magma. He is wearing a suit and horn-rimmed glasses, which apparently survived the trip through the molten interior.

His grandfather built the first steam-powered sawmill in Newfoundland in 1862, and Joey built the union with Canada, but there are other marks on the family escutcheon, including the vicious strike that took place here in 1958 because Premier Smallwood, once a strong union man, decertified the International Woodworkers of America Union without a shadow of right. Joey wanted to push his province to the forefront of development, but he could think of no better way to accomplish this than to promote growth through huge handouts — of land, money, resources, usually to foreigners, occasionally to outright crooks. He preferred to give away federal funds, when he could get his hands on them, but never flinched from opening the provincial purse to freebooters like John Shaheen or John C. Doyle. His overwhelming sense of mission convinced him that he was right, and so whatever he did was justified because of his essential rightness, even when it ended, as did the IWA strike, in deaths, beatings, appalling waste.

You couldn't shame him, shake him, or shut him up. I once interviewed him on live television for twenty-two minutes, and the only words I said after "Good evening, Mr. Premier . . ." were "but-uh," repeated at intervals as I tried to stem the flow. Another time, at a federal-provincial conference, I asked him what he was asking for, this time, for Newfoundland.

"Whatever is left when these other buggers get through," said Joey.

Come-by-Chance

I have him much in mind when we make our next nostalgic stop-off, at Come-by-Chance, at the edge of the Avalon Peninsula. This is where John Shaheen sued me for $40 million (U.S.), and I want a sentimental look at the place. We drive in down a long stretch of kidney-jarring road — later, the Driver points out that if we had simply stayed on the Trans-Canada, we could have swooped in on pavement, so I tell her that only a tissy-bristle from Upper Canada needs pavement. It is a glorious, sunshiny day as we get out of the car and find ourselves staring at signs of welcome, which read Keep Out and No Trespassing, just to make us feel at home. There is a massive pile of sulphur behind the fence, but no sign of life. The whole scene gives me a warm feeling of nostalgia, takes me back to my first visit here.

This place was planted here by Shaheen Natural Resources, which in 1969 came to one of those remarkable arrangements with Joey to build a refinery to process Saudi Arabian oil. To put it briefly, the Canadian and Newfoundland taxpayers would take the risks connected with erecting the works and Shaheen would take the gravy. The projected cost of the refinery was $165 million. It would be built by a Crown corporation, the Newfoundland Refining Corporation, and Shaheen had the option to buy the shares of that company for $2,000 at any time in the next ten years. If it proved profitable, he would get a $165-million asset for $2,000; if it didn't, he would simply drop the option, turn on his heel, and walk away.

I wrote an article in *Maclean's* magazine suggesting that this was not a good arrangement, and Shaheen dropped a libel writ for the above-mentioned sum. I wrote him a letter saying that if he could get $40 million (U.S.) out of me, I would split it with him, but that did not calm him down. He had a whole battery of public-relations experts hammering away at *Maclean's*, and he himself kept calling the then president of Maclean Hunter, our owner, to demand a retraction, an apology, a crawl-down. Donald Campbell, the president, would tell him that he had to deal with *Maclean's* directly, but every time he called the magazine he got me. (This was shortly before Peter Newman took over what was then a dying publication and breathed new life into it. At this time, early 1970, the entire working staff consisted of me, John Macfarlane, now publisher of *Toronto Life*, and Joan Weatherseed, our wonderful researcher and copy editor.)

In the upshot, I flew down to New York with a bright young lawyer, John Campbell, and we listened all day in the Shaheen boardroom while that aggrieved man marched up and down at the head of the table and told me that I seemed like a nice young lad, so why wouldn't I do the honourable thing and write a new article? He said I didn't treat him with proper dignity, and did I know that the legal work on this had been done by one Richard Nixon, not long before he assumed the office of President of the United States? Then he said this:

"Stewart, you keep on saying I can turn and walk away if Come-by-Chance fails, but it can't fail. Stewart, I've had so many Wassermanns on this thing, my ass looks like a pincushion."

At this, I leapt to my feet and told him that he would have his way — there would be another article. Naturally, I started that article with Shaheen's rather colourful quote and fired off a copy to his lawyers. They agreed to drop the libel suit if *Maclean's* would forget about the second article. For many years I thought I had won a victory, until I realized that the magazine left the entire subject alone, without a single investigative look at Come-by-Chance — for fear of setting off more lawsuits — while it sank slowly into massive debt. The refinery went bankrupt in 1976, Shaheen walked away, and Petro-Canada was lumbered with the remains in 1981. By that time, it had cost $700 million. It was sold to an Israeli company for two dollars in 1986, and soon after resold to Cumberland Farms of Canton, Massachusetts, for one dollar.

Now it has been revived, and it belongs to a New York–based firm called North Atlantic Refining Limited, which has spent $270 million since taking over in 1994 to improve and upgrade the refinery. Even so, neighbours complain about the smell of sulphur emissions — currently running at 76 tonnes a day. Despite the investment, the place we find is looking a little down at the heels, with lots of rusty storage tanks. We take a few pictures of the massive sulphur pile and drive back to the Trans-Canada.

"There is a deep, moral lesson in this whole Come-by-Chance thing," I tell the Driver.

"And what would that be?"

"I'm thinking, I'm thinking."

A Living Storm

Still numb with nostalgia, we backtrack a few kilometres westward along the Trans-Canada, then duck off up a narrow, twisting road to visit Salvage (rhymes with "rampage") on the Eastport Peninsula, a frequent port of call for us in the 1960s and 1970s. When we first visited, Salvage had only recently ceased to be an outport — that is, a village reachable only by sea — and we noticed that we could understand the women and children all right, but that the men might as well have been talking Saxon. We decided that this was because the male sector was always out fishing, while the female sector spent much of its time performing chores in front of the television set, which flattened out the language to our normal North American nasal twang. (Television reception was appalling in those days, and the usual practice was to put a large mirror in front of the set and watch the reflection of that instead. The theory was that the bounced image was somewhat clearer, but our experience was that it just looked like an inverted image in a snowstorm.) We went cod-fishing on one trip — damn near froze to death — and brought home ten dollars' worth of cod for a day's work. On another, we visited the local fishing museum and listened to Wilfred Heffern, the retired fisherman who acted as curator, as he reminisced:

> I started fishing when I was ten, sir, and I never laid off till I was sixty, and that was fishing enough. There were forty schooners went out of here at one time, sir, forty, big ones and little ones, that is, and you could walk across t' bay on 'em. I mind one time we was up off the Labrador and I was on the wheel and it was dead calm, and I looked up and saw the wind coming. Saw it on the waves, sir; she was a living storm. We was soon blowing blue water over the yards. We saw a ship go by, heeling, and she had nothing on the mast but bare sticks. The cap'n was down below, and he comes up and I says, "Should we take down the sail? She'll blow the top right off." And he says, "No, she won't," and I says, "If she doos you, she doos me," and on we come. We double-reefed and clawed into port. Everybody else hung outside. We was the only ones got in.

Heffern taught Joan how to mend a fishing net and gave her a cod jigger, so we were comforted to think that if the writing racket failed, we would have something to fall back on. Of course, that was before the cod stocks vanished. Salvage is improved these days; comparative prosperity in years of a more proactive government — the most revolutionary instrument in Newfoundland history was the mother's allowance — has not wrecked the place. The road is better, and the houses, many of which used to be little better than windblown shacks, are mostly covered with vinyl siding, less colourful than before but more comfortable. Fishing is still the major occupation, with a side dish of tourism, and the people are as warm and welcoming as ever.

From here, it is a brisk few hours down to St. John's, the capital and, hereabouts, centre of the universe. In many ways, St. John's is like any other mid-size city, except that I know of no other city of the same size where almost everyone talks to you on the street. Not the brisk youngsters who work in brokers' offices or insurance firms, of course — those who are waiting to make a dash for New York and talk only to each other — but the middle-aged couple out strolling on the waterfront who stop and want to know how you are, and where from, and do you like Newfoundland?

At dinner, our waiter, Roy from Ayreshire, says he has spoken to more people since he married a St. John's girl a few years ago than he ever had in his life before. We ask him about the fishing.

"They're fishing mad here. They stop off on the way to work and throw a line in a stream and sometimes forget to get to work at all. But the fish are going, no question. A friend of mine invited me over for a feed, because he said he had caught sixty trout earlier that day."

"'Where are they?' says I.

"'In this bowl,' says he.

"We ate all sixty for dinner."

This theme is borne out by a sign we spot on Leslie Street, a huge, homemade message of multi-hued chalk that covers about twenty-five metres of concrete wall. Pink and blue piscatorial outlines surround the central message:

WHERE'S THE FISHIES?

In St. John's, the word "fish" means cod. A friend of ours, who was here on an academic exercise, went into a local seafood store, where the coolers were packed with about a dozen varieties of delicious-looking specimens, and told the man in charge that he wanted some fish.

"Got none," said the merchant. "Come back tomorrow."

"I said I want some fish."

"And I said come back tomorrow."

Our friend thought that he was being kidded at first, then that he was running up against a prejudice because he was From Away, and a very fine shouting match got under way until another customer realized what was happening and stepped in to interpret. Our friend went home with halibut.

Collecting Newfoundland language is a small industry, with its own dictionary and all. One of my favourite phrases describes the day when a man went out onto his porch to collect some kindling, and nearly was struck by ice falling off the roof: "I was fetchin' the splittins from the broch when down come a clampeta hice damn near unshackled me head from me shoulders."

We pass the Leslie Street fishies sign — which is akin, in my view, to those brave banners the students used to raise in Beijing — on our way to Cape Spear, a magnificent lighthouse just outside St. John's, on the easternmost spit of land in North America. Our guidebook tells us that it is "closer to Ireland than to Vancouver," which understates the case considerably. It is 3,200 kilometres to Ireland and 3,141 to Toronto; Cape Spear is closer to Ireland than it is to London, Ontario (3,332 kilometres).

At the lighthouse, we climb the rocky hill with a young family from Pleasantville, a St. John's suburb — Momma, Poppa, and three boys ranging in age from nine down to six. The youngest is thrilled to come across a large ringbolt attached to a slab of cement, just to the seaward side of the lighthouse.

"Probably a treasure down there," he says.

"Probably the biggest treasure in the world," says the middle brother.

"Probably bigger than all the treasures every place in the world put together," says the oldest, not to be outdone. That settled, they walk away, leaving the putative riches undisturbed. Reminds me of those fancy notices you get from magazine sellers announcing that you have just won $11 million. Uh-huh, you say, and go on with life. The middle kid decides he is going to chuck a stone all the way to Ireland, picks up a rock, and gives a mighty heave.

"Nearly made 'er," says his big brother.

The youngest wanders off and comes back to quiz Momma.

"What does 'danger' mean?" he asks.

"It means DANGER!" shouts Momma.

"It means you can't do anything that looks like fun," I say.

"Sure, that's right," says his father.

"Ah," says the kid.

"Well," Momma says, calming down, "you can tell Mr. Blumel that you stood on the easternmost point of North America."

"Who is Mr. Blumel?" asks the kid.

"I give up," says Poppa.

"He's your teacher," says Momma.

"Ah," says the kid.

That afternoon, I wander the rambling streets of downtown St. John's — very wide streets, laid out this way after the good burghers got tired of being burnt out from time to time — supervise the loading of a container ship just in from Amsterdam, check out sales items — "Flippers, $1 Each; Also Carcass," not a sign you see everywhere — and then chug up the steep slopes of Church Hill, where the denominations range in rank from the Anglican cathedral through the United Church and the Presbyterians to the crowning Catholic basilica. They are all closed tighter than an accountant's wallet. In St. John's, as in most Canadian cities now, God is available only by appointment.

Back at the hotel, we are invaded by U.S. armed forces personnel in battle fatigues. As they clomp about the foyer, with their big boots rattling the windows, an officer shouts across to them in a parade-ground voice. "NOW MEN," he bellows, "AT SOME TIME THIS EVENING, YOU MUST ALL REPORT TO THE DESK WITH YOUR CREDIT CARDS. UNDERSTOOD?"

Napoleon's army travelled on its stomach; now the boys skid along on plastic. I ask one of the warriors what they are guarding us against.

"It's an exercise," he says.

"What sort of exercise?"

"A military exercise," he retorts, fixing me with a steely stare. He clomps off.

The troops have a plan prepared, of course. The officer is up again, sounding off.

"WE WILL ALL MEET AGAIN AT TWENTY-TWO HUNDRED HOURS," he says, adding, "AT O'REILLY'S."

O'Reilly's is a rather jolly watering hole on George Street. It will be safe for democracy this night.

When we turn west again the next morning, to recross the island, I keep an eye peeled for what the tourist information insists are its "three distinct zones." Newfoundland, we are told, is composed of three sectors whose presence is explained by the theory of continental drift. Hundreds of millions of years ago, before income tax, what was then the Afro-European and American continents became attached, stayed that way for a few hundred million years, and then drifted apart again. It will happen, even in the best-regulated families. Thus the eastern portion of Newfoundland was once part of Afro-Europe, the middle of the island consists of the ocean floor that once separated the continents, and the western part is a mélange of original America and ocean floor.

I believe it, but you couldn't prove it by me. What the Trans-Canada traveller sees is Tree and Not Tree; rock and gravel covered by evergreens, and rock and gravel bare naked. What the traveller does not see — except during the necessary visit to Signal Hill, above St. John's — are farms. From Signal Hill, you can spot small patches of rolling farmland inland, large patches of rolling ocean out to sea, and in between, snug, pocketed St. John's harbour. Along the TCH, you could form the notion that all things agricultural, and not just most things, have to be imported. Other provinces have portions where farms are scarce, but only in Newfoundland can you drive 500 kilometres without spotting anything more edible than a pine cone.

Sir Richard, Another Rogue

Back west we go, zipping along past Come-by-Chance, Gambo, Grand Falls-Windsor, and Deer Lake, until we come to Corner Brook, "the second city of the province," which boasts a large pulp mill; a major ski centre (Marble Mountain); Sir Wilfred Grenfell College, an extension of Memorial University; a handsome memorial to Capt. James Cook, who spent some years surveying hereabouts; and the Sir Richard Squires Building, ten storeys high, the highest outside St. John's. It is the seat of provincial government for Western Newfoundland, a sort of subset for the more elaborate twelve-storey Confederation Building in the capital. Here, besides the bureaucratic offices and courtrooms, there is a splendid library, where I go to refresh my memory of Sir Richard.

We honour him with a building of his very own — plus a large provincial park, with a nice memorial, just up north of Deer Lake — because he did such a truly horrible job of governing Newfoundland when it was an independent colony that it was forced to collapse into Canada's arms after a short period of commission government.

This is not, needless to say, the official version of his history, just the true one. He was born Richard Anderson Squires of Harbour Grace in 1880, was named the Newfoundland Jubilee Scholar for 1898, and went off to Dalhousie University in Halifax to obtain a law degree. Back in Newfoundland, he practised law and politics — same thing — in the firm of Edward P. Morris, who was the minister of justice and attorney general in the colonial government. He was so successful at this that he soon became one of the St. John's swells, men who lorded it over the island and pretended that they were attendees at the tea salons of London. Morris formed his own party, the People's Party, in 1908, and Squires ran in Trinity, where, after one defeat, he was elected. He became, successively, minister of justice, colonial secretary, and, in 1919, prime minister, although he had to switch parties and become a Liberal to complete his scramble to the top. One of his accomplishments was the establishment of a paper mill in Corner Brook, but to get the timber rights the government had to take over operation of the financially troubled Newfoundland Railway, then owned by Reid Newfoundland Company.

Soon after the government assumed full responsibility for both the paper mill and the railway, in 1923, a scandal broke. It involved Dr. Alexander Campbell, a friend and colleague of Squires's, whom he had appointed to his Cabinet as a member of the Legislative Council after Campbell was defeated at the polls. Campbell had used his position as minister of agriculture and mines to distribute government patronage and funds where they would do the most good at election time. Squires refused to act when the payoffs came to light, his Cabinet revolted, and he was forced to resign. A commission of inquiry, once it got a look at the government books, recommended criminal charges against both Campbell and Squires, but the new government fell, in turn, and Squires escaped unscathed. The charges were finally dropped "for lack of evidence." However, in 1925, Squires was convicted of tax evasion and fined. Oh, yes, in the meantime, he was knighted for his services to the empire.

Still, there was a certain embarrassment in the air, which caused him to sit out the 1924 election; but he came back in 1928, stronger than ever, and became prime minister again. Then, in 1932, with the Depression wracking the island, his finance minister, Richard Cashin, resigned noisily, charging that Squires was up to his old tricks, misusing government funds, falsifying documents, and dealing himself an annual stipend of $5,000 — a comfortable sum in those days — as Newfoundland's war reparations commissioner. Squires managed to avoid any sort of public inquiry; instead, he sent the whole matter to the governor, Sir John Middleton, who dismissed all charges and then retired. Prime Minister Squires, to help things along in the Depression, then jacked up tariffs and sharply reduced benefits to war veterans — about the only form of social assistance then available in Newfoundland. The veterans didn't like it much, and they descended on the legislature on April 5, 1932. A jolly riot ensured, and Squires escaped, disguised, along with one of his new political allies, a sprightly young fellow named Joseph Smallwood, who had run his campaign for him in the new constituency of Corner Brook. "When he lifted his little finger, I came running," Joey later wrote.

The House was dissolved, and both the government and Squires were defeated in the subsequent vote (so was Joey, the only time he ever lost). By this time, the provincial finances were in such a state that the British Colonial Office took over, running the province through a Commission of Government until after the Second World War, when Joey launched the short, brilliant campaign that would lead the province into Confederation on April 1, 1949. (The date was an administrative convenience, the beginning of the federal government's fiscal year, when money could be sprung for Newfoundland. But some die-hards, half a century later, still take bitter pride in the fact that the province joined Canada on April Fools' Day.)

Joey, when he wasn't otherwise occupied, spent a lot of time and effort cleaning up the image of his mentor, whom he described in his second book, *The New Newfoundland*, as "the most versatile and able statesman yet produced in Newfoundland." The standard texts usually refer to Squires as "colourful," although Joey's best biographer, Richard Gwyn, in *Smallwood: The Unlikely Revolutionary*, called him "an angular, aloof, self-made aristocrat, whose most considerable political quality was his speed of foot."

Why Are There Mounties?

I emerge from Sir Richard's edifice to find myself facing a low, modern build-ing inscribed with the symbols and titles, in English and French, of the Royal Canadian Mounted Police. Now, if there is one thing the traveller learns in Newfoundland, besides the place names — Joe Batt's Arm, Blow-me-down, Empty Basket, Little Heart's Ease, Bay Bulls, Sitdown Pond, and the rest — it is that the island is policed, in the main, by the Royal Newfoundland Constabulary, whose members keep their guns in the trunks of their cars. I march over to the RCMP building and am immediately confronted by a tall, slender, moustached man who looks quite a lot like Burt Reynolds, the actor.

I ask him why he isn't a constable, and he laughs. He is Staff Sergeant Ed North, the district commander of the RCMP. "The RCMP police all the rural areas of Newfoundland and Labrador," he explains. "The Constabulary [is] in charge of St. John's, Mount Pearl, Corner Brook, and Portugal Cove. Oh yes, and in Labrador, they look after Labrador City and Churchill Falls." In effect, the force I thought ran the joint is in charge of only a tiny portion of the province, and fewer than half its people.

"Why?"

"Well, it's a contract we have," he explains. He is too polite to tell me what I learn later — that the Constabulary was wracked by a long series of scandals involving the way it went about its work. In the delicate language of the *Newfoundland Encyclopedia:*

> In the early 1990s, a number of incidents, together with recommenda-tions of the Royal Commission of Inquiry into the Response of the Newfoundland Criminal Justice System to Complaints, called into ques-tion some of the investigative procedures of the past.

The RCMP was called in to clean up. Today, the two forces work side by side. Members of both carry firearms openly, and they get along fine, although there is some resentment among the Constabulary because its officers are paid less than the RCMP's.

North has been all over Canada, seventeen transfers in twenty-seven years of service, so I ask him whether he, a native of the province, finds the people here much different from other Canadians.

"Not really," he says. "They are very friendly, everybody knows that, but the real difference is [that] this is a relatively crime-free province. If it weren't for booze, it would be almost crime-free."

The Newfie Bullet

Our final stop in Newfoundland is Port aux Basques, now amalgamated with the nearby fishing village of Channel to form Channel-Port aux Basques. Here, we visit a museum — it is still being fitted out in the old, abandoned railway terminal — containing fond memories of the Newfoundland Railway. The famous Newfie Bullet, a.k.a. the Newfoundland Express. When we first came to Newfoundland, the Newfie Bullet was still grumbling and stumbling along, saluted by a song that related the story of a man who decided to commit suicide by lying down in front of the train:

> He must have waited quite a while,
> 'Cause I hear he starved to death;
> Waiting there on the railway track
> For the Newfoundland Express.

It was a narrow-gauge railway whose conductors would stop the train, if they felt the need, so passengers could pile out and fish while the Bullet puffed its way from St. John's to Port aux Basques. It was the kind of railway that paid a man named Laughie MacDougal twenty-five dollars a year to sound the alarm whenever the wind got so bad it was likely to blow the trains off the tracks. Laughie lived at the foot of a pass in the Long Range Mountains, near Port aux Basques, where the winds were funnelled onto the railbed with such ferocity that they literally blew cars over the edge. The place was called, ominously, Wreck House. Laughie developed a sixth sense for when conditions were such that he needed to call the dispatcher, who would order the train halted and lashed down. After he died in 1965, his wife, Amanda, became the human wind gauge, and when she died in 1972 the Canadian National Railway, which had taken on the Newfie Bullet, installed sensitive electronic equipment, for several million dollars, to do the job that Laughie and Amanda had performed for twenty-five bucks. The winds are still strong enough hereabouts to merit warning signs and a windsock along the TCH, but the Newfie Bullet is no more. The passenger service stopped in 1969 and freight in 1985.

Art Bragg, who runs the museum, regrets the passing of the Bullet, which he says was justified by "very strange accounting. . . . The CN charged this section of the line for the cost of everything that moved this side of Montreal, and then said, 'Shut her down, boys, we can't afford it any more.' They just wanted to get rid of the service."

"But wasn't it expensive to transfer freight from regular- to narrow-gauge tracks?"

Art beams; he has been waiting for this one. "Come and look at this," he says, and leads us over to a series of photographs. "They had a stretch of wide-gauge running from the ferry docks up here to a transfer shed. They would run the cars up here, lift them off their beds with a crane, and plop them onto a narrow-gauge car. It's the same method they use for container cars, and nobody says they aren't cost-efficient. No, it was the same old argument — railroads aren't stylish. The railway was doomed; they were going to shut her, no matter what."

We wander off to a nearby motel for lunch, and there I pick up a national newspaper that contains an article blasting and damning the Newfoundland government for its handling of the Voisey's Bay controversy. Everyone — well, almost everyone — outside Newfoundland thinks Premier Brian Tobin is the villain of this piece, and everyone — well, almost everyone — within the province thinks he is in the right.

The facts are not complicated. When the world's largest deposit of nickel ore was discovered in Northern Labrador in the early 1990s, a corporate cat fight broke out, ending with the giant International Nickel Company outbidding Falconbridge and paying $4 billion for the right to exploit the mineral. That was in 1996. Then the Newfoundland government began to attach conditions to the necessary permits. Instead of cleaning the ore out in six to seven years, as the company proposed to do to get its money back in a hurry, the work would have to be spread over three decades; instead of shipping the stuff, and its attendant jobs, out of province for processing, Inco would have to build a smelter in Labrador. When company spokesmen announced that they would walk away instead of meeting these terms, Tobin bid them good luck and goodbye. The financial press across the land weighed in with warnings that Newfoundland was giving up jobs, cutting off its nose to spite its face, heading to hell in a handcart.

But Tobin had worked out, and most Newfoundlanders have also finally worked out, that the value of a resource in the ground, although it may go up and down from time to time, always increases in the end. There was no longer a need to cut the kind of giveaway deals that marked the Smallwood years. The nickel isn't going anywhere. Negotiations continue, as they say, while the project works its way through a series of environmental and regulatory hearings, but Inco has already made major concessions, and will make more.

What the controversy shows, more than anything else, is how much this province has grown up since its early days, when it could be looted by every freebooter who came down the pike. Satisfied with this thought, I take my luncheon of fish chowder with a cheerful soul, and then am flummoxed when the waitress appears with our bill and an embarrassed look.

"I've taken the cole slaw and the buns off the price," she says.

"Fine," say I. "Why?"

"Because the chowder was fresh," says the waitress. "Cook tasted it, and she said it was fresh. So you get a refund."

Fearful that we are headed for one of those language ditches, I ask, "What do you mean by 'fresh'?"

"Oh." She pats my arm and speaks slowly, as if explaining to an idiot or an infant. "Fresh means it doesn't have enough salt."

Only in Newfoundland could you get a voluntary rebate for a meal that tasted dandy on the grounds that the main dish was fresh.

I think this episode says something in general about Newfoundlanders, who have a helpful attitude best explained in a joke we have heard several times over the years. It seems that during the French Revolution, an Englishman, a Frenchman, and a Newfoundlander were condemned to the guillotine. The Englishman was asked if he had any last words.

"Yes," he said. "I regret that I have but one life to give for my country."

He was placed under the blade, which slashed down and then stopped, a hair's breadth from the back of his neck. His captors decided that Fate had spoken, and let him go.

The Frenchman, asked if he had any final words, also replied in the affirmative.

"I die for my wife and my mistress," he said, adding, "and may they never meet."

He was placed under the blade, which again slashed down until it came to within a hair's breadth of the back of his neck and unaccountably stopped. Again, his captors let the man go.

Finally, the Newfoundlander was brought to the dreadful machine and asked if he had any last words.

"Yes," he said, pointing up to the guillotine. "I tink I sees your trouble, chief, right up there. . . ."

In the thirty-five years, a full generation, since we first came to this province, many things have changed. The roads are infinitely better, the economy more robust, the politics more adult, and the hotels and motels miles ahead of where they were. But nothing fundamental has happened to Newfoundlanders; they are still bright, friendly, funny, ingenious, optimistic, and outgoing.

And hard to understand.

2

Nova Scotia

FROM LOVE TO LUNENBURG

Time after time, when we thought our appetite for scenery must be sated,
we rounded a curve to find a ripple of moss green hills, a stream swarm-
ing over a ridge or a fishing village snuggled against a mountain along a
bay, and felt once more a shiver of delight and discovery.
                                    — STAR WEEKLY, APRIL 3, 1965

Our ferry between Port aux Basques and North Sydney, Nova Scotia, is the
Caribou, since the other large passenger ferry, the *Joseph and Clara Smallwood,*
is laid up temporarily with a case of the megrims. Something about the sea
doors not working properly, not a thing you want to have to worry about
during the six-hour (if you're lucky) crossing from Newfoundland. The
condition of the ferries is a big issue on both sides of this stretch of water, as
is the issue of whether the service, now operated by Marine Atlantic, a Crown
corporation, will be privatized. From Ontario west, privatization is seen
mostly as some sort of salvation that will bring the mighty engine of capital-

ism into play, but in Eastern Canada, there is not the same enthusiasm.

Crown corporations sprang up by the dozen down here because private enterprise couldn't or wouldn't do the job — especially the job of providing decent transport. Here, the populace approaches privatization the way most of us approach the dental chair. We know it's supposed to be good for us, but we doubt it. Art Bragg, the man in charge of the railway museum at Port aux Basques, was gloomily certain that Marine Atlantic would soon be sold off, and that then service would be chopped back enough to make it pay.

"They'll turn it over to somebody like the Irvings, out of Moncton," he told me. "And they'll say, 'Well, the ferry isn't full, so although she's supposed to go at 11:30 this morning, we'll just hold her until 11:30 tonight and see if we can't make a little money out of this.' The federal government has an obligation under the Terms of Union [i.e., when Newfoundland joined Confederation in 1949] to provide timely, reliable ferry service, but that isn't going to stop them."

We put all such dismal thoughts aside, however, because soon after coming aboard ship, we encounter a genuine romance. The Driver has struck up a conversation with an elderly couple who share a cosy corner of the passenger lounge with us, and they are willing, even anxious, to tell us their story. Ed and Marilyn Schmeltz live in Las Cruces, New Mexico, but they spend most of their time on the road, travelling about in a beat-up 1988 Chevy, which we noticed in the lineup to board the ferry because of its overflowing roof rack — sleeping bags, cases, a tent, mounds of plastic bags. Ed is seventy-three, a tall, handsome man with a silver white handlebar moustache, a Stetson, and a gleam in his eye that belongs to someone far younger. His ambition is to run with the bulls at Pamplona, and I have no doubt that he will do it someday. Marilyn, six years older, will not join him, but she will stand well back and cheer. Marilyn is shorter and squarer, with heavy glasses and a light smile. She wears a number of turquoise rings and a cowboy hat, but not a Stetson. They have been married only a few months.

"Met her in Las Cruces," says Ed. "Luckiest day of my life. I had been in the army, served out my full years, and then retired, but I was still pretty young, so I got a job in Washington, D.C., at the zoo. I became the reptiles acquisitions fella, because nobody else wanted to trail around the world picking up snakes and things, and I thought it was just dandy. I was married, happily married, for forty-four years, and then the wife died and I just kind of drifted for a while. Then I went down to visit my son in Las Cruces, and I went out to a dance, and that's where I met Marilyn, on the dance floor."

"The first time he touched me," says Marilyn, "it was like an electric shock went through me."

"Me too, hon," says Ed gallantly.

The next shock was when they got married within weeks of that first meeting. Marilyn's husband, to whom she had been married fifty-two years, had been dead only a little more than three months, and everybody's kids — Ed's five and Marilyn's two — kicked up a stink.

"It was too bad," says Marilyn, "but it was our lives. I told them it was no disrespect to our first mates. The reason we were getting married again was because we had such good marriages the first time. That held them."

"Before we got married," says Ed, "I only asked her two things: Did she like dancing? Which I knew she did. And did she like travelling? She said yes. So I sold my place in Washington, and we moved into a big trailer outside town on a nice piece of property."

"We have no living room," Marilyn explains. "We put in a dance floor instead."

They also have no television set. "Why do we need TV?" asks Ed. "We have a picture window." And the travel.

Ed considers himself to be almost an honorary Canadian. "It's because of Robert Service, the poet. Once, during the Second World War, I was in England on R&R and I was looking for something to read. I reached up on the shelf above my bed and pulled down a book. It turned out to be *Songs of a Sourdough,* and I plunged right in. After that, I got everything Service ever wrote, and first chance I got to go up to the Yukon with the army, I leapt at it. We spend about as much time travelling around Canada as the States."

We naturally ask them to sum up their impressions of Canada, and this is what they say:

"Fewer Canadians than Americans wear hats."

"The police have a quiet presence here, not like American cops, strutting around."

"Calgary was great. We loved the rodeo, but whatever happened to the grain elevators out west?"

"Ontario is mostly golf courses — at least, that's the impression you get driving through."

"Is Quebec losing its music? We heard a lot less music in Quebec City than on earlier trips."

Feeling uplifted, we wander off to the cafeteria, where the dreadful buffet is laid out for the captive audience. The man behind one counter steers us right. He's a Newfoundlander.

"What you want," he tells us, "is a nice bowl of beef soup." He stirs the pot and reels back in alarm. "My God, Charlie," he calls out. "Somebody's put some beef in the beef soup!"

So they have. It is delicious.

Cape Breton: Taxed Rum and Hard Times

The ferry lands at North Sydney, at the top of Cape Breton, and here we must tread warily. Once long ago, when the earth's crust was still cooling, I wrote an article describing North Sydney as a "grimy and disheartened town." The next time I came, a friend of mine with a strange sense of humour got out the word that that writer fellow from central Canada was back, and a delegation appeared at my motel, expressed a desire to have words with me, and frightened me out of a year's growth. So what I say now is that North Sydney has managed to resist the impulse to change just for the sake of change, and that it is much as I remember it. So is Sydney, the city next door and unofficial capital of Cape Breton. The Sydney waterfront has been cleaned up, and a handsome walkway lines the foreshore, where all was formerly decayed vegetation and abandoned beer bottles, but it is still a tough and homely town.

Originally known as Spanish Harbour, it was renamed in 1785 — in one of those attempts to suck up that marked the heyday of the British Empire, for Lord Sydney — then secretary of state for the colonies. The man who did the renaming was an astounding engineer, surveyor, and oceanographer, Joseph Frederick Wallet DesBarres, the first lieutenant-governor of what was then the newly formed, independent colony of Cape Breton. DesBarres was famous for the number and beauty of his mistresses, and for dancing on a tabletop to celebrate his hundredth birthday, in 1785. One of the lads.

Cape Breton was called Île-Royale when it was part of Acadie. When it was ceded to Britain at the end of the Seven Years' War, it gained its present name but was part of the new province of Nova Scotia. Then, when a flood of Loyalists streamed up from the south after the American Revolutionary War, it was split off again as a separate colony to absorb some of the influx, with Sydney, once more, as its capital. It rumbled along that way until 1816, when a British court held that the imposition of a duty of one shilling a gallon on imported rum was illegal. Because there was no representative assembly on the island to give consent, the court ruled, no taxes could be levied in the colony.

The courses of action for government were stark and clear. Give up taxes. Never! Put out the call for an elected assembly. Never! Or stick Cape Breton back onto Nova Scotia, which did have an assembly. So that was done, although it took until 1821 to get the task completed. Cape Breton, with its booze now taxed, hasn't had a day's luck since. This part of Nova Scotia has struggled with hard times, harder times, and still harder times, almost from that day to this, which is why it gradually became almost a ward of the state. For decades, it has been dominated by the two industries — Sysco, the Sydney Steel Company, and Devco, the Cape Breton Development Corporation — that still provide most of the decent-paying jobs on the island. It is becoming part of Canadian mythology that the struggles of these two giant Crowns prove that private enterprise is the only kind of industrial development that works. In fact, however, it was, in both cases, the failure of private enterprise that led to the unholy mess that confronts us today.

Sysco, whose grimy stacks I can see out of my hotel window, was a private company from 1901 until 1967, and for much of that time it made money for its owners, the British firm of Hawker Siddley. There were bitter labour relations and brutal strikes, but money was made. As soon as the profits began to fall off, however, when more modern plants took over the world's steel industry, Hawker Siddley announced that it would walk away, leaving 4,000 workers in the lurch. Faced with a choice between abandoning a substantial share of the provincial workforce or taking them onto a provincial payroll, the

Nova Scotia government stepped in to form Sysco in 1967, and it has been trying to get rid of the damn thing ever since. For some reason, no one else is anxious to take on a company that has mostly outmoded equipment, a mammoth debt load, shrinking markets, and an environmental mess that will cost untold millions to clean up. This is the result of years and years of neglect brought on by the fact that the company never seemed to be making enough money to clean up its act.

The Sydney Tar Ponds, a relic of both public and private corporate neglect, have the distinction of being named Canada's worst toxic site. The ponds cover forty hectares of central Sydney, and their outflow turns up in orange goo laced with arsenic that bubbles through basement drainpipes in the vicinity. Not something we push in the tourist pamphlets. The province is buying some of the houses as part of a three-year, $62-million cleanup plan announced while we are in town, but that is only the beginning. No one is going to take on this mess for private industry, but all that proves to me is that it would have been cheaper, smarter, and more responsible to put more, not less, money into Sysco to prevent the disaster in the first place.

Devco is a federal Crown, born at the same time as Sysco, in 1967, and for the same reason. Its then owner, the Dominion Steel and Coal Company, when faced with falling prices, brisk competition, and declining coal seams, announced that it was pulling out. After some panic and much study, Ottawa stepped in and formed Devco to preserve the 6,000 jobs thus threatened. It would not only mine coal, but also "do all such other things as the Corporation deems incidental or conducive to the attainment of its objects."

Devco Could Have Set Up Brothels and Made Money

Under this section of its corporate charter, Devco could have set up a series of brothels and maybe turned a profit. Instead, it put a lot of money into Sysco — buying its decrepit coke ovens — and then set out to provoke, inspire, and finance anybody who had a good idea for an industry on the island. What with one thing and another, it found itself in oyster farming, fishing, sheep breeding, beef production, maple syrup, boat building, wool milling, food processing, metal casting, lumber milling, and door making. Not profit making, though, never profit making. It leapt into the tourist industry and financed a steam railway, a golf course, beaches, marinas, and restaurants. Some of these were good and suitable projects and some were not, but what they all had in common was that without outside help, it is unlikely that any of these job-creating ventures would ever have seen the light of day. Even when they flopped, as many did, they represented a brave attempt to break the circle of dependence.

Now, after three decades and $1.6 billion in subsidies, the federal government is giving up. Despite a 75 percent reduction in its workforce, the coal company's productivity is still below industry standards. In January 1999, Natural Resources Minister Ralph Goodale announced that one of the two mines will be shut and the other sold, if a buyer can be found. This caused central Canadian papers like the *Toronto Star* to huff that the workers of Cape Breton, which still has an unemployment rate of 19 percent, "would be far better off today had Ottawa not tried to shield them from economic reality for the past 30 years." Actually, $1.6 billion spread over thirty years strikes me as a pretty good investment, at least compared with the alternative, which was to walk away and let Cape Breton be depopulated. Ottawa spends about $23 billion every year in subsidies to private corporations. Why is this "an investment in opportunity," while keeping Cape Bretoners in employment is shielding them from economic reality?

When CN was being privatized, Canadian taxpayers ladled out nearly a billion dollars to reduce the company's debt, to make it more attractive to new investors (who turned out to be mostly Americans). Why does it make sense to blow a billion in that way, and no sense to pay wages to Cape Bretoners? In central Canada, Sysco and Devco provoke derision; in Cape Breton, they provoke equal amounts of loyalty and despair. But without them, this part of Nova Scotia would be an economic wasteland. The calculation made in 1967 — that it is cheaper in the long run, and better in the short run, to pay people to work rather than to sit around on welfare — still holds true; it's just that nobody believes it any more. Elsewhere in Canada, governments are edging into "workfare," a program to push those who receive government cheques out to do jobs not worth doing.

At least the jobs provided here for so many years were good ones, with good pay, providing worthwhile products. The cost has been high, but not as high as the cost of simply walking away. Anyone who thinks he or she has a solution to the dilemma of producing employment on this rugged landscape with only private funds is welcome to try.

The Dog That Warred on Blankets

While we are here, we drive out to visit our favourite motel, the Île Royale (pronounced "aisle ryal"), but it is gone, leaving not a wrack behind. This is the place where, on our first trans-Canada trip, I refused to rise in the night when summoned by the Driver, who maintained that McNab, our dog, was "up to something." I wished him the best of British luck and went back to sleep.

The next day, John de Visser, the photographer, and I went out to visit Fortress Louisbourg, and when we returned to the motel, it was to find a Scene. Our kids were standing by the window, studiously examining the plant life outside; Joan was tapping her foot; the maid was wringing her hands; and the manager, a rotund little chap with a moustache, was holding aloft a blanket that looked as if it had been through the siege of Louisbourg.

"Your dog," he announced with ominous calm, "has eaten my blanket."

"Ridiculous," I retorted. "Dogs don't eat blankets."

"No, they don't," he admitted, "but your dog did. He ate this one." He shook the tattered remains.

At this point, the prop and mainstay of my life chimed in. "I told you that dog was up to something last night, but you wouldn't get up and look. Oh, no."

Triumph bloomed on the manager's face.

"All right," I grumbled. "I'll pay for the blanket. How much?"

"Fifteen dollars."

"No sir," I said. "Not for one measly blanket."

By this time, of course, he knew the drill. "Why don't we ask madam?"

Madam thought that fifteen dollars seemed most reasonable, and that was that.

Joan is sadder than I to note the absence of the Île Royale, but we both miss her. Canada's finest bran muffins were baked here.

Fortress Louisbourg, which was barely under construction when we first came to call, is now complete, reconstructed on the site of what was once the finest and largest fortress in North America, when it was held by the French. Louisbourg was the capital of Île-Royale after the fortress was begun in 1713, and its impregnability allowed sea raiders to dash down the coast, capture British and colonial shipping, and slip back home to safety. Finally, a force of New Englanders under William Pepperell — a Maine merchant who had no military experience whatever, and therefore didn't know that the fort could not be taken — took it. The motive, alas, was not patriotism or glory but loot, lots of which the invaders found when the French capitulated on June 17, 1745.

The vital importance of the fort quickly became apparent the next year, when a great armada of more than fifty ships left France to recapture Louisbourg, conquer Nova Scotia, and sack Boston. To make a long story short, the attempt was a complete disaster. The first leader of the expedition committed suicide, as did his successor, and Louisbourg remained untouched. So, of course, the British gave it back to the French, in 1748, as part of the peace treaty that ended, for a few years, the ongoing war. Gen. James Wolfe had to retake the fortress again in 1757, on his way to Quebec. He might not have succeeded, except that the garrison was so riddled by drunkenness, disease, and corruption that the defences were woefully weakened — much of the money sent out from France for work on the fort went, instead, on balls and revels. This time, the British blew the place apart, and it has had to be reassembled, as a tourist attraction, for several thousand times the money that was spent to make it a fortress in the first place.

This, I think, is progress.

The Original Ma Bell

Skimming down the pine-drenched wilderness of Cape Breton, we climb Kelly's Mountain on a series of switchbacks that afford a splendid view of Bras d'Or Lake — known as Canada's Inland Sea — to Baddeck and the Alexander Graham Bell Museum. I am here not so much to learn about Bell, whose story is hardly a secret, as to learn about his wife, Mabel Gardiner Hubbard, the original Ma Bell. She was one of Bell's private deaf pupils when he lived in Boston. When they met, Bell was teaching at the School for the Deaf during the day and in the evenings combining his own experiments into what would become the telephone with the tutoring of deaf youngsters. They were married in 1875, shortly after he first patented his invention and founded the Bell Telephone Company. Mabel, who had visited in Cape Breton, brought her husband here to look for a summer place in 1885, and they bought a lovely home on a headland overlooking Baddeck Bay. They called it Beinn Bhreagh, Gaelic for "beautiful mountain."

As well as being Bell's wife, Mabel was an enthusiastic experimenter. She was a full-fledged partner in the Aerial Experimental Association, which Bell formed with J. A. D. McCurdy and others. (This was the body that built and flew the Silver Dart, the first heavier-than-air craft to get off the ground in Canada.) She was also active in experimental horticulture and, with their two daughters, was an enthusiastic proponent of female suffrage as early as 1910, when it was very much frowned on by all the proper folk. She died within five months of her husband's death in 1822, and they are buried side by side just across the way.

Where the Painters Always Go

From here, it is a very short hop over to Arichat, on Isle Madame, a small, helmet-shaped island off the south coast of Cape Breton, not far from the Canso Causeway, which provides the road link to mainland Nova Scotia. Arichat is the largest village on the island, one of the prettiest, and most neglected, travel spots in the Atlantic provinces. Just along the road outside the village, there is a viewpoint known to the natives as the place where the painters always go. It is not hard to see why. Before you rolls the steel blue Strait of Canso, marching over from the mainland in wave after purposeful wave to a series of stepping-stone islands at your feet. One of these islands sports a lighthouse, a slash of white against the green grass and blue sea; another seems to house a colony of gulls, which wheel and dip with graceful wings and mournful cries; off a third island, an Acadian fisherman, looking suitably picturesque in his bobbing boat, wrestles with a lobster trap.

Isle Madame is ideally placed to have an oil tanker bump into it, which is what brought us here first, in 1972 — the sinking of the *Arrow*. Like so many marine disasters, this turned out to be nobody's fault — or at least, not the fault of anyone who could be brought to book or sent a bill. The *Arrow* was Liberian-registered, its ownership as evanescent as the mists that blow in from Port Hawkesbury, so when the oil tanker went adrift — its steering shot, its engines crippled — smashed into a rock, and dumped several hundred thousand tonnes of Bunker C gunk into the water, the hand-wringing was fierce and the results non-existent. The locals grumbled and got up petitions, but many of these were in French — the language of most of the island's residents — and might as well have been in pig Latin for all the good they did.

On that first visit, we looked into the history of the place. It was settled by descendants of the French who were uprooted by the fall of Louisbourg and by Huguenots from the Channel isle of Jersey. Later mingling with the Highlanders who populate most of Cape Breton gave their French a somewhat Scottish twist. *Petit,* for example, is pronounced "petty." At one time, Arichat was a considerable town, the centre of a thriving shipbuilding industry, home of the first cathedral in eastern Nova Scotia, and the original site of St. Francis Xavier University, which was moved to Antigonish two years after its founding in 1853. In those days, a local citizen went on a trip to Sydney and came back to report that "if Sydney continues to grow, it is going to become as large as Arichat."

We are staying at the Auberge Acadienne, a lovely building that we think has a faintly Norman look until we drive around the back and the Driver says, "For Pete's sake, it's Doug Shaw's old place tarted up."

On frequent visits in the 1970s, we stayed at what was then the Isle Madame Motel, owned and run by Doug Shaw, who worked for Nova Scotia Power in the daytime and as the village innkeeper at night. He charged twelve dollars for a double. We arrived, one time, the day he received his first liquor licence — and supplies — in celebration of which it was decided that we should open and sample all the products, including the champagne, to ensure that there was nothing wrong with them. Joan taught Doug, after several tries, how to make a good martini; in return, he fetched her an out-of-season lobster from his own supplier on the wharf. Today, there is no such slackness. The motel has become an *auberge,* an entire storey has been added, the same room costs more than a hundred bucks, and the pretty young woman in charge is very correct, very formal. You won't find her handing out samples of the booze.

Joan wonders what she would make of Father Poirier, one of our pals from the old days. He was one of the many priests — and many Poiriers — on the island. He divided his lunch custom between Doug's place and a smaller motel, although since he never paid, Doug said he might well have forgone the honour of his visits. After a merry luncheon one day in 1974, the good father insisted on showing us his church, an 1837 structure that still towers over the village (although it is locked up tighter than a drum these days). After a visit to Rome, he came home reeling with marble envy and had all the wooden pillars painted to look like marble. And they did.

After we admired the church, including a magnificent altar painting executed in 1854, he took us back to the manse, where he played his player piano, filled us with goblets of straight rye whisky, and told us of his Great Plan. His parishioners could not hold their heads up, Father Poirier told us, because the priest down the road was driving a Chrysler while he had to bump around in a lowly Chev. To gladden their hearts, he was going to buy a brand-new Buick and send them the bill, so Arichatians could once more march forward in pride.

Stepping through a Door into the Unknown

Isle Madame, which is off the main trading track, settled into somnolence when shipbuilding declined in the nineteenth century, but it perked along as a small, prosperous fishing centre until the cod began to disappear in the 1980s. By 1995, the fish plant, the island's major employer, was not only shut, but also demolished. Out of the rubble rose the bilingual Développement Isle Madame Association (DIMA). It was formed out of a determination to provide something to keep the younger generation from drifting away and disappearing.

Joel Bowen, a development officer with DIMA, tells us over lunch that "people were in shock and denial at first, but they realized a change had to come. For many of us, that meant stepping through a door without knowing what was on the other side — going back to school, retraining, whatever it took."

Brenda Martell, the executive director of DIMA, explains that it is a "non-profit community development group, which has, in a few short years, backed tourism ventures, the aquaculture industry, a co-op hardware store, a small-crafts manufacturing company, a local cable-television system, and a telephone call centre."

The DIMA projects create and keep far more employment than was here before the collapse of the ocean stocks. There are still a lot of unanswered questions about aquaculture, as there are about the entire Maritime economy, but on Isle Madame the populace has found a far better way to combat the uncertainties of our age than either to hope, somehow, that a suitably subsidized private firm will suddenly move in or simply to sit and curse the dark — and Ottawa.

When we leave Isle Madame, we drive across the Canso Causeway, the strip of highway that turned Cape Breton into a de facto peninsula. The causeway was opened in 1955 but is not open now. We are stopped at the swing bridge while a Canadian naval vessel, badly in need of a paint job, edges its way through the canal that divides two arms of the Atlantic: St. Georges Bay and Chedabucto Bay. Our navy would look more fierce and warlike if the sailors didn't grin and wave so much.

We swing past Stellarton, where there is a memorial to the twenty-six men who died in the Westray mine explosion that carefully avoids the role in the tragedy of the province's inept and moribund inspection system and the careless greed of the operating company. We lunch, at Truro, on lobster rolls, one of the Maritime region's most outstanding inventions since Reginald Fessenden first transmitted the sound of a human voice by radio in 1900. We munch in a window-walled restaurant, where we can watch the tidal bore barrel up the Salmon River, carting bits of wood, bushes, and even a mid-size tree improbably inland. Why it should be fascinating to see a vast, muddy ditch become a raging torrent within a few minutes I do not know, but it never loses its allure.

Halifax: Buddhists, Big Blasts, and Prince Pineapple Head

We are headed — or rather, headed back — to Halifax, the Warden of the North, capital of the province, a city that has managed to give itself a reputation for staid respectability despite a riotous, rousing, and even explosive past. The Historic Properties, a brilliant and successful redevelopment of the city waterfront, leans heavily on the respectable bits of the past, rather than on the interesting ones, although there is a plaque on one building to mark the site of John Collins's bank. Collins was a privateer who put his loot to work by lending it to the upper classes, the first, but not the last, Canadian to mix piracy and banking.

We lived here for two years in the 1980s, when I was the director of the School of Journalism at the University of King's College, so to freshen the view I have asked David Swick, one of the city's outstanding journalists and a columnist with the *Daily News,* to show me around as if I were a stranger to the place. He astonishes me.

He begins by telling me that "Halifax is booming. We are in the middle of the strongest real-estate boom since 1979."

"Why? Expansion of the film industry? Sable Island gas?"

"Buddhists."

"Come again?"

"Buddhists. Tibetan Buddhists, at that. Well, the entertainment business is expanding, no doubt about it, with Salter Street Films and television production, and some money seeps through from the development of natural gas offshore, but the real change in this city started when Chogyam Trungpa selected this place as the world headquarters of his Tibetan Buddhist organization, Varadhatu International, in 1977. He brought a whole bunch of them up from Boulder, Colorado, and they brought a lot of money, skills, and self-confidence. They transformed this place."

Tibetans have been fleeing their native land to escape the invading Chinese since 1950. The Chinese had the nation in complete subjection by 1959 (while the United Nations looked the other way), and they did not look kindly on Buddhism. The only solution for many was escape, and a large colony of Buddhists, most of whom followed a kind of spiritual training called Shambhala, sprang up in Boulder, Colorado. Their leader and teacher, Trungpa, was looking for a place that carried a little less crass materialism in its makeup than Boulder, and a friend suggested Nova Scotia as "a safe place." So he came, and saw, and was conquered.

David Swick's excellent book documenting the move, *Thunder and Ocean: Shambhala and Buddhism in Nova Scotia,* explains that the Nova Scotians were not too keen when 500 or more Tibetans practising a strange religion landed on them. At one point, a Canada Customs official phoned the mayor of Halifax, Ron Wallace, to report, "I have some Moonies wanting across. They gave your name." But the strangers turned out to be gentle, hard-working, skilled people, and the prejudice that has formed so strong a thread in Nova Scotian history was beginning to abate. Pretty soon, the newcomers were working their way into the community. They have founded the Nova Scotia Sea School, a natural-food market, the province's first stress-reduction clinic, an internationally sold magazine, and dozens of other enterprises. They have opened bookstores, cafés, bakeries, clothing stores, and a community-based alternative to banking — peer lending, a process something along the lines of that at a credit union.

"They injected into Halifax what it needed more than anything else," says Swick, "a jolt of pure energy."

He gets a précis of this out while we are driving up to the legislature, walking past the stern statue of Joseph Howe on the lawn, and presenting ourselves at the security desk. The legislature is closed — it is Saturday morning — but the guard, who knows Dave, lets us in anyway. I have been here before, but I never realized how small the place is, a tiny little cockpit of a parliament. There are a number of headless bronze birds about, a reminder of the anti-Americanism that percolated through Halifax during the War of 1812. An assembly member assumed the birds were eagles and knocked their heads off with his cane.

"That's Sir John Thompson," says Dave, pointing to a portrait. "One of the most underrated politicians Canada ever produced, and the only prime minister Halifax ever produced." (He held the office from 1892 to 1894. One of the nicest things ever said about him was intended to be a criticism. A Conservative colleague complained, "He won't even consider whether a thing is good for the party until he is quite sure it is good for the country.") Dave goes on, "Do you realize that responsible government was born in Canada here, in 1848?"

I want to point out that it came into being at the same time in the united Province of Canada, but the guard turns up in the doorway and shooshes us out. He is going off duty.

We drive out to what is now Seaview Memorial Park, along the waterfront near the Angus L. Macdonald Bridge to Dartmouth. There is a lot of grass, four men walking dogs, nothing else. This was once Africville, a black community that was formed by descendants of the black United Empire Loyalists who fled here during and after the American Revolutionary War. A ghetto community, it had all the usual problems — high unemployment, crime, alcoholism, suicides — and quite a few years were spent in searching for some sort of uplift that did not entail the white folks dipping into the till to help the black folks out. A brilliant solution presented itself with the need for a bridge to augment the ferry service across Halifax harbour in 1955.

"It was wonderful," says Swick. "This city is full of parks, right? Full of waterfront parks. So they decided they needed another one right here, at the end of the bridge, and they just wiped out the whole community, knocked down the houses, turfed out the renters — most people were renters — sent them out to find housing elsewhere, if they could. They left behind this nice memorial." He points to a two-foot slab of granite, lettered with the words "Seaview Memorial Park." Not many people, black or white, can live on this.

We leave the park, driving uphill and along the streets that bore much of the blast of the Halifax Explosion in 1917.

"My grandfather slept right through it," says Dave proudly. "Of course, he was only nine at the time. A Norwegian freighter and a French munitions ship collided and caught on fire early in the morning of December 5. When people woke up, the first thing they saw was the fire, so they came out of their houses and stood looking at the blaze. That's why thousands of people were blinded when the explosion took place — they were looking right at it."

The blast killed 2,200 Haligonians, injured thousands more, and flattened a huge swath of the city.

"They found bits of wreckage as far inland as Truro," Dave says with awe. Truro is about one hundred kilometres from where we are standing.

One odd outcome of the explosion was the creation of a whole new neigh-bourhood, with wide boulevards, sturdy hydrostone houses, its own shops and boutiques. At the time, it was considered to be a disgraceful place to live, because the houses were built with government help; now it is one of the most desirable areas of the city.

We drive haughtily past the standard tourist stops, such as the Citadel, St. Paul's (Canada's oldest Protestant church), and the Maritime Museum — although they are well worth a call for anyone visiting Halifax for the first time. Instead, we drop in at St. George's Church, the so-called Round Church, on Brunswick Street, where for decades the top ring of seating was reserved for blacks (closer to God, but smaller seats). We also, of course, have a look at Sir John Thompson's grave and at the Armdale Yacht Club, off the North West Arm of Halifax harbour. Many of the buildings here were originally used to house French prisoners during the Napoleonic Wars; now they offer shelter to stockbrokers and lawyers.

Alas, there is not time to visit the site near Bedford where Prince Edward, the second son of the sons of King George III, installed his mistress, who rejoiced in the name Alphonsie Thérèse Bernadine Julie de Montgenet de Fortisson but was known to pals as Julie. When the United Empire Loyalists came pouring into Halifax at the close of the American Revolutionary War, it was to find a town garrisoned by "one regiment of artillery, two of infantry and three of whores." Two of the highest-paid and most respectable whores were Julie, who bore Edward two illegitimate children, and Frances Wentworth, wife of Sir John Wentworth, Nova Scotia's lieutenant-governor of the time. She was paired with Edward's younger brother, William — the man who would become William IV. At this time, he was a naval captain, and was generally known as Pineapple Head because his dome came to a point and he was not overly bright. His other nickname was Silly Billy.

The two mistresses became fast friends, and it was a sight to delight the hearts of Halifax when Frances had herself rowed, in a galley powered by slaves owned by her hubby, up Bedford Basin to call on Julie at the swell new joint Edward had built for her in lieu of the official residence provided for him at Citadel Hill. This was a two-storey love nest, with gravel rides, a path laid out to spell "Julie," and an artificial pond shaped like a heart. There was an enormous ballroom, a vast central hall in Italian rococo style, a bandstand that took the form of a Moorish cupola surrounded by Greek columns, and a Chinese temple hung about with windbells. Quietly tasteful, in other words. Edward departed Halifax in 1800, leaving behind eleven of his soldiers under sentence of death for mutiny and desertion.

He was needed back home, to marry and beget offspring for the Crown in case his two older brothers, George and William, botched the job. Which they did, so that after Edward himself died before he could succeed to the throne, his legitimate daughter, Victoria, copped the crown. She never visited Halifax, which is probably just as well; she might have wanted to check out Daddy's old haunts. All of this lovely history is buried now, and the good burghers of the city look as if their ancestors knew nothing of such goings-on. Pity.

The South Shore, Next to the Eastern Shore

Peggy's Cove, about an hour's drive down the South Shore, lures us next. (If you merely nod your head when someone tells you that you drive up the South Shore until you hit Halifax and then drive up the same road along the Eastern Shore, you have the soul of a Maritimer.) Peggy's Cove is one of those touristy places — like Niagara Falls; Magnetic Hill, near Moncton; Grouse Mountain, B.C. — that are always crowded because they deserve to be. There is the lighthouse, white and red; the rocks, which look to be grey at first but turn out to have every hue of the rainbow; and beyond, the incredible blue of the sea, with wheeling gulls, paid no doubt by the chamber of commerce to add an authentic touch, and gambolling families.

Right up against the lighthouse itself, staring landward, stands a young man with a cellphone soldered to his ear. He is talking: "Harry, that's not what I said. Harry, if that was what I said, it was not what I meant. I said try him at fifty thou, Harry. Harry, we can't make a dime at forty thou. Try him at fifty thou, Harry. I'm sorry, Harry, I can't hear you for the goddamn waves."

He claps shut the phone, glances briefly around — where the hell am I? — scrambles over to a car parked (illegally) along the entrance road, and disappears with a roar. "Have a nice day," I say.

We stop for lunch at Chester, where the swells live, at our favourite motel, the Windjammer. There is a special on the menu: Dom Perignon, with Our Own Home-Cut Fries, $157.50. Our waitress offers to throw in gravy on the fries for free. "We've had a couple of bottles of Dom Perignon for quite a while," she says wistfully, "but no one has ordered it yet." The Driver points out that for a good year, $157.50 is a steal for this champagne, but we resist the temptation anyway.

It is only another hour or so to Lunenburg, home port of the *Bluenose* and a town whose streets are enlivened by some of the most brightly painted, best-kept houses in the Maritimes. When we check into the Boscawen Inn, we encounter a man who has been sailing for twenty-nine hours straight — coming up from what the locals call the Boston States — and who wants to know how long he can sleep in tomorrow morning.

"When is your back-out time?" he asks the innkeeper. Noon. He staggers off.

Lunenburg was settled in 1753 by "foreign Protestants" from Germany, Switzerland, and France. They were brought over as part of a British colonial policy to introduce more Protestant settlers into the heavily Catholic Acadian population. The original intention was to place them in the Minas Basin, off the Bay of Fundy, but the French and aboriginals were still fractious there, so they were simply dumped on Halifax, 1,500 indigent people huddled together in barracks behind the town. They quickly became an affliction and an expense to the authorities, whom they were always besieging with petitions to find them some land, farming implements, and seeds, and let them become an asset, instead of a cost, to the Crown. A brief respite from war in 1753 provided the opportunity, but the idea of sending them anywhere near any settled area was now abandoned.

The fear was that they were so disaffected that they would join any local uprising. Instead, they were hoisted off to Lunenburg, where they were given axes, some supplies, and cheerful good wishes. The industrious newcomers quickly made a livelihood by selling firewood to Halifax, and by 1760 the provincial governor was able to report to England that they were already reimbursing the Crown for "the heavy expense incurred" in shifting them to this new land.

Their descendants are still here, still industrious, neat, and prosperous.

They became wonderful shipbuilders, sailors, racers — the schooner *Bluenose* first won the International Fishermen's Trophy in 1921 and defended her title successfully four times against American would-be usurpers of the crown. She came to an ignoble end, however, clapped out, converted to cargo, and sunk off the coast of Haiti with a load of dynamite aboard. Then she was resurrected, both on the back of the dime and in the form of *Bluenose II*, a replica of which cruises the waters off Nova Scotia to promote tourism. She is in harbour this day, drawing oohs and aahs, but I cannot convince a gaggle of visiting Americans that the original *Bluenose* ever defeated a Massachusetts schooner.

"Not a Canadian ship beating an American ship," scoffs a large, pink gent from Boston. "You made that up."

I offer to get him documentary proof.

"Don't bother," he says. "I wouldn't believe that either."

I do not offer to sock him in the nose, not because he is so pink but because he is so large.

Power from the Moon

The next day, we ramble across the waist of Nova Scotia, along a lupine-lined highway that skirts Kejimkujik National Park, to Annapolis Royal. It used to be Port-Royal, so named by Samuel de Champlain in 1604 because he found the setting so pleasing. It was the oldest permanent European settlement north of Florida — St. Augustine, its elder, was founded in 1565. Port-Royal, being so handy to the sea, was captured by the British, then retaken by the French so often that the historian William B. Hamilton wrote that it "has probably changed hands more frequently than any other parcel of real estate on the continent." (One of the many forts built, and then destroyed, here was thrown up by Charles de Menou d'Aulnay in 1636. We will meet him in chapter 4.) Finally, the British took it permanently in 1710 and promptly renamed it Annapolis Royal, either in honour of Queen Anne or to confuse the French the next time around — take your pick.

We are here not to visit the many historic sites (I pause here to recall the story of the Nova Scotia public-school boy who wrote on an exam paper,

"Nova Scotia has few industries; its main product is history"), but to visit the nearby Tidal Power Project, which Harry Bruce, one of Nova Scotia's, and Canada's, finest writers, used to refer to as the Great Tidal Bore. Since the beginning of this century, Canadians and others have looked at the masses of water that slosh back and forth in response to the tug of the moon's gravity, and said, "Hey, here is a huge source of untapped power. How about it?" Here is the theory:

Twice every day, as the tidal current surges against the east coast of North America, two billion tons of water pour into Passamaquoddy Bay, a twenty-five-kilometre inlet off the Bay of Fundy, next to Annapolis Royal. This tidal thrust lifts the bay eight metres in places, and the poised water represents a fantastic storehouse of untapped energy; this is energy, moreover, that is unaffected by floods, droughts, ice jams, or silting, the bugbears of river-placed hydro plants. Schemes to tap this power have appeared since 1919, and I wrote an article in the *Star Weekly* in 1963 announcing that the dream was on the verge of fruition — "Next spring, if all goes well, scows will begin chugging across Passamaquoddy, and the massive engineering job will begin." Wrong again.

Actually, it began in 1980, was finished in 1983, was opened (by Prince Edward) in 1984, cost $33 million to build, and is now returning $1.5 million to Nova Scotia Power every year. It produces 20,000 kilowatts when it is running at maximum capacity, and a total of 35 million kilowatt hours annually, or about one percent of Nova Scotia's electrical needs. The cost per kilowatt is still slightly higher than that for oil-produced power, but the margin narrows every year, and there is no contribution to global warming from tidal power. The facility, which looks a bit like a spaceship poised to jump over a dam, contains only one huge one-way turbine. Water flows through on the high tide, is blocked off by the dam, and is dropped through the turbine at low tide. (Two-way turbines can take off power when the water rushes up and again when it rushes back down, but they cost more.) It works about six hours a day. Well, what do you expect? It's a public servant. However, the thing to bear in mind is that this project proves the feasibility of tidal power, which is all it is designed to do. It was installed here in the first place to pave the way — or prepare the water — for a really humongous tidal project that would string 128 two-way turbines straight across the entire Minas Basin, between the towns of Cove Road, on the north side, and Minasville, on the south, site of the world's highest tides. When completed, if ever, this project would produce 20 billion kilowatts of power annually — three times as much as Nova Scotia needs — take twelve years to build, and cost a nifty $33 billion. That is presuming a historic first: that a project this size comes in on budget.

And there's the rub. "We don't seem to be able to find the investors," explains Eileen Rice, the young woman delegated to answer questions from Nosey Parkers like me. "You have to be able to show you have secure markets for the power we don't need." It seems a pity that in a world where folks will plop down billions for Internet investments floated on little more than faith and folly, we cannot round up enough suckers — pardon me — *investors* to plunge into this baby. If people will buy unicorn horns, why not shares in the Miracle of Minas Basin? Tidal power appears to be a good thing — clean, economical, environmentally friendly — in the main, and it is never going to run out. As long as there is a moon, there will be tides. But no one wants a series of small projects scattered about the place, soaking up mere millions. The "Doers and Dreamers" (Nova Scotia's new motto) want to redraw entire sections of the landscape, whack dams across twenty-five kilometres of open water, sign contracts for billions and billions of dollars; it is the modern way.

As we pull away from the Passamaquoddy Tidal Power Project, I have a feeling that decades from now, people will still be saying what a wonderful thing it would be if only we could tap into the potential power of the tides hereabouts.

Another Romance: Fake but Fortunate

If you come out of the Annapolis Basin, turn right, and drive along Highway 101 past Wolfville, you soon find yourself within minutes of another of the historic sites that make a mockery of the notion that Canada's history is dull. I speak of Grand Pré National Historic Park, the site of what was once an Acadian village, before the expulsion of 1755. This was a form of ethnic cleansing — similar to the treatment accorded the Beothuk of Newfoundland, come to think of it — centuries before the term was invented. The Acadians first moved into Grand Pré ("great meadow") in 1680, threw up dykes to allow them to work the rich lowlands, and prospered and multiplied. By the middle of the eighteenth century, cleared lands around the village extended for twenty kilometres, and the Acadians were producing wheat, cattle, sheep, peas, flax, barley, and babies. By that time, there were more Acadians at Grand Pré than there were British at Port-Royal.

In 1713, when Acadia was ceded to the British, the residents were asked either to take an oath of allegiance to the Crown or to leave. The vast majority decided to stay, but most would take only a conditional form of oath — the condition being that they never be asked to take up arms against the French. Life became more complicated for them when, in 1744, Britain and France once again declared war, and the French, from Quebec and Louisbourg, once more tried to take what was to them Acadie.

A mainly peaceable people who wanted nothing more than to get on with the business of raising crops, the Acadians were caught between the demands of the French governors of Quebec, who warned that any of them who refused to support France would be "dealt with by force," and the British, who regarded them as a potential enemy within.

The solution proposed to this problem by, among others, William Shirley, the governor of Massachusetts, was to expel the Acadians entirely, get rid of them, scatter them on the wind. He saw himself as governor of the joined colonies of Massachusetts and Nova Scotia, and he didn't want to have to look after a bunch of French. One suggestion was to replace the Acadians on the rich farmland with displaced Highland rebels, but Shirley was not in favour; he wanted the land for his New Englanders. In 1747, Shirley dispatched a force of 450 New England soldiers up to establish a blockhouse in the village, but an early winter prevented that, and the soldiers were quartered with resentful villagers. A handful of young Acadians slipped away in the dead of night to Chignecto, where the French garrison was wintered, and the result was a surprise attack on Grand Pré on the night of February 7, 1747, during which many of the New Englanders were slain.

However, the survivors rallied, beat off the attack, and a truce was called; under its terms, they were able to march back to Port-Royal. Now the cries to expel the Acadians became louder and fiercer, but the British feared this would lead to a wholesale insurrection, so the decision was taken to do nothing until there was a peace with France.

Then British policy changed again, to one of incorporating the Acadians into English Nova Scotia by settling British farmers among them, but this was never done. Instead, leaders of the Acadian community were summoned to Halifax by Col. Edward Cornwallis and ordered to sign a new and stronger oath of allegiance, which would force them to take up arms against their fellow French. They refused and were imprisoned.

By this time, the French were in general disarray and retreat; the time had come to act against the Acadians "with perfect safety," as a contemporary document put it. They would be dispersed among the English colonies to the south. Lt.-Col. John Winslow was dispatched with 400 New England troops, and they took up headquarters in Saint-Charles Church on August 19, 1755. Then, on September 5, 418 males from Grand Pré and vicinity obeyed his summons to meet in the "masshouse."

Once there, they were told that they were under arrest, their lands and goods all forfeit to His Majesty; they were to be expelled. It was, Winslow told them — a copy of his proclamation is right here on the site — "His Majesty's Final Resolution to the French inhabitants of this his Province of Nova Scotia." Now there is a phrase with an eerie modern ring.

It took the rest of that year to deport more than 6,000 Acadians, not only from the Minas Basin, but from all over Nova Scotia. Families were torn apart, their members never to see each other again. Their villages were razed to the ground. Thousands more were expelled from the area right up until 1763, when peace broke out once again. Most of them were shipped off to the southern colonies, where they were sometimes refused entry. The House of Burgesses of Virginia sent its quota off to England, and they wound up on the outskirts of St-Malo, in France. Others wound up elsewhere in Europe, in the West Indies, as far away as the Falkland Islands. When the deportation was done, the Board of Trade Commissioners in London explained the heavy financial charges incurred with a phrase that might have come right out of Bosnia or Kosovo. The removal of the Acadians was "absolutely necessary for the security and preservation of the province."

Some of the locals escaped and took to the woods, and a few joined the

French forces at Chignecto, making all the dire predictions about them seem valid.

The site today is one of idyllic beauty, with rolling lawns, deep meadows, a reconstructed church, and the dykes marching solemnly across the landscape to the sea. There is also a handsome statue of Evangeline — who was never here, never existed, but "whose fictional tale," Mike Charlton, one of the guides here tells me, "brought a forgotten reality to life."

Evangeline Was a Socko Hit

Indeed, even the story was forgotten, beyond a minor mention in Thomas Chandler Haliburton's *History of Nova Scotia,* published at Halifax in 1829. Then, in 1839 or 1840 — the date is uncertain — the Rev. Horace Lorenzo Connolly, rector of St. Matthew's Episcopal Church in South Boston, told the poet Henry Wadsworth Longfellow a story he had heard from "a French Canadian." It concerned a young couple, Acadians, who were separated on their wedding day at Grand Pré and shipped off to New England. The bride spent the rest of her life searching for her lost husband, and at last, when she was old, found him on his deathbed, in Louisiana, of all places. She died, of shock, beside him. Well, it was a tearjerker, right?

In 1847 — the mere blink of an eye in poetical terms — Longfellow published *Evangeline: A Tale of Acadie.* He gave the bride and bridegroom names — "gentle Evangeline" and "Gabriel Lajeunesse, the son of Basil the blacksmith" — found himself a lolloping rhythm, and got the thing off with a line ("This is the forest primeval") that became one of the most famous in the English language. And never mind the fact that the forest primeval had been knocked down, wiped out, burned up by the Acadians long before. Longfellow never went near the place.

Evangeline was to its day what the movie *Titanic* is to ours: a box-office smash. And it did, indeed, revive the story, with all its pain and glory. In 1907, a local jeweller, John Frederic Herbin, an Acadian by descent, purchased the land believed to be the site of the original church of Saint-Charles so that it might be protected. He erected a cross to mark the cemetery of the church, and later sold the land to the Dominion Atlantic Railway on condition that

Acadians be involved in the preservation of the site. A statue to the (non-existent) Evangeline was erected in 1920–21, and a memorial church was finished in 1930, with funds raised through the Société l'Assomption.

While I circle the statue of a grieving Evangeline, two elderly women from Quebec make the sign of the cross before it. This strikes me as rather weird, but not as weird as the time Joan and I, on a visit to St. Martinville, Louisiana, were confronted by a plaque on a tree that marks the very spot where Evangeline stepped ashore from a riverboat and saw Gabriel for the first time since the expulsion. There was just no use in telling folks that it never, ever happened, that Henry made it up.

Soon after we leave this place, thousands of local Acadians, and hundreds of thousands of others from all over the world, will be descending on New Orleans to join in the second Congrés Mondial Acadien, part of what has become a huge international celebration of the Acadian way of life. I hope they have a good meeting; it seems to me fitting that what took place here nearly two and a half centuries ago has not been allowed to wither away, almost solely because of the power of literary imagination.

3

Prince Edward Island

ANNIE, I HARDLY KNEW YE

We spent a day browsing the island — it's only 140 miles long by 40 wide — and swam in the sea by the soft-swelling sand dunes along the north shore. Red clay and green grass cover most of PEI; about 85 per cent of the province is open country, and there are no great forests. Tourist booklets like to call it the Million-Acre Farm, and the atmosphere is rural, peaceful and pleasant.

— STAR WEEKLY, APRIL 3, 1965

Confederation Bridge, the thirteen-kilometre span that lifts us across to Prince Edward Island, is a bane and an abomination — and a beautiful thing. We used to ride the ferry from Caribou, Nova Scotia, to Wood Islands or from Cape Tormentine, New Brunswick, to Borden; either way, it was a short drive after our arrival at the ferry terminal along the Trans-Canada to Charlotte-town, the capital (named to honour Charlotte, King George III's wife, after the

British took over from the French in 1763; before that, it was Port-la-Joie, a much more evocative name).

Our favourite ferry was the *Abegweit* (pronounced "a big wait," because that is what she so often entailed). In the tourist season, you couldn't get on the ship until you had put in a few hours of restful contemplation on the seashore, breathing carbon monoxide from the waiting cars and trucks. In the off-season, you could get on easily enough, though whether you would get all the way across was another matter. Still, there was the romantic idea of a ferry ride, the tang of the salt air, the cries of the gulls, the possibility — it happened to us, twice — that you would get caught in the ice and hang there in the middle of the Northumberland Strait, singing a chorus of "Stormy Weather" and hoping for spring. Now, you just wheel onto the handsome bridge that arcs overhead and seems to disappear into the sky, and before you can say "Bud the Spud," you are rolling down the ramp on the other side, ready for fun and frolic.

You don't even have to pay on the way over; the canny folks in charge wait until you are on your way back, crammed with Malpeque oysters and goodwill, before handing you a bill for $35.50, cash or credit card, for the two-way passage. You can, if you wish, still ride the ferry — but only the one from Caribou, and I don't know why you would. It takes about three hours when you work in the waiting, loading, and unloading, and it is available, special for you, for the knock-down price of only $47 a car. The ferry company asks you to calculate what you save in gas and wear and tear to make the price look better.

Agitation for a bridge went on for more than a century. In 1885, Sen. George Howland, one of the delegates who arranged PEI's entry into Confederation, proposed either a bridge over or a subway under the Northumberland Strait, but nothing came of it. Every few years thereafter, someone would produce a study showing that a fixed link — a bridge, a tunnel, whatever — would pay for itself, if looked at in the right way. This allowed politicians at both the federal and provincial levels of government to promise action on the matter every time a vote was called — the Pearson government actually went so far as to spend a few million on planning, which resulted in a handful of concrete abutments outside Borden, but nothing more came of it, and during next election the project was trotted out for enticement once again. Indeed, the bridge to PEI was one of this nation's earliest and most successful recycling projects. Will R. Bird, in his first edition of *Here Are the Maritimes*, published in 1959, quoted a PEI islander as saying, "They've spent millions without number up on the St. Lawrence Seaway to help a country already rich. Why can't they spend a few dollars down here and build us a causeway?"

The short answers were that it would take more than a few dollars — about $1 billion more — and that everyone, pro and con the link, knew that it would change PEI forever. A 1994 newspaper column contended that "a bridge or a tunnel would be Confederation's equivalent of AIDS." A more thoughtful view, in *Islands Magazine*, was that "the sense of being an island influences everything you do. But once you have a bridge, it is no longer an island. We will be like everywhere else. And if we are like everywhere else, you won't have any reason to come."

As to costs, the structure was projected to come in at $630 million when it was approved in 1987; that was the estimate of Public Works Canada. Well, you know how these things go. In the end, according to Strait Crossing Bridge Limited, the private consortium that owns it, the bill was $840 million in 1992 dollars; more than a billion in today's currency. The deal involved three development firms, one from Calgary, one from Montreal, and one from the Netherlands, which run the business, collect the tolls, and take the profits, if any. At the end of thirty-five years (in 2032), ownership reverts to the government of Canada.

As to the changes bound to come to the island, this was no inconsiderable point in all the years while debate raged; tourism is not the only industry on PEI, but next to agriculture it is the main one. Accordingly, as soon as we pull off the bridge, I charge into the information bureau — which is nestled among a neat little flock of shops that wait, like a catcher's mitt, just in the right spot — to ask Joanne, one of the guides, how the visitors, and the islanders, are taking to the new structure:

A number of people have come in to tell us they're afraid of it; they say it's too high and too windy. But most people say it is a lot handier than the ferry. Sometimes the winds are high, but the bridge has never been completely closed to cars; once or twice, the traffic has been one-way only, because of winds, and trucks have been banned entirely from time to time. But that's rare. . . .

The locals were resentful at first, because of the lost jobs on the ferry. But there are more jobs now; there are about as many jobs in this little area alone as there were on the ferry, and they go all year round.

Finally, as to staying away because Prince Edward Island is "like everywhere else," this crack could come only from an islander. It is one of the glories of our nation that none of its provinces is "like everywhere else," and the old magic of red soil, rolling roads, splendid sea views, and lush, green countryside exerts as strong a pull as ever. The Driver and I were sure we would (on behalf of the islanders, of course) resent Confederation Bridge, until we ran into several couples who said they had been heading for Quebec City, or Halifax, or Saint John, and had decided at the last minute, since it was so easy now, to run over to PEI instead. Moreover, a waiter in the dining room at the swish Prince Edward Convention Centre in Charlottetown reported, "I was afraid it would change things too much, but what really happened is that my wife and I can take our kids to see their grandparents in Sackville, New Brunswick, a heck of a lot easier than we ever could on the ferry."

In the first full year of the operation of the bridge, from June 1997 to June 1998, PEI tourism increased by about 20 percent; the next year, it went up another 30 percent, and the grumbling has come down a lot since then. However, the essential complaint that the new link will change the island forever is doubtless true. The hope is that it will make it easier to create jobs here, not only in tourism, but also in the manufacturing sector, with a road to market so swift and handy; the reality is that the tourism season will be extended, and the place will get more crowded.

When you pour 1.3 million visitors onto about 135,000 locals, on an island of 5,600 square kilometres, you begin to run out of elbow room. Driving down Queen Street, the main north-south drag in Charlottetown, we find ourselves in a mini-traffic jam, made slightly worse by the fact that everyone, seeing our Ontario licence plate, stops to let us by, which somehow seems to prolong things. They'll get over that.

Confederation: Lustful Smiles and Stern Denials

The tourist literature likes to boast that Charlottetown is "where Canada began," and the city motto is "The Cradle of Confederation." In a way, it is true, and we mustn't snicker. The theme of harmony is very much emphasized at Province House, cheek by jowl with Confederation Square, where they hand you a nice little pamphlet containing "A Brief Account of Confederation," which begins thus:

> Canada dates its birth from July 1, 1867, and its conception from September of 1864. The occasion was a conference to discuss the desirability of union of Britain's North American colonies. The place was Province House, in Charlottetown.

This leaves out the best part: at the time, PEI said, "Include us out, brothers, and we don't mean maybe." When the Canadian delegates disembarked from the *Queen Victoria* in Charlottetown harbour on September 1, 1864, Prince Edward Island was, in the words of P. B. Waite, the eminent historian, "a small, isolated, violent little bailiwick." It had agreed to a meeting with the other Atlantic colonies because it would have been rude to refuse, and suddenly it found itself lumbered with a proposal from John A. Macdonald to create a grand union of all the British North American colonies. Again to quote Waite:

> However, the truth was that no party or group [on PEI] could have taken up Confederation and survived. Personal recriminations, changes of heart, visions of a united British North America all had to bow before the fundamental fact that Prince Edward Island did not want to join any unions, and [it] had no intention of being forced to do so.

The islanders, of whom there were about 87,000 in 1864, were taken up with their own battles, then almost a century old. The root cause was the generous gesture of George III, who held a lottery on July 23, 1767. The prizes were sixty-seven townships of 20,000 acres each — virtually the whole of what was then the Island of St. John (the name was changed in 1799 to honour

Prince Edward, Julie's pal, whom we met in the last chapter). The parcels went to royal hangers-on, lords, military officers, politicians, high-ranking civil servants, wealthy merchants, and business adventurers. They were given 999-year leases for land that they could divide up into farms and then rent out for prices that began, for a hundred-acre farm, at five pounds a year — "the value of one steer or milk cow." With luck, a landlord could collect a thousand pounds a year — an enormous amount of money at that time — for land for which he paid nothing. And did nothing.

When Walter Patterson, an Irishman from Donegal and a palpable rogue, was appointed governor-in-chief and captain-general of St. John in 1769, only a handful of parcels had been developed, although they were all supposed to have been settled and quit-rents paid on them. A quit-rent was a fee paid by the freeholder in lieu of services he might otherwise be called upon to perform. Such rents were almost uniformly charged on Crown lands in the eighteenth century. The absentee landlords of St. John, while they refused to pay such rents themselves, tried to collect them from their tenants.

At this time, the island contained 271 inhabitants, 68 of them English and the rest French. When Scots were imported — shoved off their Highland holdings to allow sheep on, as part of the enclosures — they quickly discovered that they could not own any land. It was all taken, and all they could do was pay for it. Most of them decamped. The absentee landlords in England, meanwhile, would neither send in settlers — and they certainly were not going to go themselves — nor pay the rents. This meant that there was no money to pay for public servants, and the first chief justice of the island, John Duport, apparently starved to death, according to W. S. McNutt, the noted historian and author of *The Atlantic Provinces: The Emergence of Colonial Society.*

Sir Walter Patterson called a general assembly to take some action on the matter of the non-paying landowners in 1773. It met in a Charlottetown tavern, consisted of eighteen delegates representing the island population, and was described as a "damned queer parliament." Its first piece of legislation was an attempt to either roust the absentee landlords or make them pay quit-rents, but it was disallowed by the Colonial Office. Seeing that he could not lick the landlords, Patterson decided to get into their racket himself.

In 1780, he appointed his brother-in-law as receiver of quit-rents and his private secretary as deputy receiver, and he brought escheatment proceedings against the absentee landlords — he would take away their land for not fulfilling their obligations. As a result, six whole and eight half townships — 230,000 acres in total — were marked for sale at auction. To keep this from falling into the wrong hands, viz. any other than his own, Patterson kept shifting the time and place of this auction. In this way, he and his friends managed to grab up about one-sixth of the island at bargain-basement prices.

By this time, the first of the 500 Loyalist families who would eventually seek shelter in St. John had arrived, and when they found out that the rich acres they thought had been ceded to them were instead in Patterson's control they raised hell in London, where it mattered. Patterson was ordered to give back the land, and he agreed to do so. But he didn't. Instead, he called another election to put a new assembly in place to validate his land grab. Alas, the whole plan came unstuck, not on the legal merits of the case — there were none, on either side — but because Patterson had made a powerful enemy of Peter Stewart, the chief justice, by making Stewart's wife his mistress. Stewart put up his son, John — a.k.a. Hellfire Jack — to lead the opposition to Patterson, and their faction won a majority of the assembly seats.

Next, Patterson hit on the idea of luring in enough Loyalists to overwhelm the Stewart faction by offering them land owned by the absentee landlords. The Colonial Office went so far as to forgive the quit-rents on this land to help things along. But the landlords would not cede the necessary titles. The Loyalists moved in, all right, but the landlords hung on to the deeds. And they kept on trying to collect from the Loyalists the quit-rents they refused to pay themselves. Oh, yes, and Patterson refused to give up the land he had grabbed for himself, though he was repeatedly instructed to do so. Finally, in 1786, he was ordered abruptly home, investigated, disgraced, and chucked into Newgate Prison for debt. His successor, Col. Edmund Fanning, a Loyalist, succeeded in having a law passed to escheat the neglected properties, but the paperwork was somehow "lost" in the Colonial Office and no action resulted.

At the time of the Confederation initiative, this battle was still raging between and among the factions on the island and their lobbyists in London. The absentee landlords' dilemma would not be settled until new legislation escheated almost all of the original land grants in 1877. Thus when the

Canadians landed, full of hope and expense-account champagne, in 1864, the whole idea of most Prince Edward Islanders was to throw off the old landlords, not to take on a new one in Ottawa. They were also — at least some of them — distressed, or said they were, by what they claimed was the debauchery of the Canadian delegates during the conference. One newspaper, describing a ball held on September 7, 1864, broke into the kind of stuff you expect to see these days — albeit in less fanciful prose — in *Frank* magazine:

> *Pleasure panoplied in lustful smiles meets and embraces exuberant Joy. . . . The fascinating dance goes merrily, and the libidinous waltz with its lascivious entwinements whiles in growing excitement; the swelling bosom and the voluptuous eye tell the story of intemperate revel. . . .*

Well, you get the idea. There are no lascivious entwinements in the Province House pamphlet's version. Instead we get this:

> *When the Maritime colonies agreed that their own union should be the subject of a conference, Canada seized the opportunity and her governor wrote to as [sic] if the Canadians might attend. The Maritimers set a date, September 1, 1864; the Canadians were invited to attend and the rest is history.*

In this version, the delegates next met in London, England, in 1866. "Once again, there was agreement. . . ." Well, there was, but not among the PEI delegation. They stayed home and sulked. Prince Edward Island would have nothing to do with Confederation until her own economic problems grew so huge that she was faced with a stark choice: Confederation or bankruptcy. In addition to a general economic depression, the island faced its own financial problems, most of them connected with the building of a railway. The province had guaranteed the bonds for construction, but these could not be sold, and the result was likely to be ruination.

By this time, 1873, it had become fairly established policy to demand trinkets from Ottawa as the price of union, and PEI wrung a number of concessions out of the process. One was an increase in the annual subsidy offered by Ottawa; another was the provision that the island would always have as many senators as members of Parliament, and never less than four of each. Ottawa also took over the railway guarantees, and it provided $800,000 to get the process of buying out the absentee landlords under way. And of course, there was the promise of year-round communication with the mainland — the ferry service.

When Lord Dufferin, the governor general, arrived in Charlottetown to receive the island into Confederation, he was greeted by an arch of welcome on which were carved these words: "Long Courted: Won at Last." Reporting his visit to Prime Minister John A. Macdonald, Dufferin wrote:

> *I found the Island in a high state of jubilation and quite under the impression that it is the Dominion that has been annexed to Prince Edward.*

Maritime Union: Popular Everywhere but the Maritimes

Exalted and uplifted by the version of smooth unity that flows around the hallways of Province House, I begin to ask people I run into how they feel about Atlantic Union. If Confederation has been so good for you, I wonder, how about a mini-Confederation, which is how the whole process started anyway? I am willing to exempt Newfoundland, which has rebuffed the notion so often it has become boring, and contemplate merely a threesome of Nova Scotia, New Brunswick, and PEI. This was not a scoop; I wrote my first article on this subject when I was but a slip of a boy, in 1969, for *Maclean's* magazine. The argument hasn't changed one whit from that day to this. I wrote then:

> *By welding three scattered economies together, union would provide bet-ter markets and a magnet for industry — more jobs for those whom farming and fishing can no longer sustain. The political muscle that could be exerted on behalf of the nearly 1.5 million people of a united Maritimes — it would be Canada's fifth-largest province — would be far greater than the combined muscle of today's Nova Scotia, New Brunswick and PEI. It would mean better public service, paid for from*

savings made possible by ending the pointless duplication of provincial governments. The Maritimes today groans under the weight of more officialdom than any area in Canada — 136 provincial legislators, 38 cabinet ministers, three lieutenants-governor and 24,106 civil servants look to the needs of a population two-thirds the size of Metropolitan Toronto.

In the pocket of my jacket as I prowl the hallways of Province House is a copy of an article from the May 1999 issue of *Atlantic Progress,* which begins, "The time has come to unite into one Atlantic Province," and ends:

The Atlantic provinces can't continue down the road they're on. It only leads to greater political marginalization and squabbling among our governments. The difficulties inherent to political unification are a small price to pay for better government, more political power, and fewer impediments to business.

Trevor Adams, who wrote the 1999 piece, and I both made arguments that were cogent but irrelevant. In the first place, any proposal for union, whether Maritime or Atlantic, is essentially a proposal to ask the vast majority of the provincial politicians, and the civil servants who advise them in such weighty matters, whether they would prefer cyanide, hanging, or a shove off a steep cliff on a dark night. Most of them will be put out of work. Why should they bust a gusset trying to bring that about? In the second place, there is not — how shall we say? — a groundswell of opinion in favour of banging all the heads together and hoping for the best. My little survey draws this kind of response:

"Is this a TV stunt? Where's the camera?"

"Who gives a fart?"

"It isn't going to happen, so why worry about it?"

"My God, I thought the subject was dead and buried years ago."

"If you expect us to want to be swallowed in a union bound to be dominated by Nova Scotia and New Brunswick, forget it."

And:

"Only a mainlander would go around asking a dumb question like that."

I get a rather better response when accidents lead me to people who are not from PEI itself. Two Japanese businessmen who say yes to every question I ask them, and bow a lot, go into the "For Atlantic Union" column. So do three visitors from Britain — two men, one woman — to whom it is clear that "it doesn't make sense to have three governments for such a tiny population." A young woman tourist from Halifax says, "One province makes sense, because the leader would be speaking for more people, and maybe then Ottawa would stop screwing us." But her companion, an earnest young man with a slight stutter, disagrees bitterly. "You have a premier's meeting. Instead of four spokespeople from the Atlantic area, you have one. Then you'll see some screwing. T-t-talk s-sense."

Overall, on the subject of Maritime Union, I wind up with seven for, about twenty-seven (hard to read my own jottings) against, and a dozen non-committal shrugs. If any sort of Maritime, or Atlantic, union ever takes place, I conclude, it will be in the same circumstances that drove Confederation forward — not dreams of glory, in other words, but fear of collapse. It seems that when outside forces threaten the nation — when the separation of Quebec becomes headline news, for example — Maritime Union arises anew, like the phoenix. Otherwise, it lies among the ashes. In the 1970s, when the Quebec Question was on the front pages, a regional study strongly recommended the union, with these words:

> At the present time, the uncertainties which confront the Maritimes arise from two dangers: the possible political disintegration of the nation and continued substantial economic disparities in relation to the rest of the nation.

The only result of that study was the formation, four years later, of the Council of Maritime Premiers, which was to meet four times a year, positively and without fail, to edge forward the process of interprovincial co-operation. It meets once a year, if that, and deals with such subjects as a lawsuit filed by PEI against Nova Scotia, in which it's alleged that the larger province promised to have its police officers trained at the Atlantic Police Academy in

Charlottetown and isn't doing so, and that Nova Scotia wants to pull out of the Atlantic Lottery Corporation, the region's most profitable sucker-sifting operation, because it thinks it could make more on its own.

This whole region is on an economic upturn; disasters like the collapse of the cod fishery are more than offset by such other developments as the huge offshore energy projects and, in PEI, the Confederation Bridge itself, which brought in $1 billion in construction costs and is now bringing in more tourists and making it easier for local industry to compete with the rest of Canada.

This Story Is a Potboiler

We run across more and more signs on this trip that the regional economy is improving to the point where the young folks who once couldn't wait to strap on their running shoes and get the hell out of here — by ferry, bridge, or broomstick — are now finding it worthwhile to stay home instead. Let me confine myself to one single example of many.

Scott Chandler is twenty-four, young, bright, energetic, holder of a degree in business marketing — just the sort who used to bail out of here as fast as possible. When I go out to meet him at the Paderno Kitchenware Factory in the West Royalty Industrial Park on the outskirts of Charlottetown, he is wearing a grey shirt, a very wide, very bright tie, a cheerful smile, and a pair of shorts. He looks as if he is auditioning for the Michael J. Fox role in *The Secret of My Success*. He is the sales manager for Paderno, a very classy, very costly ($123 for a small frying pan, at full price) line of hand-finished, stainless-steel pots, pans, braziers, double-boilers, sauté pans, and steamers.

If that name, Paderno, sounds Italian, it is. The business was started by an Italian pot-maker who came here in 1979 to take advantage of a low-paid, highly skilled workforce. But the timing was wrong, and the business lost money. In 1985, a local group bought in, and also ran into problems. They decided to hold a going-out-of-business sale in downtown Charlottetown, shipped most of their goods down there, slashed prices, and the merchandise "went like gangbusters."

Chandler speaks in awed tones. "Now we hold clearance sales two or three times a year, and they represent 70 percent of our business. We expanded; now we own four outlets in PEI, sell through 350 other outlets in Canada, plus one we own in Maine, and we're selling on the Internet." Because Paderno is still going, the PEI company cannot use the name outside Canada, so in the United States the kitchenware is sold as Chaudier, and that has become a second, and slightly costlier, line in Canada. Today, Paderno sometimes runs three shifts, usually two, and employs a workforce that is never lower than fifty here, plus hundreds in the outlet stores.

"I always wanted to work here, meant to work here," Chandler says. "And I can."

Since he seems to be in a good mood, I ask him to take part in my provincial union poll; his eyes go blank. "I have no reaction to the idea of Maritime Union at all," he says.

Did Somebody Say Green Gables?

Of course, the *really big* industry in PEI is not in Charlottetown, but along the island's north shore, near Cavendish. This is where we find a national park (since 1987) in memory of another heroine who, like Evangeline, never existed — but don't say that out loud. *Anne of Green Gables,* L. M. Montgomery's classic tale of a spirited little red-headed orphan sucks in tourists from Japan, Germany, the United States, Britain — all over the world — and they will buy almost anything connected with the tale. They are known as "Anne" products, and I count 269 of them in one catalogue alone.

In one Anne of Green Gables store, which sells books, records, tapes, jams, relish, tea bags, dolls, cut-outs, clothing, and quilts, you can lay out $1.50 for a bottle of A of GG Raspberry Cordial (too sweet) or $2,900 for a rocking horse. The Japanese, in particular, can't seem to get enough of this stuff, and while we are lolling about one of the museums at Cavendish — museum, forsooth — refusing to pay to see the artifacts of a girl who never knew corporeal form, people keep rushing hither and thither, getting ready, it turns out, for a giant double wedding of Japanese couples who have come here to tie the knot. It will serve them right if they have red-headed kids and have to explain *that* to Tokyo.

Could the fascination with Anne have something to do with Shinto, do you suppose? After all, one of the great principals of Shinto is Amaterasu-o-mikami, who, though not a redhead, "emerged and restored light to the world." Always the aim of our Anne. "Oh, beech tree," she trilled in *Anne of the Island,* "what a wondrous thing you are!" Old Man Beech Tree, he don't say nuthin', but Anne, not discouraged — it was one of her best things, not being discouraged — went on to tell the tree her most intimate secrets, and what a sap Gilbert was. What gets me, and this is purely professional jealousy, you understand, is that aside from *Anne of Green Gables* itself, I don't believe Lucy Maud could write a lick. Her books were turned into a wonderful musical and then a magnificent television series, that's all. Hell, if I had Megan Follows to play a principal role in one of my books — say, *Shrug: Trudeau in Power* — well, watch my smoke is all I can say.

In accounting for the wild popularity of Anne, we must acknowledge that the setting is half the battle. The entire north coast of Prince Edward Island (now, officially, so help me, Anne's Land/*Au Pays d'Anne* in the *Prince Edward Island Handbook*) consists of pretty little towns flung into dappled dales beside the sea. Seagulls wheel and mourn, and great blue herons stalk with dignified decorum among the bulrushes, then flap with slow and awful majesty up and away above the sandbanks. There are pretty copses, flower-filled meadows, wandering streams, sunny glades — it softens the brain and makes us swallow a line of story sweet enough to cause cavities on contact.

The folks in charge have made serious attempts to keep some sort of grip on what can be turned out under the Anne label — we have been able to avoid Anne vibrators and Green Gables garbage bags — but you can still buy Marilla's Pizza at Matthew's Market in the Avonlea Plaza. You can pay eighty dollars (eighty, that is not a misprint) for the Anne of Green Gables Treasury Experience — lunch is thrown in — during which you can "make a straw-bedecked straw hat like Anne's, create fragrant sachets, paper lace ornaments and button crafts," and "re-enact Lady Elaine scene from *Anne of Green Gables.*" (Presumably, you lie down in a leaky punt and get wet.) And here is something I would like Anne's views on — right next to the farmhouse in Cavendish that inspired the setting for the original book (built in the mid-1880s, once the home of cousins of Montgomery's grandfather, Alexander Macneill), we now have the Green Gables Golf Course. I do not recall anything about Anne playing golf, but we might have a go:

> *The perky little redhead swung at the ball, missed, swung again, missed again, swung a third time, and sent the ball fourteen feet to the left, into a gooseberry bush.*
>
> *"Oh, Marilla," she sobbed. "This is just the most tragical thing that has ever happened to me! Goddamit."*

When the Driver and I first rambled through here, Anne was not a big item, as you can tell from the epigraph at the opening of this chapter. Not among the top ten. However, the (deserved) success of her musical and the TV series have made her into something of a monster, and while I do not blame PEI for cashing in, whenever we come across another tourist trap festooned with red hair and a gaping grin, I wonder if the world would really have been worse off if she had missed the damn train for Bright River.

L. M. Montgomery's Harrowing Life

Her creator, Lucy Maud Montgomery, had a hell of a life herself, what with one thing and another. Born in 1874 at Clifton, PEI, a village near Cavendish that is no longer on the map, she was left behind after her mother died of tuberculosis in 1876 and her father moved to Western Canada.

Lucy was brought up by her mother's parents, in the house that became the setting for *Anne*. She was a very lonely little girl, with no siblings and few playmates, so, like Anne, she made up imaginary companions. She went to Prince of Wales College in Charlottetown before going west in 1889 to join her father and his second wife in Alberta. She hated the second wife, of whom she wrote in her diary, "Mrs. Montgomery — I cannot call her anything else, except before others for father's sake."

That wasn't going to work, so she returned east to finish her education at Dalhousie University in Halifax, then worked briefly as a journalist. She came back to PEI in 1891 as a teacher, and promptly fell in love with Herman Leard, the son of the family with whom she boarded at Lower Bedeque, outside

Summerside. What made this awkward was that she was already engaged to her second cousin, Edwin Simpson. She didn't love Edwin, but she didn't think Herman, a farmer, was really her kind of people either. She had been working at writing from her youngest years, and by this time had managed to sell a few items to the Charlottetown paper. Herman did not approve.

She broke her engagement to Edwin, dumped Herman, and after her grandfather's death in 1898 became a housekeeper to her grandmother for nine years, all while continuing to pour out stories. In 1906, she became engaged to a dour Presbyterian minister named Ewan MacDonald; she didn't love him either, but he was considered a "suitable match," and she was, after all, creaking into her thirty-third year. Her first novel, *Anne of Green Gables,* was completed in 1908, but it was turned down by five publishers in a row before it was finally accepted by L. C. Page of Boston. It became an almost-instant triumph, selling 19,000 copies in five months. She began work at once on the first of seven sequels, none of which ever came anywhere near *Anne.*

After her grandmother's death in 1911, Lucy Maud married MacDonald, who whisked her off to do her duties, as a minister's wife should, in Norval, Ontario, the first of a number of postings for him. Her husband suffered from severe bouts of depression, not improved when one of their three sons died at birth. Lucy Maud spent most of the rest of her life juggling her duties as a housewife, Sunday school teacher, and minister's helpmate with writing twenty-four books and hundreds of short stories, essays, and poems, as well as active involvement with writers' groups.

In 1939, under the many constant strains, she ceased writing, even in the journal she had begun when she was fourteen. She quarrelled with her publisher, withdrew from her friends, and ceased correspondence with the pen pals she had built up over the years. She died two years later, sad and bitter. While she sold many copies of her books, Montgomery was ignored by the critics and never treated as a serious artist. They may have had a point, but you could not expect her to see that, and it added greatly to her sense of grievance. It was not until the 1970s that she was rediscovered (at least, *Anne* was; the rest of her works were dragged along in its wake), and her first novel was turned into a musical, a ballet, and a TV mini-series. To say nothing of a cult industry. She has now been translated into seventeen languages and sells by the millions. People probably make more on Anne T-shirts than Lucy Maud ever made on the novel.

Needless to say, you will get no more of this real story in the cradle of her island than you will get the lowdown on Confederation. Hereabouts, life is all gas and gaiters, and they will sell you the gaiters with an Anne logo on the side.

There Is More to PEI than Anne — Honest

Despite what it seems to say in the tourist brochures, there is no law compelling you to go anywhere near Green Gables, or the Lucy Maud Montgomery Birthplace, or the Anne of Green Gables Museum at Silver Bush, or the Lucy Maud Montgomery Heritage Museum, or the Lucy Maud Montgomery Cavendish Home Site, or even the golf course. Instead, you may choose to put in your time at Prince Edward Island National Park, where the sand dunes are high, the beaches splendid, and the walks wonderful. There is swimming, of course, but the chill water sweeping in from the Gulf of St. Lawrence often puts me in mind of James Joyce's line about the "scrotum-tightening sea," and you may choose to paddle along the shoreline instead.

There are splendid places to stay, including and especially Dalvay-by-the-Sea, a Victorian inn perched on its own lake within a clamshell throw of the ocean. Prince Edward Island is so small, and her roads so fine, that you can sweep from end to end in a couple of hours, so you may wish to visit the only homely town on the island, which is O'Leary, up past Summerside, straight south of Tignish — it makes a nice change.

The browsing and sluicing are of a generally high standard, and one of the island's very prettiest towns, Stanley Bridge, also houses the Spot O' Tea restaurant, owned and run by Catherine McKinnon, whose husband, Don Harron, may be on hand to join her in a dinner show. He wrote the original book and lyrics for the stage production of *Anne of Green Gables* and can tell you all you want to know, or even more, about the redhead.

On our way back to the Confederation Bridge, I am grousing about the way PEI seems to bend itself into a pretzel over Anne when the Driver says, sternly, "No. Stop complaining about Lucy Maud and remember about Paderno, and people coming home to work instead of drifting off, and the way the place looks, and how cheerful everybody seems compared with earlier visits. Smile!"

It hurts, but I smile, right up until they ask me for $35.50 just to drive over a bridge.

4

New Brunswick

SWEET (DEAD) MARIE AND OTHERS

New Brunswick is a tourist's delight; accommodation is plentiful, the road is smooth and fast, the scenery is superb. At Moncton, we watched the tidal bore and rode Magnetic Hill; at Fredericton, we visited the Beaverbrook Art Gallery and Christ Church Cathedral. We watched the nut-brown Pokiok Falls step daintily down to meet the St. John River at Pokiok, and crossed the world's longest covered bridge at Hartland.

— *Star Weekly, April 3, 1965*

The Trans-Canada leads you off the Confederation Bridge and past Cape Tormentine to a key junction at Aulac, New Brunswick. To your left is Nova Scotia, to the right opens the entire Loyalist Province, as it likes to call itself. We turn left, not to go back to Nova Scotia, but to call in at the provincial tourist bureau, where, in the high season, there is usually a kilted piper, in full regalia, marching up and down and playing "Road to the Isles," "Scotland the Brave," or "Will Ye No' Come Back Again." The last of these gents I interviewed, years ago, was named something like Boris and came from the Highlands of Kiev. Never mind, it is the plaid that counts.

We are too early for this treat, if that is the right term for bagpipes, so we turn right and head down a narrow road to Fort Beauséjour. We are after lunch, not lessons, but we are out of luck. For many years, the Drury Lane Steakhouse, Alvira Smith, Prop., stood here and dished up some of the finest steaks, chops, lobsters, and clams in the region. Gone, alas, with the snows of yesteryear. I go into the fort instead.

This star-shaped structure overlooking the Bay of Fundy was built by the French in 1751 to defend their interests in the area. A look at the map shows why — it dominates the Cumberland Basin, and thus Chignecto Bay, key to control in a day of sea transport.

In 1754, Beauséjour was a considerable thorn in the side of the British, and as we saw in chapter 2, sorties from this area could prove deadly. Besides, the expulsion of the Acadians, already in contemplation, was not going to mean much if they could simply hike up here and seek shelter. Accordingly, Charles Lawrence, the British commander at Halifax, sent Col. Robert Monckton down to Boston to arrange a joint foray against the fort with Governor Shirley. "Shirley loyally cooperated," says the text. Let me rephrase that: Shirley could see in the project large profits from military and naval construction contracts, as well as loot and glory, and he wouldn't even have to risk his neck, so he sent Col. John Winslow of Plymouth up with 2,000 troops in a fleet of thirty-six vessels to join 500 British regulars at Fort Lawrence, five kilometres north of Fort Beauséjour. The two nations were not at war, by the way, but this was a detail overlooked by either side from time to time.

The siege ought to have failed. The French fort was built according to the very latest European plans, with nice, thick walls, underground casements to protect against heavy artillery, a pentagon shape to ensure that enfilading fire would greet invaders no matter where they came from, its own deep wells, and lots of food and ammunition for its defenders — 200 French regulars and hundreds of Acadian and Native allies.

But the British, I am sorry to say, did not play fair. Instead of marching up to the gates, knocking, and taking their medicine like men, they, on the morning of June 4, 1754, slipped through the swamp next door in small boats and clambered up the slope overlooking the fort.

When you walk over the ground today, this slope seems to have been raised here for this very purpose; we are not to know why the original designers didn't see this. The invaders soon had their heavy artillery in place, and proceeded to bombard the fort from the wrong side. *"Mon Dieu!"* said the French, and they meant it. On the morning of June 16, a shell burst through one of the casements, which was thought to be proof against such things, and killed four men, upon which the French commander, Duchambon de Verger, said to hell with this and surrendered. For which action, of course, he has been excoriated by every right-thinking military historian, although he was merely exercising common sense.

He knew that no reinforcements were to be sent; he knew that there was no way to escape, and now his supposedly impregnable fortress was proving to be pregnable after all (in part, it is suggested, because he diverted some of the funds that should have gone to defence construction to building himself a château in France). So he very sensibly lined up the lads and marched out beneath his colours, and the British marched in. (Fort Albany, on Hudson Bay, is another of our historical forts where common sense overcame military custom; the British would get all settled down inside, look out on the water and see arriving a French fleet they couldn't lick, and surrender. A few years later they would bring their own, bigger fleet, and the French would surrender. And so on. I like to think that these historical precedents explain how Canadians came to be such a peaceable and commonsensical people.)

Fort Beauséjour became Fort Cumberland, and Lawrence, the British commander, saw all those New England volunteers sitting around, eating their heads off, and with months left to serve — they had signed up for a year — so he gave the nod to Colonel Winslow to march off to Grand Pré and expel the Acadians.

The Mary Celeste

I wander around the fort in the sunshine, admire its casements, now reduced pretty much to rubble, and visit the little museum attached to the place, where I am astonished to come across the answer to a maritime mystery that has puzzled me for decades. I refer to the fate of the *Mary Celeste* (often wrongly spelled "Marie"). It really had very little to do with this place, except that the ship, a brigantine, was built nearby, at Spencers Island, and christened the *Amazon*, in May 1861. Then it was bought by an American, renamed the *Mary Celeste*, and on November 7, 1872, cleared New York harbour for Genoa, Italy, carrying 170 barrels of alcohol. The ship's complement of ten consisted of Capt. Benjamin Spooner Briggs, his wife, two mates, a cook, a steward, and four seamen. The ship was found nearly a month later, on December 4, drifting aimlessly between Portugal and the Azores. Not a soul was on board, but three sails were set. The captain of the ship that found her, the barquentine *Del Gratia* (a barquentine has three masts; a brigantine, two) told a wondrous tale of overhauling the *Mary Celeste* as she wandered over the open ocean.

When he looked through his glass, he could see no one on board, so he sent a mate across to investigate. The mate reported that he found everything as if the ship had been abandoned only moments before. There was breakfast on the cabin table and the tea still seemed to be warm. The cargo was intact, the cash box untouched; one ship's boat was gone (the other hung in her davits), yet no survivors were picked up. There was a metre of water in the hold, and bedding was wet from water washing in through an open skylight. At least four men would later present themselves as survivors of the mystery vessel, but none could describe her interior details.

The *Del Gratia's* skipper put a crew on board, and both ships went to Gibraltar, where a court of inquiry was unable to plumb the mystery. According to the law of the sea, the *Del Gratia's* captain and crew were awarded salvage of £1,700 — a small fortune in those days.

That was that, for about forty years, until there appeared a magazine article that claimed to solve the mystery. It stated that the captain and his first mate had been engaged in a swimming race while everyone else watched. A sudden shift in the wind sent everybody overboard, where they were eaten by sharks — except for one man, who was washed ashore in Africa. One problem with this story was its claim that the reason the gang got swept overboard was that the ship's carpenter had built a special little "quarter-deck" for the captain's two-year-old daughter, and it was from this contraption that the swim-meet spectators were swept. The problem with that was that the captain and his wife did not have a child. There was a baby mentioned in the ship's log, but it was a baby grand piano, not a baby person. Ah, well.

A literary cult built up around the renewed mystery; it produced a number of articles and books, even a movie, all providing wonderful explanations. My favourite was the one that said the booze on board threatened to explode, for some reason, so everybody jumped into the sea and drowned. Another story explained that a cloud of poison gas welled up from the sea, somehow, and that made everybody decamp, dying. There was even one in which an angel with a sword took over.

As recently as 1991, a local writer, Stan Spicer, wrote:

> The reason for the disappearance of all on board the Mary Celeste *will never be known. The brigantine sailed the seas until 1885, when she drove ashore on a reef off Haiti. She carried her secret with her.*

And then some spoilsport came along with a new investigation based on interviews made years earlier in England with an old man who turned out to be the ship's cook. He told an horrific tale. Captain Briggs, he said, was a weak and foolish man who could not handle the crew. His first mate could, but he was frequently drunk, so that didn't help. During a storm, the piano came loose, sheared across the deck, and killed the captain's wife. Distraught, he hurled himself into the sea. Then another crew member was killed in a fight, and the second mate and two seamen decided to get out while the going was good, so they took one ship's boat and left. This left on board the cook and three seamen, who were — guess what? — actually members of the *Del Gratia*'s crew. An arrangement had been made to lend these three to the *Mary Celeste* in New York; they were to be taken back when the voyage was finished.

When the *Del Gratia* came up to the *Mary Celeste*, her captain, seeing an opportunity to collect a little salvage money, decided to declare that he had found her derelict, and he made up all the stuff about breakfast on board and warm tea to add a touch of verisimilitude, as W. S. Gilbert says, to an otherwise bald and unconvincing narrative. His crew members, who stood to share in the booty, were not about to spill the beans, any more than the deserters — presuming they ever learned what happened.

Got away with it, too, the son of a gun. It is a little disillusioning to come across so mundane, and evil, an explanation for one of the great mysteries. I preferred the angel with the sword. But I am left with another puzzle. Why is all this stuff — articles and artifacts from the *Mary Celeste*, in their own extensive corner of the display area — sitting in a museum in the bowels of Fort Beauséjour? That's easy, a museum guide explains. One of the men who made generous donations to the museum happened to be a nut on the subject, so he left his collection here.

The Kid from Hell Meets His Match

Back on the road, we follow the Trans-Canada past Moncton — home of Cy's Seafood Restaurant, the tidal bore, and Magnetic Hill. We skip these this time, with reluctance. We have not tried the gravity-defying slopes of Magnetic Hill since the days when it cost about a quarter, instead of two bucks. It was always fun to slip the car into neutral and watch it seemingly roll uphill.

Moncton is a city full of energy and, in the winter, full of snow; seated astride a series of hills about midway between the Bay of Fundy and the Northumberland Strait, it attracts every storm in the area. We are sorry to skip on past with the weather so clement; it would be nice to lunch at Cy's — great rolls and a lobster stew made in heaven — but we are on our way to Sussex instead. Sussex, the so-called dairy capital of the Maritimes, produces, along with about fifty delicious flavours of ice cream, one of the world's finest peanut butters (Baxter's), and it is also the home of the Bluebird Motel and Restaurant. We are here for the fish chowder, coleslaw, butter tarts, and the bittersweet memory of one of the Driver's great triumphs.

This happened a few years ago, on one of our continental swings. We had just started to tuck into lunch when a commotion at the doorway announced the arrival of the Kid from Hell. He was about four, wore shorts, a shirt, and a snarl. He was accompanied by Momma, Poppa, and two sisters — ten and twelve, at a guess, nicely dressed, beautifully behaved. The K. from H. didn't like them, didn't like the waitress, didn't like the table by the window where she put them, didn't like anything. And he made the mistake of sticking out his tongue at the Driver on his way past us. Within minutes, the joint rang with his complaints, laments, and criticisms while Momma offered the weak, and pointless, explanation that the little bundle had been a surprise and, you know, with two girls to see to him, he seems to have become somewhat spoiled. He was the fault of Mother Nature, apparently.

The K. from H. knocked over his water glass, knocked over one sister's glass, punched the other sister, screamed when Momma said, "Now, dear . . ." and tried to kick the waitress. Finally, Poppa decided it was time to do the big, manly thing, and he leaned over and said, "Now, if you act up one more time, I'm afraid I'm going to have to take you straight out of here."

The K. from H. gave him a calculating look.

The Driver called out, "Don't worry about it, kid. He's bluffing."

The K. from H. kicked his sister. Poppa, his bluff called, picked him up and huffed out of the restaurant to sit on the front stoop, where the K. from H. blubbered — but offstage, bearably — and Poppa sulked while the rest of us had a lovely, quiet lunch.

We passed them on our way back to the car — the kid was stuffing a chocolate bar into his face by this time, but Poppa had nothing at all.

"Such a sweet little boy," the Driver murmured as we walked by. "Why don't you take him inside?"

Benedict Arnold and Other Loyalists

On this visit there is no uproar, just the cheerful gabble of a local service-club luncheon. It is only about an hour from here to Saint John, a soul-lifting drive along the Saint John River valley, past places with names like Apohaqui, Nauwigewauk, and Quispamsis. The Loyalists, who came pouring into the province during and after the American Revolutionary War, kept many of the First Nations names. This province, like PEI, Ontario, and Cape Breton, was formed specifically to hold these refugees from war, many of whom had already suffered at the hands of patriot mobs in Boston, Charleston, and New York. Most of them were dumped unceremoniously on the shore at the lower cove of a town-to-be called Parr Town (named for the then governor of Nova Scotia, John Parr, who hoped, in vain, to add this area to his own province). They were expecting to find ready-made homes, cleared lots, and supplies.

Instead, they found tents, axes, and trees. They were mostly urban dwellers or small-town folk, and they had no notion how to fend for themselves in a wilderness. That winter, many of them died of cold and hunger. Mary Fisher, a Loyalist who wrote of living in tents in two metres of snow along the river, added this:

> How we lived through that awful winter I hardly know. There were mothers, that had been reared in a pleasant country enjoying all the comforts of life, with helpless children in their arms. They clasped the infants to their bosoms and tried by the warmth of their own bodies to protect them from the bitter cold. . . .
>
> Graves were dug with axes and shovels near the spot where our party had landed, and there in the stormy weather our loved ones were buried. We had no minister, so we had to bury them without any religious service, besides our own prayers.

To make things worse, many of the Loyalists who cleared land, erected makeshift shelters, and put in crops at Parr Town in the spring were later told that they would have to give up their land to make way for other Loyalists with better connections, and that they would have to shift themselves a hundred kilometres upriver to St. Anne's — the settlement that was to become Fredericton — with winter coming on. They might have rebelled — some thought of it — but they had seen enough of revolution, so they moved. Some of them ate poisonous weeds and died; it must have been a bitter ending to escape the wrath of mobs and armies and be felled by a trailside berry or root. Some had planted potatoes when they first arrived, and then dug them up again to eat. And everyone waited for spring, when provisions would arrive. By a miracle, they did. That first winter ended with many dead and many embittered, but with many others ready to forget the trials and tribulations and get on with the business of planting crops and beginning a new life.

The Loyalists who survived all these upheavals gradually became adapted to the new land. They learned to catch fish and shoot pigeons, and they made the fiddlehead into a provincial delicacy. One of the most extraordinary of this extraordinary bunch was Benedict Arnold, the former head of West Point, who offered to sell that fort to the British for £20,000. They paid him only a little under £7,000, but then, they didn't get the fort. Instead, he became the archetypal traitor to his country. He appears to have been motivated mainly by pique. A trader and hardware merchant in his native Connecticut, Arnold raised his own regiment early in the Revolutionary War and helped to take Fort Ticonderoga with Ethan Allen.

Although, or perhaps because, he had little military training, he proved to be a brilliant soldier, and he invaded Canada in 1775 by way of the Maine forests. He was wounded at the battle for Quebec, in the unsuccessful assault on December 31, 1775, when Richard Montgomery, his co-commander, was killed. Arnold kept up the siege until spring, then retreated with his army to Lake Champlain. There, he built a small fleet of vessels, so the British obligingly stopped long enough to bring up their own shipping. By the time they arrived, the American army had melted away south and escaped. Despite his successes, Arnold was not popular, in large part because he had a head the size of Carpenter's Hall and an insatiable appetite for money. (He would later put in a claim for war reparations from the Crown; it was pointed out that he had already collected his share when he was paid to betray West Point.) George Washington recommended him for a major generalship, but Congress balked and the rank went instead to five brigadiers of junior rank; lesser soldiers, but better politicians.

Arnold continued to run up a series of brilliant victories, especially in the Saratoga campaign, where his relief of Fort Stanwix played a significant part in the American success. However, when he was made commander in Philadelphia (and married Peggy Shippen, of Loyalist family), he was court-martialled for a series of battles with the civil authority. Washington reprimanded him but, by way of compensation, made him commander of West Point. By this time, Arnold was in a permanent snit over the way he had been treated, so he arranged to let the British march in, in return for a commission in the British army and some cash. The plot was discovered, and his go-between, Maj. John André, was caught and hanged, but Benedict Arnold was tipped off and escaped. Later in the war, fighting for the British, he led two savage raids against Virginia and New London, Connecticut.

Arnold went to England after the final British defeat at Yorktown, but he was not comfortable there. He had never been to England before. He moved to Saint John in 1787, and received a grant of land as a Loyalist. He lived there for four years but was not able to either make a fortune or get along with his neighbours, so he returned to London in 1792. The next year, he fought a duel with a British nobleman who called him, correctly but not very tactfully, a traitor. At the duel, Arnold, who was now fifty-two, a little past his prime, fired one shot and missed; his opponent did not fire back.

He lost much of his money in various stock swindles and died in modest circumstances in 1801, leaving behind a wife, a mistress, five legitimate children, and two bastards, who had stayed behind in Canada. They were mentioned in his will and left sizeable amounts of money, but there was not enough in the estate to meet all the demands on it, and his wife scooped the lot instead.

An Invasion of Killer Commandos

It is not surprising that I have the military much in mind after we check in at the Delta Hotel in downtown Saint John (which, in Saint John, is called uptown — go figure). I am standing in a little lobby on the fourth floor, by the elevator, waiting, fairly patiently, amid a gaggle of pre-teen boys wearing red jackets, white shirts, grey slacks, and wide smiles. Not a gaggle, it turns out, but an out-of-town choir, here for a performance at the New Brunswick Museum. The elevator still hasn't come.

"Somebody forgot to feed the hamster," cracks one kid, and they all fall about.

"What do you think of Saint John?" I ask them.

"Neat," says one kid.

"Cool," says another.

"Dumb," says a third.

"Why dumb?" I want to know.

"Aw, Billy thinks everything is dumb," one of the older kids explains.

"Yeah, especially you, Fraser," Billy retorts.

"Cheese!" says another kid, and silence descends. He looks behind me, where four soldiers in combat fatigues march noisily up the hallway in arm-swinging, boot-stomping glory, wheel smartly, clang to a halt, and snap to attention. This is purely for the kids' benefit; last time I saw these warriors, they were slouching around downstairs, looking for postcards to send home. They are British troops, here for an exercise at Camp Gagetown, sixty kilometres away. As we saw in St. John's, soldiers apparently don't forage out from tawdry tents or grim barracks when they invade foreign lands any more; they stay in hotels. The elevator arrives, the door opens, the soldiers march in, about face and stand there, glaring, as the door seethes shut on them.

"Ta, lads," says one, and they disappear.

"Wow!" says a choirboy. "Those were commandos!"

"They can kill with their bare hands," exults another.

"Or feet," I say. "Did you see the boots?"

Another elevator arrives, and we ride down in awed silence. I can tell that Saint John has gone up considerably in Billy's estimation, thanks to the killer commandos.

Or possibly, clerk-typists.

I wander down the hill to the waterfront, to look in at the Market Square, which houses, along with several fine restaurants, the provincial museum, the Saint John library, and a tourist kiosk. Market Square is not where the market is — that would make things too simple. That is up the hill, on King Street, the oldest continuously operating farmers' market in Canada. There are six separate stands at that market selling dulse, or to put it plainly, seaweed. Locals swear by the stuff, which, although it tastes like something off the bottom of a rubber boot, is reputed to be good for everything from keeping cats out of your garden (it would certainly work on me) to keeping you healthy. I promise to visit this market again another time, but today I want to look over the new market, where there are boutiques, milling crowds, and high up on one wall, an illustrated plaque that reads:

In 1631, Charles La Tour established a trading post and fort on the Green Mound. The fort was captured by a rival trader, d'Aulnay Charnisay, in 1645. La Tour was away in Boston at the time of the attack and his wife was in command of the fort. By her heroic defence Madame La Tour became known as the heroine of Acadia. It was said that she was impris-

*oned by Charnisay after the battle and in less than three weeks Madame
La Tour died of a broken heart.*

I am so incensed by this mistelling of one of our great stories that I charge
into the information booth at the corner of the square and ask the woman
who trembles at me over the counter whether she believes this tripe.

"It is the generally acknowledged story," she says. "I learned it in school."

Marie La Tour: The True Story

Françoise-Marie Jacquelin, daughter of a doctor in a small town about 200
kilometres south of Paris, married Charles Amador de Saint-Étienne, sieur de
La Tour, through a marriage contract signed December 31, 1639. They were
not in love, had never met, and the ceremony itself was conducted by proxy,
in Paris, while Charles remained in Acadia. He was forty-six, and needed a
wife and heirs; Marie was picked out for him by his agent, Guillaume
Desjardins, who had written orders to "seek out and request for us in marriage
a person suitable to our condition." (This lovely quote is from M. A.
MacDonald's book, mostly about Charles, called *Fortune & La Tour*.) She was
comely, young, and available, since her family lacked the means to provide her
with the kind of dowry that would have made her a better catch. Marie stood
to gain wealth from the deal — she was promised an inheritance fund of at
least 10,000 livres. Soon after this, La Tour, who described himself as "governor and lieutenant-general for His Majesty in all the coast and province of
Acadia, country of New France," obtained, by means of a handsome bribe,
paid in 1640, a monopoly on all fur-trading rights in the Bay of Fundy.

By one of those errors in bookkeeping that crop up from time to time when
money changes hands, the same rights were also given, via another bribe, to
Charles de Menou, sieur d'Aulnay Charnisay. The two men set up shop right
across from each other; La Tour built a fort on what is now the waterfront of
Saint John, and Charnisay, as we saw in chapter 2, built one at Port-Royal, just
across the water. They then settled down to snarl at each other and see who
could cheat the Natives more.

In 1643, Charnisay decided to settle the issue, and he sailed across with a gang of mercenaries to attack Fort La Tour. Charles was not much use in the subsequent battle, but Marie rallied the troops, personally raised the family flag, and led the defence. A doggerel poem later recorded Charnisay's reaction as the flag went up and a cheer broke out at Fort La Tour:

> *The dark-brow'd d'Aulnay heard it as he paced*
> *his deck in pride;*
> *And cursed the sound, and cursed La Tour,*
> *and cursed the adverse tide.*

You don't hardly get poetry like that any more.

Charnisay had obtained papers ousting La Tour from his fur-trading rights and possessions; he was able to do this because he had better connections at court than La Tour did. He read the condemning documents out and set up a siege, but Marie and Charles slipped past in a tiny boat and legged it for Boston, where they hired their own gang of mercenaries. Marie was a Huguenot, although Charles was a Catholic, and this helped them to round up allies among the Protestants of Massachusetts, as long as they were paid. When they returned to Fort La Tour with their own little army, Charnisay exited, stage left, snarling, "Curses, foiled again."

Then Charles sent Marie over to France to enlist aid among the Huguenots of La Rochelle and see what she could do about getting his trading rights back. But Charnisay had also gone back to France, and he had her proclaimed a rebel by the Queen Mother and set out after her with a writ of arrest. Marie escaped again, this time to England, where she chartered a vessel for home. Charnisay managed to intercept and search this ship off the coast of Acadia, but Marie was hidden in the hold and escaped once more.

The ship went on to Boston, after making a couple of trading stops along the way, and did Marie thank the captain brokenly? Did she hell. She sued him for dawdling on the way, and a Boston court awarded her £2,000 in damages. With this, she was able to buy and outfit three small ships for the final leg of her trip back to Fort La Tour.

In February 1645, while Charles was again away cheating the First Nations people, Charnisay attacked once more, and again Marie led the defence. (She is pictured dressed in a breastplate and helmet, looking like a Valkyrie, but apparently there was no historic basis for this. Pity.) After four days of battle, it became clear that her outnumbered garrison could not hold out, and when Charnisay promised to spare all the inhabitants Marie surrendered the fort to him. Should have known better. Once inside, Charnisay hanged every man in the place and forced Marie, with a rope around her neck, to watch.

The authors of *An Historical Guide to New Brunswick* would have us believe that "the shock was too great for her, and her noble spirit was completely broken. In three weeks she died, and was buried near the scene of her heroic fight." If you believe that, I can sell you shares in Bre-X. Does she strike you as the wilting type? The librarians at the New Brunswick Archives, where I first heard this story, harboured a dark suspicion that, in the words of Eliza Doolittle, "Oi think they done the old girl in."

Charnisay drowned in 1650. Served him right, too. He was travelling in a canoe with a servant whom he had earlier ordered beaten. When Charnisay begged for help, the servant obligingly towed him ashore, but carelessly neglected to keep his head above water.

In the meantime, Charles La Tour had decamped to where the air was safer. First, he went to Boston, where friends and allies loaned him money and a ship. He took the money, dumped the crew of the ship on the ice-bound shore of Cape Sable, and sailed up to Quebec, where he stayed for four years, trading and, no doubt, avoiding any visitors from Boston. However, once he heard that the coast was clear, owing to the attempt of his foe, Charnisay, to swim ashore underwater, La Tour hurried back to Port-Royal and married d'Aulnay's widow, Jeanne Motin. This settled all the questions about trading rights, and may have been our first corporate merger. The couple had five children, and La Tour succeeded in having himself reappointed as governor of Acadia. When the British took over in 1654, he was allowed to retain his post, and was given a grant of land by Oliver Cromwell. He retired to Cape Sable, dying either there or at Port-Royal in 1663. La Tour's biographer calls him a "survivor." I guess you could say that. Also a louse and a crook, as well as a fine figure in official history.

And Marie, according to this same history, was such a wimp that she perished of shame and fright, but — and here is the part that modern libera-tionists might note — she was never even called Marie La Tour. As was the custom of her time and station, she kept her own name and signed all documents "Françoise-Marie Jacquelin."

I give the woman behind the desk at the information kiosk the ten-second condensation of this, and then ask her for a map and directions to Fort La Tour. Thus armed, I stomp out of the place and go looking for the Green Mound. Bad move. It is raining lightly as I trudge along Water Street, cross the Harbour Bridge on Main Street, and duck back under the bridge on a tiny, dirty, windblown street called Fort La Tour Drive. Then it really begins to rain. Ah well, it is all part of the pity of the thing, for what I find at the end of Fort La Tour Drive is a bit of chintzy palisade, a chunk of snow fence slung across the road, and, beyond, two flags — one Canadian, one New Brunswick — drooping mournfully over a little square of logs. Not a fort, mind, just lengths of logs, four each way, to make a little pile beneath a sign that says Fort La Tour.

Behind me, up the hill, is Fort Howe, a splendid reconstruction devoted to the good name of Gen. William Howe, commander-in-chief of the British army that lost the American Revolutionary War. I do not begrudge Howe his memorial, even though he spent most of his war in Boston with his mistress, Mrs. Deborah Loring, known as the Sultana. After the British defeat at Saratoga, a patriot wag wrote:

Sir William, he, snug as a flea,
Lay all this time a snoring,
Nor dreamed of harm as he lay warm,
In bed with Mrs. Loring.

It was Saratoga, you may remember, that convinced the French the British could be beaten during the American Revolutionary War, and thus brought them in on the rebel side. Howe was withdrawn to England, where a some-what captious critic wrote that his reward for his services "ought to be a hangman's noose." Instead, he got a nice fort named after him, while Marie Jacquelin gets four lousy logs and a lot of dandelions. Is this right?

K. C.

The next day, when the sun shines, I am over my crankiness and we drive out to look at the Reversing Falls. Should have stayed away. The Reversing Falls, between the Trans-Canada Highway and Bridge Road in Saint John West, are formed, as every schoolchild knows, when the tide pours up and overwhelms the normal flow of the Saint John River on its way into Saint John harbour. They work their little trick in the very shadow of a huge paper mill, property of the Irving empire. It stinks. Well, paper mills do, don't they? The Irvings have spent a lot of money cleaning this one up, but it hasn't worked, and the stench is palpable as I walk around the little area marked out for visitors to look at the falls. A middle-aged gent is chewing on the end of a ragged cigarette and looking over the falls, so I ask him what he thinks of the stink.

"What stink?"

I wave my hands about.

"Oh, that." He leaps to the instant defence of the Irvings. "They're okay, you know. They make jobs. Outsiders may be down on them, but we like 'em."

"Where do you work?" I ask.

"Over there." He waves across the road to the mill.

Silly me. In this province, deference to the Irvings and their works is ingrained, which is possibly no surprise when you realize that the family founded by the tycoon K. C. Irving owns almost every media outlet in the province. It helps to create an atmosphere.

"Everything in New Brunswick that is worth owning belongs to either God, the government or the Irvings." That's not me, that is the late Alden Nowlan, poet, journalist, shrewd observer, and occasional admirer of Kenneth Conlin Irving, the boy from Buctouche who turned a family store into an international empire by hard work, shrewd dealing, and a ruthless disregard for anything or anyone who stood in his way. A Saint John lawyer who made a list of Irving holdings some years ago wound up with a chart more than a metre long, which is truly impressive when you realize that the secretive Irvings have always hidden as much as they could from the rude public gaze.

The holdings included pulp mills, paper factories, refineries, a chain of gas stations, a fleet of tankers, shipbuilding firms, a tugboat company, a bus line, sawmills, control of millions of hectares of forest land, radio and television stations, magazines, a book-publishing company, and every one of New Brunswick's five English-language daily newspapers. At the height of his power, the soft-spoken K. C. was accustomed to telling governments what to do, and to having them bend themselves into pretzels to comply. In return, he sent every member of the legislature a giant wheel of cheese at Christmas, as a goodwill gesture and a reminder. It was Irving's serious view that, as he put it, "New Brunswick is too small for politics." Instead, he would tell the boys what to do, and they would do it, avoiding all the mess, expense, and untidiness that democratic government brings in its wake.

When Gordon Fairweather, the liberal, if Conservative, politician from Rothesay, was attorney-general of New Brunswick, he annoyed K. C. by refusing to outlaw another pulp mill on the Saint John River, which Irving regarded as his own personal stream. That Christmas, Fairweather was left off the cheese list. He was always going to write his autobiography and title it *No Cheese for Christmas,* but he has yet to fulfil this promise.

When Liberals (gasp) got in, under Louis Robichaud, sweeping reforms were introduced, much to K. C.'s annoyance. At that time, the municipalities ran and financed schools, hospitals, and welfare programs. One result of this was that the poorer areas of the province — for which read, in the main, the francophone areas — were ill-served indeed. Robichaud introduced what he called the Program of Equal Opportunity, which had the province take over all these programs. Many anglophone New Brunswickers called the reforms Evangeline's Revenge, because they brought a measure of equity to provincial life, which was not welcomed everywhere.

The newspapers attacked the program, root and branch. The Saint John *Telegraph-Journal,* whose official and embarrassing motto for years had been "The Maritimes' Greatest Newspaper" — embarrassing because, if true, it said something ominous about the quality of Maritime newspapers — now adopted a new, unofficial motto, which the then premier Richard Hatfield put this way: "If there's a government here, we're against it."

The editorials, which for years had consisted of variations on the theme of "no comment," suddenly became daily diatribes against not merely the Robichaud government, but every sort of government interference into the public weal. New Brunswick's emergence as a modern, bilingual province was achieved in the teeth of almost every shred of advice, cajolery, admonition, argument, and defiance that K. C. could bring to bear. And when he lost, he took his bat and ball and went away.

Irving was a man of many talents, no doubt about that, but he held his province, and country, in such contempt that once it was clear that he could no longer command governments, he departed for Bermuda, where falls not either sleet or snow, or — more important — the heavy hand of the taxman. When he ducked out in 1971, the *Telegraph-Journal* defended him this way:

> *Mr. Irving has not escaped to a hideaway taking tax-free millions with him. Instead, he has apparently left the province to assure that industries will continue to exist and to operate, providing jobs for thousands of New Brunswickers.*

When Ottawa removed succession duties in the 1970 budget, New Brunswick imposed estate taxes. The empire was going to have to disgorge some of the immense fortune amassed during K. C.'s lifetime, and he wasn't having that. He might have been down to his last few hundred million. His heirs might have had to sell some of their companies to competitors, and it was one of the standing rules of K. C. that while his newspapers might trumpet the glories of free-enterprise competition, his own business technique was to acquire a stranglehold on whatever field he went into and either gobble up his competitors or render them harmless. Worse, the government, which was known to be profligate, spendthrift, and wasteful, except when it was giving a leg up to one of the Irving concerns, was likely to fritter away a percentage of K. C.'s hoarded millions on medicare, schools, and other fripperies. When Irving ducked out of town, it was naturally a matter of great interest to New Brunswickers, so the bold journalists of his own papers tracked him down in Bermuda and returned with this bulletin, quoted with approval in Douglas How and Ralph Costello's hagiography, *K. C.*:

> *I am no longer residing in New Brunswick. My sons are carrying on the various businesses. As far as anything else goes, I do not choose to discuss the matter further.*

Case closed. For this bold stroke, the province of his birth, whose pockets he had just picked to the tune of many millions of dollars, fell right down and worshipped him. Still does. At his memorial service in 1992 (he was not buried here, but rather in the Presbyterian cemetery in Warwick, Bermuda), the Rev. Philip Lee said, "All New Brunswick weeps today." Not quite all. There were former employees, environmental watchdogs, government regulators, and media critics who were able to keep their tears in check. But he beat them all, and here is the proof of it: the Irving mill astride the Saint John River in the middle of the city, stinking its blooming little heart out.

A Duel Dried Up the Church Funds

K. C. was not the only mogul produced in this province — the place seems to have been run by barons from time immemorial. It breeds tycoons the way Victoria breeds roses. This is borne in on us when we duck up Highway 7 to Fredericton, the provincial capital. We do not go via the Trans-Canada, because Irving's spiritual heirs have turned a sector of this road into a toll highway, which so enrages the Driver that she cannot pass by without telling the money-collectors what she thinks of it. They don't care. By going this way, cutting across country instead of following the Saint John, we also avoid one of the worst stretches of driving on the Trans-Canada. Pretty, though. The narrow two-lane roadway from Jemseg through Maugerville to Fredericton is dangerous at the best of times, hideous when there is fog or snow, and drivers continue to race along as if they were on the 401.

The tiny settlement of St. Anne's Point (formerly, Fort Nashwack) was renamed Frederick Town in 1785, in honour of George III's second son, and made the capital of New Brunswick. Fredericton became a city in 1848, not because it deserved the status on the basis of its population, but because only a city could hold a cathedral, and the Anglican Christ Church Cathedral, begun in 1845, deserved the honour. This magnificent building, one of the best and earliest examples of Gothic revival in Canada, was modelled after a fourteenth-century church in Norfolk, England.

During the construction, as Colleen Thompson notes in her *New Brunswick Inside Out*, funds dried up as the result of a duel. This was fought between one of the officers stationed here and the brother of a Fredericton lady whose honour had been impeached. The Anglican bishop, John Medley, was incensed, and banned the duelling brother from his services; in retaliation, he was able to get funding cut off, and things looked bad until "Bishop Medley spent the night in prayer, and miraculously, the next day, adequate funds arrived from England."

This lovely church has its own ghost, said to be the widow of Bishop Medley — though why she is still wandering about is anyone's guess — and the wrong statue. In 1906, the Fredericton Society of St. Andrews asked the then bishop for permission to erect a statue of "the bard" on cathedral grounds. The bishop gave his assent because he thought they meant Shakespeare, or possibly Browning, but when a statue of Robert Burns suddenly sprouted on his lawn, he declared that he would not have that drunken lecher soiling church property. So the statue was moved across the road to the riverbank, and Robbie Burns stands with his head turned away from the cathedral.

Everybody loves Fredericton, which Bruce Hutchinson once called "the last surviving Home Town of America, uncorrupted and innocent as your grandmother." (His grandmother, not mine, who had her days.) It reflects this totally misleading air of innocence even today, fifty metres away from a provincial legislature that has perpetrated such nifties as the Bricklin Car Project, one of the smellier episodes in corporate finance.

Lord Beaverbrook: Contempt and Charity

Probably it is the sweeping green of the riverside walks that exudes the air of innocence — that and the magnificent homes set back on the stretch of waterfront known as the Green. Even the statue of Lord Beaverbrook, in the middle of the town's main square, seems to reflect solidity and integrity, although he was really a man of mercurial temper, arrogance, and contempt for most of his fellow creatures. "I always dispute the umpire's call," he said once.

Born Max Aitken, at Newcastle, New Brunswick, he made his first fortune in Canada by merging blocks of companies together to crush competition — banks, a cement conglomerate, and a steel conglomerate, formed with Sir

James Dunn. Then, at the age of thirty-one, he moved to Britain as secretary to Bonar Law, the only Canadian-born prime minister of Britain, eventually becoming an MP and then minister of information. He made a second and much larger fortune by sinking journalism to what was then a new low, in the London *Express*. When he was raised to the peerage, he took his title from Beaver Brook Station, near Newcastle, and adopted a motto that was all too apt: *Res mihi non mihi res* (Things for me, not me for things).

Once he had amassed what he considered to be enough wealth, Beaverbrook, unlike K. C. Irving, the most grudging giver God ever strung guts in, showered gifts on his native province. Within a stone's throw of his statue are the Beaverbrook Art Gallery and the Playhouse (built with funds from the Beaverbrook and Sir James Dunn foundations), just across from the Lord Beaverbrook Hotel.

The Beaverbrook Foundation, established with money from his estate, has been involved in literally hundreds of charitable, educational, and cultural projects around the province, as well as in Fredericton. The best thing about the statue, by the way, is that it was built by the nickels and dimes of New Brunswick schoolchildren, and when the Beaver unveiled it in 1957 he was moved to tears by this gesture.

Kings Landing

Our next stop, back up the Trans-Canada, following the Saint John River once more, is at Kings Landing Historical Settlement, the largest, and possibly the best, historical reconstruction in Canada. It began in the mid-1960s, when the building of the Mactaquac hydro project threatened to flood many of the oldest homes and farms in the river valley.

Some were moved, and more were recreated with money that came from both federal and provincial coffers during the 1967 centennial spending spree. The result is not just a museum and a few houses and stores, but an entire village, including stores, a church, a sawmill, a gristmill, a cooper shop, an inn, a farm, and, of course, a smithy. There is even a dock and a small schooner — called a woodboat because they were used to transport planks (called deals, which is where the name deal table comes from). The *Brunswick Lion* was built by hand in 1975 as an exact replica of a woodboat registered in Saint John in 1837.

All of these treasures are laid out exactly as they were in the eighteenth century, in the patterns of a typical Loyalist settlement of the time, and staffed by students and locals who dress in authentic costume and know the period from soup to nuts. (Many of them are bilingual, and I was entranced to discover, standing by while a young woman did her preliminary pep talk with francophone youngsters here on a bus tour, the French term for the Loyalists. It is *les Loyalists*. We live and learn.)

At the orientation building, I plunk down my ten bucks, pick up a pamphlet, check out a few exhibits, and walk out the door, smack dab into the middle of colonial New Brunswick. Every historical settlement tries for this effect, but I know of none that succeeds as well as Kings Landing. (And with this wonderful side benefit: while everything else is old-fashioned, lots of modern washroom facilities remain within easy scamper.)

As I trudge down a dirt path, off to my right is the Agricultural Hall, crammed with exhibits; farther along, I see a bonneted young woman hoeing in a field. She must be hot — the sun is blazing down — but she works industriously away, obligingly stopping long enough to let me take a picture and then bending to work again. Across the way, behind a rail fence, a mother and a girl of about five, also bonneted and costumed, are planting potatoes, and up the lane in front of me comes a large, lumbering horse-drawn wagon, speeding along at about two kilometres an hour at the urging of a large, behatted, genial driver. Anyone who wants to ride all or part of the way — there seem to be a couple of kilometres of trail — is welcome to board the wagon.

I amble down through a cool woods where I hear the sound of falling water, and I come upon a sawmill, water-driven, shingle-sided, and topped by four huge barrels. As I come up, I am greeted by a handsome, grey-bearded man with these words: "Do you know what the barrels are for?"

"I presume that's where they kept the booze," I say.

"Nearly right. Three of them are full of water, in case of fire. The fourth is full of rum, to make sure there is always someone on hand to fight the fire."

Harold Sanderson has been guiding here since retiring from a job selling real estate, and he loves it. He takes me on a tour of his mill, shows me how everything works — still works. This mill, built on the model of an early eighteenth-century place just up the river, provides all the lumber for the settlement's needs. Motion is transferred from the stream by a large watermill through huge gears that move a log carriage that shunts the tree trunks into position, where a vertical blade, driven by a different set of gears, does the work. Sanderson is as proud of it as if he had invented everything himself, and it is with great reluctance that I tear myself away.

However, thirst calls, and I have not the ambition to climb up on the roof, so I cross the river and find the King's Head Inn, which has a taproom downstairs and a fine dining room upstairs. I stay downstairs.

Climbing the hill beyond the inn a decent interval later, I hear the sound of horses, chuffing and clinking, and a saw, and as I turn the corner I come upon the damnedest sight: saw horses. Literally. Two horses are yoked together in the middle of what looks like a wagon. But the floor of the wagon is a treadmill. The operator lifts a lever, the floor of the wagon tilts up, and the horses, to keep from slipping backwards, walk forward; this turns the treads, which are geared to a saw that goes through a twenty-five-centimetre pine log in fourteen seconds by my watch. I tell the two young men operating this wonderful contraption that Rube Goldberg would be proud of them.

"This is how they sawed wood, no fooling," says one young man. He points out that all the wood burned on the site — several cords a day — comes courtesy of this ingenious machine.

"Looks great to me," I say. "How do the horses feel about it?"

"They don't mind," he says. "But if you'd care to spell them off a while, it can be arranged."

"Alas," I tell him, "I cannot tarry." Slipping quickly down the path, I round another corner and come upon another young man, this one leading two yoked oxen, Lion and Bright, hefty critters but not the flash-in-the-pan type.

"Are they good workers?" I ask.

"Anything a horse can do," their handler answers proudly, "they can do slower."

I have not left myself enough time — a day, not a few hours, should be the minimum to explore the wonders of Kings Landing, which shows us not merely how our ancestors worked and lived, but also what clever people they were and how they made ingenious use of everything that came to hand.

Another Romantic Tale

Taking a back road to the Trans-Canada the next morning, we come across two signs that sum up the bitter battle about toll roads in the Maritimes. The first, a neatly printed placard, reads:

STOP PRIVATE ROADS
1-800-END TOLL

The second is a crude, hand-lettered effort stuck on a post just beyond the first:

4 lanes
better than dead

We follow the Saint John River again, this time up to Grand Falls, where the rushing water plunges twenty-five metres into a beautiful gorge, and where, if you are of a credulous nature, the following wonderful events took place.

A beautiful First Nations maiden — well, of course she was beautiful — named Malabiannah, or possibly Malabeam, or even (who is to say?) Mabel, was walking along the riverbank one day with her lover when they were beset by raiding Mohawks, who demanded that they — Mabel and friend — lead them — the wicked Mohawks — to Mabel's village for a little rapine, spoils, scalping, etc. When the young warrior refused, the bad men killed him. Then the maiden, plotting revenge, said she would lead them to the village in her canoe, and they were to follow in their canoes.

Sure, said the Mohawks. Sounds good to us.

So they all got in their canoes and rushed towards the falls, and the dumb Mohawks, instead of saying, "Hey, what's that huge noise? Sounds kinda like a cataract?" kept right on paddling and went over the falls to their dooms, while the maiden slipped into a side stream — they didn't follow her into this, although they were supposed to be hard on her heels, pardon me, paddle — and escaped. Or else she went right over the falls, sacrificing her own life to save the village.

Just about every place in Canada that has a fall of water of more than ten metres has a version of this story, and it is a good one; we must not mock it, even if it assumes that First Nations people were all very hard of hearing.

With this uplifting tale and a lobster roll under our belts, we turn north once more. This is the road to Edmundston, but we are cutting across country towards Quebec on this trip and so are forced to miss, for now, the Republic of Madawaska, which was once a sort of no man's land.

Quebec once claimed the territory right down to Grand Falls, the Americans claimed it was part of Maine, and Fredericton didn't seem to care much either way, so there was a sense — still is, for some locals — that this pulp-mill town would be better off setting up shop for itself, under the county name, as a republic. It is an odoriferous town, thanks to its means of earning a living, but Americans swarm across the river to sample its fine seafood and to stroll through a splendid park in the middle of town, which is enchanting at night.

Another time. Today, we turn off at St-Léonard, where many Acadians settled after the expulsion, and which is now the centre of a bustling weaving trade, and plunge into the woods towards Quebec.

5

Quebec

THE LONG FAREWELL

The Trans-Canada Highway touches the ancient grandeur of old France and the modern splendour of new Canada; it stirs the silence of centuries-old settlements and rattles the windows of brand-new ones; it follows a route laid down by country lanes, city streets, superhighways and a bulldozer chugging through the bush.

— STAR WEEKLY, APRIL 10, 1965

The road from St-Léonard, New Brunswick, to the Gaspé region of Quebec is not part of the Trans-Canada; instead, it is Provincial Highway 17 that we follow as it plunges into what was once the forest primeval and is now, thanks to the woodlands conservation programs of the province of New Brunswick, mainly tree stumps. The logging industry has decided, no doubt from the best of motives, that what Canada really needs to make it a nation fit for heroes is to have a landscape bald as a billiard ball — possibly to facilitate traffic. The lumber companies seem to exercise a certain restraint along highways where their devastation is likely to provoke curiosity, even meddling, but give them a stretch of road where travellers are infrequent, and they let you know what they can do with their tree-chomping, landscape-levelling machinery. Not a pretty sight.

Along the road, we are overtaken, and in turn overtake, a number of large trucks — thirty-two wheels, some of them, real monsters. What they are doing here, we have no idea, unless, as we guess, they are avoiding any embarrassment that might crop up at an inspection station on the Trans-Canada by nipping down this side road. When one of these giants wants to pass, it comes up so close that its front bumper disappears in our mirror, and then the driver leans on the air horn. When we want to pass one of them, because a hill has taken its oomph away, the trucker moves out to straddle the centre line and hangs there. Time was when the big trucks carried large notices that read "I'll Help You Pass." Now there is a slight change in the motto — to "I'll See You in Hell First."

Near Campbellton, we cross a wide bridge, then turn west and north to run up the Bay des Chaleurs. We are now cutting across the base of the Gaspé Peninsula, along the Matapédia River, a gorgeous, tumbling stream that glints and splashes in the sunlight. We are back into dense spruce forest, which is interrupted by pretty little towns mostly named after saints, such as St-Tharcicius and St-Vianney, whose deeds are no doubt written somewhere in letters of bright gold, but who mean nothing to us.

The Driver wants to know why the French stick a hyphen in the middle of a saint's name, and I reply that she should instead inquire why we short-shrift St. George and St. Joan, rather than giving them their orthographic due. She says, "Huh?" Just then, we pass one of those Quebec signs that always delight me by mixing up the languages: Course de Stock-Car. We have learned two new French words on this trip already: Loyalist and stock-car. At this rate, we will soon be bilingual.

We are headed for Matane, on the St. Lawrence (Saint-Laurent), a fishing-cum-tourist town famed for good eating, scenic views, and windmills. Most of the windmills are not in Matane but about seventy kilometres beyond, at Cap-Chat, a village of 3,000. Highway 132, the main route to Ste-Anne-des-Monts, Roche Percé, and all the glories of the Gaspé, runs right smack dab through a score of towns and villages without bothering to slow down.

The posted speed is ninety kilometres per hour, and the locals obviously feel that it would be sissy to go any slower than this, manly to go faster, so we endure some heckling and honking when we decline to run right over villagers who wander across the highway, heedless of consequences. We assume the residents must achieve either adroitness or death by their teenage years.

The Answer, My Friend, Is Blowin' in the . . .

We come over a hill north of Capucins and there they are: scores of vertical-axis windmills spread over the slopes ahead of us. They look like three-bladed, pure white propellers that have somehow become detached from their parent airplanes and wound up on poles. Don Quixote would go crazy — between here and Matane, there are 133 windmills for him to tilt at. Alas for his lance, they are sixteen storeys high, with blades forty-eight metres long. This is Le Nordais Windmill Park, Canada's largest wind-driven electrical power project, one of the largest in North America.

This is not a patch on other wind-driven projects we have driven through — in the Mohave Desert of Southern California, you can drive for miles and miles while the windmills atop the hills wave at you and pass messages to each other. They stand silent until you approach, and then, one at a time, they begin to spin. "Here they come," they say, and the next batch on the next hill gets the message. "We see them," they reply.

The wind farm here in Quebec is nothing so grand as this — just a few score white propellers slung at intervals over the hills. Nevertheless, this is a good beginning to what could be, should be, one of the many small solutions to Canada's future energy needs.

Wind power has been known, and virtually ignored, throughout our history, possibly because it seems so simple and inexpensive. Give our engineers and contractors a nuclear plant — or even a tidal power project — that costs a few billion, and they leap into action. But to harness the wind, like so many Dutch tulip growers or Canadian agricultural pioneers, seems desperately dull to them. Where are the lush contracts, the scientific breakthroughs, the engineering challenges? All you have to do is stick a cleverly designed blade in front of the twenty-eight-kilometre-an-hour breezes that blow night and day along the St. Lawrence shore, hook the generators to turbines, and the result is 100 megawatts of power. Enough to provide the needs of a town of 10,000 people.

It is absolutely clean, totally renewable, environmentally friendly energy. It is not as cheap as producing electricity by oil — not yet, anyway — because the projects employing wind power are so small, and have not attained the efficiencies of scale that are bound to follow. There is another wind farm, near Pincher Creek, Alberta, that produces a minuscule 23 megawatts; but that's about it for Canada. In Germany, where there are a number of such projects, prices are coming down every year. Le Nordais, owned by the private company that built the $106-million facility, sells its product to Hydro-Québec, which has had such disasters with nuclear power that it is more broad-minded than many other provincial energy providers.

After gawking at the array of towers, we drive up the hill, over a ridge, and down a small side road to find the Big Daddy Windmill, 110 metres high. This one does not have propeller blades, but has instead two curved vertical shafts — it looks like an egg-beater on steroids. This is the largest single windmill of its kind in the world, and it may turn out to be the prototype for future developments. I am standing beneath it, wondering what kind of hurricane is needed to propel these monster blades, when suddenly, in a mild-mannered breeze, they begin to move. Soon, they are beating the air with a soft sibilance that is really rather eerie.

"Let's get out of here," I tell the Driver. "I think Big Daddy is trying to tell us something. In French."

A Moment in Matane

We drive to Matane, back down Highway 132, which has more thrills than merely the possibility of running over the populace. It reminds us of the country north of Lake Superior, where the road swoops and dips, and looking ahead you see nothing but an expanse of diamond-studded water, glistening in the sun. And then, just as it seems certain that you will tumble off into the drink, the road makes a shift, like a halfback hitting the line, and you are on dry pavement after all, hurtling down on the next episode. We check into our rather dumpy chain motel, and soon set off in search of somewhere more elegant to eat.

We find it in the motel where we should have stayed, the Belle Plage, plunked right on the St. Lawrence shoreline in downtown Matane. While we dine deliciously on fresh salmon and gaze out through huge windows across the river, our eyes are caught by an eruption of kids from the motel winging out onto the grassy knoll beneath the building beside us.

There are a dozen of them, ranging in age from about twelve down to perhaps three, evenly divided as to sex. They are dressed up, arrayed in their finery, the girls in long dresses and high heels that threaten to pitch them into the water at any minute, the boys in clean white shirts, with ties yet, and pressed pants, shorts for the tads, slacks for the oldsters of eleven or twelve. They are here for some relative's fiftieth wedding anniversary — golden balloons held aloft advertise this fact; they are marked, simply, "50me." Obviously, we have come to the time for long-winded speeches in the banquet hall inside, and some kindly, or wise, person has decided that things will go more smoothly if the young fry are given their freedom.

No one has thought to tie the array of balloons to the kids' wrists, although they are filled with helium and as bent on liberty as the kids. The first one breaks loose before the youngsters have been outside a minute, and when it streams skyward across the broad St. Lawrence its owner, a little boy of about five, lets out a wail that must be audible at Cap-Chat. An older girl promptly lets her balloon go, too, to make it into a lark, and soon every one of the balloons is aloft and away.

The kids swarm all over the place, find a beach where they can dabble in the river and soak their shiny shoes, clamber over two anchors — one a real iron anchor, about two metres high, off a ship; the other a stone replica, at least a metre higher — and then they find the hill.

This is a greenswarded knoll, five metres in height, quite steep, down which you can roll and get quite a thrill. The girls do not roll, of course, that would not be consonant with their high dignity; besides, it would rumple the duds. Instead, they stand at the top, rocking back and forth on their high heels for about a minute, and then plunge shrieking down the slope, waving their arms to keep their balance, and collapse at the bottom. Hook them up to a turbine, and the energy would match anything the windmills up at Cap-Chat can produce. The boys eschew such soft stuff, and lie right down on the ground and roll. Trouble is, the hill is so steep that they get going too fast, so they swing around and perform the last bit on their bums, sliding without decorum to the sand.

Then you have to clamber back up the slope to do it again. One of the older girls decides to help one of the younger lads, a sturdy youngster but small. He tries to get away twice, but she has him firmly by the arm, and she is going to be a help to him if it kills them both, so he rolls his eyes, gives her his hand, and they scramble up the slope. She runs down, he rolls down, and a glorious time is had by all.

After a few minutes of this, Poppa — somebody's poppa — comes wandering out of the motel. He has been told off to keep an eye on those kids and whatever you do, don't let them get their nice, new clothes dirty. Yes, dear. He is greeted by welcoming shouts, waves at the kids, and helps a couple of the larger boys, who have decided the grass slope doesn't offer enough scope. Instead, they climb up to the top of the stone anchor, slide down one side of it, and drop to the ground. If they slip, they will crack their little skulls. Poppa, who, whatever else he is, is not an insurance salesman, hands one kid who is too small to mount the pedestal below the anchor up to an older brother, or pal, and then catches him as he comes hurtling off the stone. This sport, while it clearly impresses the little girls, is perhaps a little *too* daring, and soon everybody is back to hurtling, howling, down the hill.

Poppa trudges away to watch the ferry from Baie Comeau, almost directly across the river, come putting into the terminal. It is a slow and absorbing process, and Poppa obviously feels that the clumsy ship sliding backwards into the dock needs his insight and direction to avoid calamity. Behind him, the kids are turning themselves into a joyous, sodden — the grass on the knoll appears to be damp — mass.

Then Momma appears, young, pretty, energetic, and mad as hell. She takes one look around and begins to bellow — at the kids, at Poppa, at the world. The kids stop, freeze in place, prepare to meet their doom. Poppa comes wandering back, and Momma tells him what she thinks of him, *nom d'un nom,* waving her arms to get her point across. He reaches out, pinions her arms, and gives her a kiss that quite literally takes her breath away. She gives a lovely, Gallic shrug, grins, and, arm in arm, they wander back into the motel while the kids go back to gathering grime.

Shortly before we came out to dinner, we were watching the news on television, watching pictures of kids just like this in Kosovo, tearful, frightened, cowering, with nothing behind them but tragedy and nothing ahead of them but hopelessness, and the contrast between those scenes and the one of these giggly little rats rolling down the hill at Matane stirs emotions too deep for utterance.

After a long silence, the Driver speaks. "I suppose that Poppa really is married to that Momma?" she asks. *Quel cynique.*

Danger, but Don't Tell the Stranger

The next morning, we take Highway 132 south, past lush, riverbank farms. Near St-Ulric, we spot two moose, a male and a female, peering over a farm fence, intently watching a flock of black-and-white ducks that have just settled down in a pond surrounded by hay. They look like a middle-aged couple, and I swear they nod as we whisk by.

Once we pass Rivière-du-Loup, we are on the Trans-Canada again. While we deserted it to check out the Gaspé, it went straight across from Edmundston to Rivière-du-Loup, then turned itself into Highway 20, the Autoroute Jean-Lesage, a wide swath where anyone foolish enough to observe the speed limit of one hundred kilometres an hour is liable to be run right over.

Decades ago, you ambled down the south shore of the St. Lawrence on a highway that strolled through every village and hamlet, so that the inhabitants could gather on their front porches, about fifteen centimetres off the pavement, and tell each other what fools these outsiders were, speeding past at twenty miles an hour instead of stopping to enjoy life as *le bon Dieu* intended. The villages and hamlets are still there, but they're a couple of kilometres away, along the riverbank, while Highway 20 plunges a little inland past St-Germaine, St-Pascal, and La Pocatière. Signs implore the traveller to turn in and sample the maple syrup, sugar pie, and woodcarvings, but who has time?

This is *Kamouraska* country, and the land I remember from public-school French novels like *Maria Chapdelaine,* in which young ladies went berry-picking in the woods and did things with young gallants that they were never allowed to get away with in English school literature. The highway signs are all in French; it is as if the authorities don't want anyone who cannot speak the language to know where they are, or what lies ahead, or what dangers lurk over the hill.

Tourism may be important, but that doesn't mean we have to tip the tourists off to danger. This policy, which is exactly the opposite of bilingual New Brunswick's, is mirrored in Alberta, where, outside the national parks, anyone who reads only English can run over a cliff, so far as the sign-makers care.

"*Risque de Brouilliard sur 500 Metres,*" bellows a warning, but no Anglo is to know that a fog bank may roll down over the next 500 metres. Strangers are not let in on the fact that right turns are prohibited at this intersection, or that the road is closed ahead, or that high winds pose a danger. Most of these warnings can be made out by anyone with even a minimum of French, so we conclude that withholding translations is aimed at the Americans. Let them come up here trying to shower dollar bills on us, and we'll kill the buggers off.

Finally, near Trois Pistoles, we hit our first bold English-only sign. It reads:

Yes 60%
Here We Are Ready!

Apparently, this town voted heavily Yes in the last referendum on separation.

For auld lang syne, we drop down to the river at St-Jean-Port-Joli, at the heart of woodcarvers' country, about halfway between Rivière-du-Loup and Quebec City. At the Auberge du Faubourg, at the west end of town, I learned many years ago how to order dinner in slightly peccable French, for myself and *madame* and *les enfants,* and we nearly always got what we thought we'd ordered. It forms a bond, so we drive in to find to our relief that everything is as it should be, as we remembered it to be — except for an industrial park — and the town is still crammed with beautiful old houses, antique stores, woodcarving shops, and friendly people who will neither sneer at your French nor switch to English.

Anger along the Grand Allée

About ninety minutes later, we have crossed the river into Ste-Foy and are heading for the heart of Quebec City. Ste-Foy is just a suburb like any suburb, but soon we are heading, with mounting excitement and narrowing lanes, into the Old City, past the city wall, past the National Assembly, into the Grand Allée. We never take this route without my mind flashing back to a time, nearly three decades ago, when we came this way and were abruptly stopped by a huge demonstration outside the legislative buildings.

There were thousands of angry Quebecers on every side, waving placards, punching fists in the air, threatening mayhem and chaos. The signs made their demands clear — they wanted the English out, they wanted Quebec for Quebecers and nobody but, and they expressed themselves, in rough and ready French not taught at Berlitz, on the subject of how they meant to deal with interlopers such as ourselves.

"What do the signs say?" asked the Driver.

"They advise us to turn around and go back," I replied.

"Turn around? I'm not going to turn around. We have to get to the hotel."

While I crouched on the floor of the front seat — to protect her, do you see, by drawing their fire — the Driver lowered her window.

"You there," she commanded a large, beer-bellied thug waving a sign that read *A Bas les Anglais!* "Move to one side, please, my good man. I must get through."

The thug stared at her, stupefied.

She honked the horn. "I don't have time for this," she exclaimed impatiently. "KINDLY ... GET ... OUT ... OF ... MY ... WAY."

Like the Red Sea parting for Moses, the multitudes split asunder and we rolled through.

"Thank you so much," said the Driver. And then, to me, "What are you doing down there?"

My Farewell to Quebec

That was the trip that resulted in an article for *Maclean's* magazine called "My Farewell to Quebec." It began with an argument I had one night, all in French, with a young separatist on Dufferin Terrace, the boardwalk that fronts on the river outside Quebec's — and possibly Canada's — finest hotel, the Château Frontenac.

He explained to me, as one would to a child, that the English of Canada had always been oppressors of his people, that they always would be oppressors of his people, and that he and his generation had had enough. They wanted out. He said that Canada had been pulled together by a compact linking two separate but equal partners, the two founding peoples, but that English Canada would never accord French Canada equality, and now the French were being drowned in their own province by an influx of Europeans, and Asians, who turned to the English side, wanted to go to English schools, would soon see Quebec swamped with English culture and lose everything worthwhile. And every time the French population tried to protect itself by enacting language laws, the English howled bloody murder and tried to strike them down.

I skipped the historical argument that, as a matter of fact, Canada was never a union of two peoples; rather, that canny old fox John A. Macdonald, who found his legislature deadlocked every time by French bloc voting, hoped to stamp out the French by enlisting the Maritimes to outnumber them. This was, I believed, and still believe, historical fact, though it's neither flattering nor useful. Much better to embrace the polite fiction that Confederation was indeed meant to joint two disparate groups of people (our ancestors actually called them races in those days) in a continent-wide federation in which the rights of all would be protected.

This erroneous but useful interpretation had been placarded as *deux peuples fondateurs* in the early 1960s, and if it wasn't true, it should have been. Instead of getting into this, I agreed that French Canada had indeed been abused, and that the increase in federal power did indeed represent a threat to the provincial powers that lay at the heart of French culture.

But, I argued, the fact that we were having this discussion in French showed that at least some lessons had been learned; that we, on the English side, realized the necessity of building a bilingual nation where all our people could be at home, a notion embraced not merely by Pierre Trudeau, then prime minister, but also by his predecessor, Lester Pearson, by his opponents in the

Conservative and New Democratic parties, by almost everyone in English Canada under the age of fifty.

And the young man stunned me by telling me that he didn't want bilingualism, couldn't care less about bilingualism. It was not a help but a danger. That way lay assimilation, lay the end of *la francophonie,* lay the collapse of French culture in North America.

He didn't want equality in Quebec — equality meant that the English would have to be accorded equal rights in school, in higher education, in politics, everywhere. The immigrants would then continue to join the English, and soon it would be *finis.* We went at it, back and forth, for a couple of hours, racking up every old score from the Manitoba Schools Question (where, indeed, our side's idea of equality very soon turned into laws barring the teaching of French), to the Royal Visit of 1964 (when francophone kids were bludgeoned by cops wielding two-foot clubs because they dared to line the routes where Her Majesty would go, and the possibility that they might boo was raised), to the ousting of René Lévesque from the Liberal Party.

We avoided the Battle of the Plains of Abraham but not the visit of Charles de Gaulle. (In 1967, the president of France stood on a balcony not far from where we argued now and shouted "*Vive le Québec! Vive le Québec libre!*" He sent a shiver of delight through French Canada and a shudder of outrage through English Canada, and no one, anywhere, was unmoved.) And in the end, I said, "*Vous avez raison.*" You're right. If the French, the young French, have decided in overwhelming numbers that they want to be on their own, out of Canada, I wrote in the subsequent article, there is no point in trying to make them stay. They are smart enough, and numerous enough, and rich enough, and well-trained enough, to form a nation on their own, and if that is what they want to do, they will do it. I wrote that, Canada being Canada, they would not do it by going to war with the rest of us — people who move out of the way when you ask them to do so are not warriors — but that they would gradually take, or take back, federal powers into their own hands.

They would start to set up their own embassies abroad; they would gain control over their own immigration flows; they would take control of the education system entirely into their own hands; they would pass language laws to protect themselves from absorption; and they would pay absolutely no attention to protests that this was not right, not constitutional. They would sign national deals, from time to time, to get better financial arrangements from Ottawa, and they would break the deals as soon as it made sense to them to do so. I concluded:

> *History shows that when a people has decided that it is a people — a separate state — only force of arms can reverse the decision. Quebec has made such a declaration, to itself, and we are not about to take up arms. So we simply have to accommodate ourselves to what the separatist paper* Le Jour *calls "the legitimate aspirations of the people."*

It did not take a whole lot of insight to write this article — many others were making the same predictions, although usually in French, about what in fact came to pass — but when it appeared in *Maclean's,* it created something of a stir. At the next board of directors meeting of our owner, Maclean Hunter, my scalp was demanded on a platter. Lloyd Hodgkinson, who was then the vice-president of the magazine division, said that it was the duty of writers to describe the world they saw, not what they wanted, and that was that.

Baseball, Yes; Separatism, No

Now here we are, back in Quebec City, back at the Château, so I go back onto Dufferin Terrace, and I cannot get a single soul to talk to me about breaking up Canada. Baseball, the young men will talk about baseball, even admire the Blue Jays, but either they have decided that it is pointless to argue with an Anglo, or they are as sick of the subject as the rest of the nation and want a truce, for a time at least. We were to discover this same kind indifference everywhere we went in the province.

In the 1960s, we used to get honked at, especially in downtown Montreal, for the sin of having an Ontario licence plate. (And later, when we lived in Nova Scotia, for the sin of having a Nova Scotia licence plate.) The Driver always honked back, which often led to an exchange of views, the French side of which I either could not or would not translate. Now people stop to give us the right-of-way, and they wave.

A few years ago, in stores, we were addressed first in French; in restaurants, we were handled with chill politeness when we consulted the English side of the menu. The Driver and I have different interpretations of this sea change. Hers, briefly put, is that the French are beginning to come to their senses and realize what a good deal they have in Canada, and that they don't want out any more. Mine is that they realize that they have won; they have, in fact if not in name, established their own nation by exactly the kind of gradualism you would expect of an essentially conservative people. When Premier Daniel Johnson renamed the legislature the National Assembly three decades ago, every Quebecer knew what it meant. And almost no one demurred.

Whoever has the right interpretation of it, there is no doubt that much of the tension and outrage is gone. It is stored away and taken out at mass rallies, but for the rest of the time it is either mothballed or evaporated, it doesn't matter which. Waiters don't care which language you speak, and in a Quebec City store, when I am having trouble finding the word for "bookmark" (*signet*), the clerk keeps smiling while I keep trying, and when I pantomime it and we both get it, she hugs me.

I amble along the Dufferin Terrace in the late-afternoon light, then skip up — with stops — the 310 stairs that carry you to the top, where, according to the signs, you will be able to see the cove where Wolfe led his troops ashore the night before the Battle of the Plains of Abraham. No such luck. L'Anse au Foulon has been built over; the whole shoreline is changed.

Halfway up the steps, I come across a family from New York gathered around a giant and disreputable-looking St. Bernard dog. The little girl, about eight and lugging a sucker about the size of her head, wants to hug the dog, but he is having no part of it.

"Come here," commands the little girl. "Come here and sit down!"

"He speaks French, dopey," says her brother, a kid of about six or seven.

"Say '*Ici*,'" I suggest.

She says, "*Ici*," and the dog comes to her.

"Say '*Assais-toi*,'" I tell her.

"Say toi," says the girl. The dog sits, the girl hugs him, and the dog takes a giant bite out of her sucker. We depart, all feeling satisfied.

At the top of the stairs, there is a bandstand, and gathered below this a gang of tourists surround their tour guide, who wants to tell them all about the Battle of the Plains of Abraham. She has prepared her little spiel and wants to deliver it, but her audience is onto other things.

"What's that bridge?" asks one of the gaggle, pointing upriver.

"That's the old Quebec Bridge," says the guide. "It is interesting that you should ask about it. This bridge is in the *Guinness Book of Records* as the longest cantilevered bridge in the world [the span between the two main pillars is 549 metres long]. It was the site of a great tragedy. In 1914 [wrong — it was 1916], the south section [wrong — it was the centre span] fell down during construction, and seventy-seven workers were killed. The accident happened just fifteen minutes before quitting time. However, seventy-eight other workers escaped unharmed."

"They were Newfoundlanders," comes a loud voice from the back of the pack. "And they all buggered off early."

"Now I've lost completely what I was going to say," moans the guide over the laughter of the crowd. "Oh, yes. They built the Citadel just below us here, and do you know what it was to guard against?"

"Americans," says a tourist.

"Newfoundlanders," says the guide, getting her own back.

"Aw, luv," says the man who had interrupted her, "I've been away from the island for four days, so I can't come up there and hug you."

The guide flaps a hand in defeat.

"Look at it this way, dearie," comes another shout from the crowd. "You've only got to put up with my Charlie for another fourteen days."

The guide slumps against the man beside her, and everybody roars.

The French Beat the British after the Plains of Abraham

I cross the wide park where the battle was fought and reflect that it means such different things to our two solitudes in Canada, although it really didn't settle anything at all. Some English Canadians talk as if Wolfe's victory in September

1759 was the end of all things French, and what are those sore losers still grousing about anyway? Some French Canadians talk as if it was the beginning of an age of darkness when Montcalm slumped to the ground and his stricken aides — who didn't know that Wolfe, too, had been mortally wounded — sued for surrender.

The British marched into Quebec, all right, but they would have marched right out again were it not for the fact that it was a British, not a French, fleet that first appeared in the St. Lawrence in the spring of 1760. The British army was not invincible, and was, in fact, dealt a stunning defeat by François Gaston, duc de Lévis, at the battle of Ste-Foy on April 28, 1670, months after the Plains of Abraham.

The British, under James Murray, were bottled up in the fortress with nowhere to go when the British navy came rolling up to the front door in May, like the U.S. marines coming to the rescue. The French retreated to Montreal, where they were surrounded by converging British forces from Quebec, Lake Champlain, and Lake Ontario, in September 1760. That was when Philippe de Rigaud, marquis de Vaudreuil, the governor of New France, concluded that he had no course but to surrender, and all of New France, not merely Quebec, passed into English hands. The British navy was at least as much to blame — or praise — as James Wolfe.

As I come out of Battlefield Park, I am confronted by huge hoardings stretching as far as the eye can see. They are covered with lavish illustrations of the Colline Parliamentaire du Québec, Phase I, and behind this, bulldozers are bulling, trucks trucking, steam shovels digging at the splendid new edifice, fit for a new nation, that will rise here one day. The people may not be ready, but the building will be. It looks gorgeous.

I recollect that exactly this sort of grandiose cement-chucking is going on back in Ottawa, where Prime Minister Jean Chrétien seems determined to outbuild and outspend this lot in fashioning a new centre for *his* national capital. Can it be, I wonder, that we are to have all this architectural splendour as part of a pissing contest?

When I return to the Château Frontenac, I am ordered into my finery, such as it is, for we are to go to the main dining room for dinner. This is a test. We have stayed at the Château perhaps fifty times over the years, but we gave it up about fifteen years ago. It was all right, but at these prices ($315 a night puts a roof over your head), you expect more than all right. The waiters were not surly, but they were not friendly either; the staff seemed to treat English callers as a necessary nuisance, and that was it.

No more. We are swept in, complimented — well, not me (I look, as usual, like an unmade bed), but Joan is *arrayed* — and turned over to a waiter who says, "Now, shall we do this in French or English?"

"*Comme vous voulez,*" I reply.

"Okay, English," he says, having had enough of my accent.

We are fussed over but not bustled, cosseted, made to feel that our arrival was just what this place needed to give it a little class, and fed a meal of such splendour that when we're handed a bill for $147 in any language you choose, I don't even choke and roll on the floor, but instead pay it with a hefty tip and a broad smile. I will cry later, at credit card time, but even then I will know it was worth it.

The next morning, I walk down to Old Town, down the very hill where steps were first emplaced in 1635, the year Samuel de Champlain died here, and wander through the Quartier Petit Champlain, at the foot of the hill. Stooging through the lovely little shops that line the streets, I keep bumping into a couple from Boston on their first visit to the city. They keep saying, "Isn't this marvellous!" "Isn't Quebec wonderful?" and I realize that, yes, it is, dammit, but no Canadian is going to boast out loud about it.

The woman — in her fifties, portly, with a camera, a shopping bag about the size of the Albert Hall, and a pleased grin — finally decides to impart her gathered wisdom to me.

"You English," she says. "You wouldn't want to lose this."

Well, no.

L'Île d'Orléans Has Gone Uptown

When we check out of the Château, right on the dot of 11 a.m. — we are taking no chances of being landed with an extra night's lodging — we drive north from Quebec to visit another favourite haunt, Île d'Orléans. Our memories are of a place where they sawed off a piece of Normandy, plunked it down on an island outside Quebec City, and peopled it with peasants. The peasants run boutiques now, or restaurants quaint and costly. Passing the *club de golfe*, the first thing we see as we turn along Highway 368, the one that circles the island, is a grey-haired lady in shorts bowling across a farm field on an all-terrain vehicle, with her pedal to the metal and her face split by a grin.

There are still farms, of course, still lovely old buildings, still beautiful views of the St. Lawrence, but the Île is a big girl now. About thirty years ago, you stopped every few hundred metres to buy fresh-baked bread or panniers of strawberries that had to be tasted to be believed; pull off the road now, and you are likely to be run over by a Mercedes-Benz belonging to a Quebec City lawyer who comes down here to enjoy the simple life in his $2-million chalet. Well, good luck to them; we do not grudge the island its new richness as a dormitory suburb for the provincial capital, but we do miss the strawberries and bread.

When we duck back through Quebec City to pick up the Trans-Canada again on our way to Drummondville, we come upon signs inviting us to visit Montmorency Falls. Well, of course we will. The highest, most beautiful falls in the province. But here's the rub: they have been privatized. You cannot get within viewing distance of the tumbling water without forking over seven dollars for a "parking fee" to a concessionaire who has built the longest stretch of fencing I have ever seen. I want to walk the mile or so it would take to get a peek at the falls, just on principle, but the Driver is not in favour, and we grumble on our way.

Along the TCH, and indeed, along every highway we have travelled in Quebec, we keep seeing signs that say, simply: CLSC. And point. This stands for Centre de Loisir et Santé Communautaires. In Quebec, almost every town has a place where you can go if you need help — mental, physical, whatever. It is also the place where there is a community swimming pool, if such exists, meeting hall, sports centre. The CLSCs do not replace the churches — they are often connected to, or right around the corner from, a church, in fact — but they provide a much broader, if less spiritual, range of services, and we think every province should have them.

We are not going to Montreal, not yet; in keeping with the theory that much can be told about people by the heroes they choose to honour, I have decided to look at two Quebec figures, one from the early days and one from my own day: Madeleine de Verchères and Joseph-Armand Bombardier. Accordingly, when we reach Drummondville, we leave the Trans-Canada for Highway 55, the autoroute to the Eastern Townships. At Richmond, where the waitress in the coffee shop tells us in great detail what a lousy job the hired photographer did on the pictures for her recent wedding — we have no useful counsel to offer on this — we turn onto a much smaller road and aim for Valcourt, where Bombardier was born, raised, and invented the snowmobile.

The Deer — or Chevreuil — Did It

But we run into a snag, or possibly, a stag — some variety of deer, anyway. We are cruising through the countryside, admiring the rolling green hills and dense woodlands, when it begins to rain. Not heavily, but enough to make the Driver ease back on the gas pedal. Then a deer pops out of the woods in front of us and crosses the road in three bounds. Joan slows still further, not that it does a fat lot of good; suddenly, there is a flash of reddish brown from the left side of the road and then a thunk! The flash disappears.

By the time I get ready to say I think we may have hit something, we are stopped and Joan is out examining the damage — severe to us, fatal to the deer, which lies, with open, faintly accusing eyes, in a roadside ditch. I had no notion it could happen so fast — it never does in the movies, does it? One second we were proceeding sedately down the road, and the next examining a banged-up front end and contemplating the mortality of a fellow creature.

The van will still move, not happily, but steadily, so we drive into the next town, Racine, and Joan pulls into a garage. A mechanic, wearing overalls and a welcoming smile, engages her in conversation while I get on the car phone to the insurance company. Joan gets out of the van so she can wave her arms better, and out of the corner of my eye I can see that she and the mechanic are having a fine Canadian conversation, she entirely in English, he entirely in French, and understanding each other perfectly. I get through to the insurance company, expecting the kind of response you see on television in those ads put out by the kindly insurers:

"But are you all right, Mrs. Jones? Fine, fine. Now we'll just get you and the little girl home."

Our insurance company has not seen the ad, and instead I got something like this:

"If you have hit a wall, please press 1 now."

"If you have hit a tree, please press 2 now."

"If you have hit a small Frenchman with a moustache . . ." *Und so weiter.*

Finally, I get through to Sean. Or possibly, Shawn. I think he is somewhere in Kansas. Sean doesn't want to know if we are all right. What he wants to know is where the heck is Racine, Quebec, and how soon can we get the van to a town where he can have an appraiser come and look at it before parting with any dough?

I say we can probably stagger to Granby, about fifteen kilometres away, and Sean says to go there and call again. Don't ask for me, though, he emphasizes; just whoever answers the phone will do. Possibly, he is afraid of breaking down under the worry about our fate. Or possibly not. I emerge from the van to find that Joan and the garage gent have made a deal. Lots of gestures does it.

He is arranging for a friend of his, who has a body shop over in Richmond, to come and get our vanquished van. So I have to tell him that that is all off, and that we are going to Granby to wait for an appraiser. But I can't think of the word for "appraiser." (I can't even think of the word for deer. *Chevreuil* — that's the baby. But what's the use of knowing it now?) I tell the garage gent that "the man who makes the guess" is going to meet us in Granby, and he knows at once what I mean. (I should have said the *évaluateur.*) Joan wants him to fix up a light that is hanging by the wires and likely to cause a short, so I try explaining this to the mechanic in French while he scratches his head and rolls his eyes and wonders what in the world I am getting at.

Thereupon, Joan holds her hands up with the index fingers pointing at each other — like two wires, see? — and makes a short-circuit noise, "Zzt! Zzt!" while pointing to the light. Then she wraps her finger with imaginary electrical tape and the mechanic slaps his forehead — *Zut alors,* how could I be such a noodle-head? — rushes away and gets some electrical tape, and fixes it up.

God, it's great to be fluent in French. And then I give the gent a five-dollar tip, to cover the tape, and he thanks me gravely and takes the five bucks inside and *puts it in the till.*

We stagger to Granby, check into a hotel, and telephone the insurance company. This is great fun. You get to play punch the telephone for a few hours, as you are shifted from one voicemail station to another while a tin voice explains, in the language of your choice ("If you wish to be served in English, please press 1 now"), that Mr. Jones is not at his desk right now, any more than Miss Smith, Mr. Eydenfall, or any of the rest of the gang.

They are down at the television station, making a commercial about their swift and courteous service. Joan, who does all the family shouting at official-dom, leaves a number of urgent messages. *Quelle blague!* The next day, she manages to get through to a human person, who has no idea where we are, where Granby is, possibly even where Quebec is, but who, in the fullness of time, is able to sort through the right list and tell us that an appraiser will be getting in touch with us about arranging a time suitable to his convenience to come and look at the vehicle.

So we sit around for a few more hours until the Driver, possibly a trifle fed up, phones back to the insurance company, keeps growling until she gets a supervisor, and announces that we are going to limp home and have the repairs effected by our own garage, in Lindsay, Ontario. The insurance company knows where Lindsay is. They hope we make it there.

So we do that, and five days later, with the van repaired and pretending that nothing whatever has happened, we drive to Valcourt, fit for any fate. I announce that I am going to call our little contretemps *tripus interruptus,* and Joan says she wouldn't put it past me.

A Man for Snow Seasons

Valcourt is a pleasant little town of about 5,000 souls in the Black River valley of the Eastern Townships. Everybody in every town around mostly works for Bombardier, and there is a nice little museum, built right next door to the garage where it all began, to tell you all about it.

Joseph-Armand Bombardier was the son of Joseph-Alfred Bombardier, a well-to-do farmer and a descendant of André Bombardier, a soldier who came to New France late in the seventeenth century. Alfred, a skilled mechanic as well as a knowledgeable farmer, married a local girl, Anna Gravel, in 1906; they had ten children, four of whom died. Among the survivors was their first son, Joseph-Armand, born on April 16, 1907. (You can buy a biography, by Roger Lacasse, right at the museum for an astonishingly modest ten bucks.)

Poppa thought it would be a good thing if his oldest son were to go into the priesthood, and he pressed this upon the boy as soon as he was old enough to understand. Joseph-Armand was willing enough, in theory — he was certainly not one to defy his father, in any event — but his mind was always full of other, less spiritual things. A tinkerer and taker-apart of toys, clocks, machinery, anything he could get his hands on, he spent all the money he earned serving at mass on dials, ratchets, gears, and springs, which he incorporated into toys.

By the time he was thirteen, he had achieved a modest local fame constructing tractors, trains, boats, and locomotives that actually worked, actually moved by themselves with the aid of homemade, spring-driven motors. Then he persuaded a friend of his father's to give him an old shotgun with a broken butt, and he made it into a cannon in his father's workshop. When Armand set it off with a roar that rattled neighbouring windows, Poppa decided it was time to get serious, so he bundled him off, at the age of fourteen, to the seminary of St-Charles Borromée, in Sherbrooke.

A bright lad, and a fervent Catholic, Joseph-Armand was nonetheless a poor student of theology, and his father finally gave up and brought the boy home to work on the farm — and his inventions. In December 1922, Alfred bought an old Model-T Ford, which was apparently harmless, the engine beyond repair, and gave it to his son. Soon, Joseph-Armand, with his younger brother, Léopold, was hard at work in his father's shed, banging and clanging away with boundless energy on something new — but no one had any idea what it was.

On New Year's Eve, there was a thundering noise from behind the workshop doors, and they suddenly burst open to reveal a strange new machine that went banging down the drive and out onto the street. Joseph-Armand had always wondered why, if people could ski downhill, they couldn't ski uphill as well, and this was his answer to how they could. With Léopold's help, he had taken the Ford apart, mounted the engine on two homemade sleighs, and hooked an old wooden propeller, which he had scrounged, onto the back. It made a gawdawful noise, frightened the village horses, and astounded the populace who came out to watch as it slipped, banging and backfiring, down the street.

Alfred Bombardier was certain the boys would kill themselves or, with that whirling propeller, someone else, and he ordered his sons to dismantle the machine immediately. He was impressed, however, as who would not be, that his fifteen-year-old had managed to design and build a machine like this on his own.

But a boy, a good boy of a good Catholic family, should be a priest — everyone knew that. Or since that did not seem to be in the cards, a lawyer, a doctor, even a merchant (Alfred had recently bought a store in town). Still, the boy didn't seem to want any of these things; he wanted only to tinker, and finally Poppa decided to let him have his way. Joseph-Armand was apprenticed to a mechanic in nearby Stukely. In 1924, when he was seventeen, he moved to Montreal to live with relatives and work in a garage while taking correspondence courses from Ford.

Two years later, he moved back to Valcourt, where his father had bought a piece of land near the town bridge to turn into a garage for his nineteen-year-old son. In mid-1926, the Garage Bombardier, a small, white, single-storey building marked by a red sign and three Imperial Oil pumps, was open for business.

And the rest, as they say, is history. Joseph-Armand became a noted mechanic, one to whom other garages were happy to send problem cars they could not fix. He was also a clever businessman, who was soon buying and selling vehicles; a good boss, whose workforce soon included many family members; and an able accountant, since he realized that the money was as important as everything else.

Despite working fourteen-hour days to keep the garage profitable, he managed to find time to work on his inventions, especially the snowmobile. It was not until 1936 that he was able to patent his first working model, called the B7. The patent was accepted on June 27, 1937, and Bombardier built eight of the vehicles that winter, when garage work had slowed down. All eight were quickly sold — for about $1,400 each.

In 1937, the sign over the garage was changed to L'Auto-Neige Bombardier. Joseph-Armand had decided to go into the snowmobile business full time. That year, he sold twelve B7s; the next year, twenty-five; and the next year, fifty. Soon, Joseph-Armand's little factory could not keep up with the demand, and the first of many expansions was under way.

During the Second World War, Bombardier vehicles were built to the specifications of the Canadian army; they were built in a new factory that opened in January 1941, in the midst of a general celebration in the town. After the war, he developed huge industrial machines to travel through muskeg, through swamps as well as snow, for oil exploration and timber harvesting. Along the way, he developed a vulcanizing machine and a tractor called the Red Ram, which was designed to pick up and cart entire tree trunks from the cutting site to a truck-loading site, as well as a twenty-five-seat snow-bus for schoolchildren.

The Ski-Doo, the machine that was to make him a household name, came about after a priest in Northern Manitoba wrote Bombardier in 1956 to complain that what were needed in isolated parts of Canada were not huge machines, but small, lightweight, practical vehicles that would not break down — and that people could afford.

The result was the launch, in 1959, of a sort of snow-going motorcycle called the Ski-Dog. In a brochure printed for a company convention, a typographical error turned this into Ski-Doo. Bombardier realized at once that this was a far better name, and that is what it became. The Ski-Doo was the first of his inventions to be marketed by a vigorous advertising campaign — word of mouth had done most of the work up until this time — and when Bombardier was told that $32,000 was to be spent on advertising, he was taken aback. "Don't you realize," he said, "that $32,000 is the price of a house?"

The Ski-Doo, a noisy but useful beast, transformed not only winter sport but also northern travel. Dogsleds became relics. By this time, Joseph-Armand had married, had children and grandchildren, had formed a company that was becoming a giant corporation, and was gaining a national and international recognition. But the patterns he had established in early life never changed; he still worked sixteen- to eighteen-hour days, drove his colleagues almost as hard as he drove himself, and exhibited a constant impatience with anything that threatened to interfere with the most important thing in life — making more and better snowmobiles. However, he would not go into debt or allow his company to go into debt or, better still, go public and sell shares to expand, as he was constantly urged to do.

His biographer, Roger Lacasse, wrote that he could have sold many more Ski-Doos than he did, but he "deliberately slowed down promotion of the Ski-Doo to prevent the product from draining the company's resources at the expense of its other activities. He decided to retain control of the company, rather than give in to the demands of the euphoric market."

He was an insomniac, a demanding employer — he would never allow a union in his factories, because he believed his workers were well paid and well treated — and a generous donor to church and charity. But he was also impatient, bad-tempered, brusque, and moody; a man who knew he should spend more time with his growing family but never managed to do so. He remained a devout Catholic, never tolerating swearing in his presence, and a French-Canadian nationalist who had nothing but contempt for fellow francophones so greedy that they sold their businesses to Americans and moved to Florida.

He was mistrustful of wealth, even his own, and spent much of his last years worrying about ways to pass his company on to his wife and children; he was still worrying away at this when cancer struck in late 1963. He died on February 18, 1964, at the age of fifty-six. In hospital, he was still working on plans for yet another factory, and for ten new patents that he had under development.

Bombardier Inc. today would be unrecognizable to Joseph-Armand. It became a public company in 1969, launched a massive diversification program in 1974, and began to build mass-transit systems, railway equipment, and dozens of new, mostly recreational, vehicles. Bombardier Inc. won a $1-billion contract to build subway cars for New York City in 1982.

Five years later, it acquired Canadair, Canada's top aircraft manufacturer. Today, it is one of Canada's largest corporations, with 40,000 employees, $14 billion in back orders in its aerospace division alone, factories in six countries, and an enviable reputation for smooth management and efficient operation. In the 1990s, its steady profits propelled the stock from $3.63 to $18.65 per share, and it has so much money sloshing around its innards that it has formed Bombardier Capital, a new group, to invest the stuff.

It has the same relationship to the company Joseph-Armand knew as an oak does to an acorn. The garage-born critter of his time has become a muscular giant that receives huge government handouts — pardon me — development and research grants, and seems to be signing another billion-dollar contract every time you pick up the newspaper.

In the meantime, Valcourt is still doing very well, thank you, turning out recreational vehicles in a huge factory just down the street from Joseph-Armand's original garage. Something that looks like a cross between a golf cart and a Hummer zips past us as we pull out of town, and the Driver says, "I'll bet that's a new machine they're testing out." Probably a UFO.

Madeleine de Verchères

It is a short hop — by van or snowmobile — from Valcourt in the Eastern Townships to Verchères, a lovely old tree-lined village on the St. Lawrence, within fifty kilometres of Montreal. And here, on the foreshore, we find another Quebec hero, this one standing on guard with a musket, a hat, and a haughty expression from atop a pillar in her own park.

In the days when Canadian schoolchildren learned the rudiments of Canadian history, everyone knew who Madeleine de Verchères was. Today's youngsters may suspect that she sings lead for Doug and the Slugs. She was the fourth of twelve children of François Jarret de Verchères, a seigneur of New France who had a large farm and a small fort here in the seventeenth century. Madeleine was born in 1678, and in 1692, when she was fourteen, her parents were absent on a visit when a raiding party of Iroquois struck.

They seized a number of the people working in the fields, including Madeleine, but she escaped, rushed back to the fort, and took command. She ordered everyone inside to make as much noise as possible — banging pots, shouting back and forth, and firing off muskets — to indicate that there was a large and belligerent defence force within. The Iroquois eased back. There might not have been a half regiment of soldiers inside there, making all that noise, but on the other hand, there might have been.

They hung about all night, and the next morning, when the racket continued, they decided to beat a strategic retreat, leaving Madeleine triumphant within. It took a week for rescue to arrive, by which time there was no need. As an adult, she wrote two accounts of her exploit, and these passed into history when a Jesuit priest, Pierre-François-Xavier de Charlevoix, used the story in his history of New France, published in 1744.

Madeleine had only one other run-in with Iroquois. When she was a matron and mother, she came home one day to find a First Nations citizen rifling through the drawers in her kitchen, and she beaned him with a frying pan.

I like to think that Madeleine and Joseph-Armand had a number of characteristics in common that make them worthy heroes for Quebec in their separate times; both were courageous, resourceful, devout — and handy with their hands.

Montreal Is Singing Again

We walk the narrow, memory-soaked streets of Verchères, drop in to one of the restaurants on the main drag, which is also the shore highway to Montreal, for a delicious luncheon highlighted by much pantomiming with the waitress as an aid to translation, and within an hour are at our hotel, just off Sherbrooke in downtown Montreal, several centuries away from Verchères. Montreal is still our most cosmopolitan city, and one that, after years of economic blight, has come booming to life again.

In the streets, sidewalk cafés are jammed to overflowing, and I note what is to me the amazing sight of grown men and women standing in line, waiting to sit down in a chair on the sidewalk to consume coffee, croissants, and carbon monoxide from the passing traffic. Hotels that languished with 50 to 60 percent occupancy rates a few years ago are now crammed — and of course, raising their rack rates.

True, much of the industrial activity that built this city of 3 million is going or gone, but it has been replaced by aerospace, pharmaceuticals, and information technology — there are more than one thousand firms in the advanced technology industry, from tiny one-man outfits to international giants, in and around Montreal, and fourteen new international financial centres have set up shop here in recent years.

Rue Ste-Catherine, which was pockmarked with empty storefronts during a visit we made here in 1995, is jammed with busy shops where Montrealers, and Americans, and Germans, and Japanese buyers are grabbing the stuff off the shelves. Not me, of course; disdaining these wonderful brand-name boutiques, much to the Driver's disgust, I spend my shopping time in the largest everything-for-a-dollar store I have ever seen.

It is a lovely thing to see Montreal singing again, to see the streets bustling, business blossoming, wallets opening, credit cards sliding across hotel desks and store counters and the well-greased palms of restaurateurs. But does this mean that prosperity will melt the dismay and dislike of former years and that separatism will perish, like a Strasbourg goose, on a diet of fat?

I doubt it. We are no longer honked at in Montreal — just as, I hope, no one who tries to speak French in Calgary is invited to "speak white" — but the problem of survival of the French language and culture has not disappeared. It may even have worsened in some ways.

While the overwhelming majority of Quebecers are French-speaking today, a smaller and smaller proportion of these give French as their mother tongue. Immigrants are now directed — you could say forced — into the French educational system, but they are Italians, or Germans, or Hong Kong émigrés who constantly dilute the pool of Quebecers who consider themselves French first, Quebecers second, and Canadians a dim and distant third.

Moreover, because Quebec has the lowest birthrate in Canada, the population of the province itself, now about 24 percent of Canada's, will drop, unless something drastic happens, to about 16 percent over the next century.

How Many Solitudes Was That?

Despite all the victories of recent years, and despite the certainty of most of Canada that Quebec, the spoiled child of Confederation, is making a lot of fuss over nothing, French language and culture are still under threat. Faced with a tragedy that would be national, not merely provincial, Quebecers, not surprisingly, continue to press demands on Ottawa that the rest of the nation simply cannot comprehend.

If I were a Quebecer, faced with a choice between the extinction of my culture or separation from the rest of the country, I would be up at the National Assembly, kissing the foot of that small, weird statue of René Lévesque, before you could say Meech Lake.

The mood of Quebec today, to the extent that anyone from outside can measure such matters in visits of a few days at a time, is decidedly upbeat, most of the time, on most subjects. And as the rest of the nation has grudgingly given way on a few of the language issues — some of us can still remember the days when the payrolls of the giant firms here, whose employees were overwhelmingly French, were universally discharged by cheques written in English — there is more civility in the air.

However, as long as the underlying problems remain, as long as Quebec's security depends on belligerent defensiveness on the one side and uncomprehending anxiety on the other, there will continue to be a strong measure of anything from indifference to unease to outrage running through this society. Things are better here; they are far from ideal.

6

Ontario

FROM BY'S TOWN TO MARY'S LAMB

We found that along the north shore of Lake Superior — an inland sea larger than the Adriatic — the Trans-Canada is an asphalt lifeline. Before it was opened in 1960, supplies for the mining and logging towns carved into the wilderness were brought in by plane or rail; travel into and between the stranded communities was tedious and rare. The highway has changed all that, and brought a late-blooming boom to the countryside.

— STAR WEEKLY, APRIL 10, 1965

When the late Jean Marchand was a prominent member of the Trudeau Cabinet, he used to say that the best thing about Ottawa was the train to Montreal. That was when there were good, frequent trains to Montreal, of course, but even then it wasn't true. When we zip down the Trans-Canada from Montreal — in less than two hours — we enter what is probably the most verbally abused city in Canada — Lotusland, Fogbound on the Rideau, and all the rest of it. As a symbol of all the things Canadians like to bitch about in government, the whole National Capital area is fair game, but looked at as a city it is a credit to us all. It is clean, comfortable, easy to get around, peaceable, and decorated with a network of parks — many of them the playthings of the National Capital Commission itself — that are jammed with the citizenry almost every day of the year.

Then there is the Rideau Canal, arcing through downtown. In spring, summer, and fall, the walkways on either side of this stretch of (rather murky) water throng with people. Bureaucrats, hatted and attaché-cased, stride purposefully along beside visiting businessmen; tourists; and Ottawa families, kids, dogs, and all. In the winter, thanks to the common sense of Douglas Fullerton, when he was chairman of the National Capital Commission, the canal is scraped free of snow and turned into the world's longest skating rink, which starts just below the Château Laurier and unrolls all the way back to Dow's Lake, about six kilometres upstream.

When we lived here, in the 1960s, we could strap on skates on the front porch, walk half a block down to the end of Allan Place, hop the low fence onto Patterson Creek, and be set for a four- or five-mile (pre-metric) skate. Well, not us, you understand — the kids covered the four- or five-mile part. The tourist guides tell the visitor about all the highlights — the changing of the guard on a summer morning on Parliament Hill; the eternal flame, on ditto; the Parliamentary Library, the Canadian Mint, the National Archives, the National Art Gallery, and across the river in Hull, the Museum of Man. All well worth seeing, of course.

Bureaucrats on Blades: A Capital Sight

But the capital's finest sight, available most winter mornings, is the battalion of bureaucrats, briefcased, mittened, and mufflered, skating down the canal to work. You can tell the lower ranks from the upper because, even though they may be better skaters, the lesser fry dare not pass. Gawking at them on a winter morning's walk, I often try to guess their departments by the skating styles. I like to think the long-legged lady who sweeps and swoops with such panache works at the art gallery; the lawyerly looking chap who has trouble holding onto his hat with one hand and a bulging briefcase with another is a justice department mandarin; and the fat little fellow who goes over on his ankles is stumbling and sliding to work at Revenue Canada.

However, the Ottawa I know and love, with all its bilingualism, its first-rate restaurants, its amateur and professional theatre, music, and art, looks and feels about as much like the city that started here as Jean Chrétien looks like Bambi. This was Bytown, a brawling, crude, rude lumber town that took its name from Colonel By, the man who engineered the Rideau Canal, and its manners from the gangs of thugs who, in 1837, very nearly turned it into a hellhole utterly without law and order. The story of Peter Aylen, King of the Shiners, and the Bytown riots he helped to foment and prolong, has been elided from our history books as not consonant with the high character we like to believe we possess as a nation. (My late father, Miller Stewart, wrote about these stirring days in "King of the Shiners," a chapter of *The Flamboyant Canadians,* edited by Ellen Stafford.) But this tale is as much a part of who we are as the annual Tulip Festival or Winter Carnival.

Them Bytown Days Was Fightin' Days

The city began as a series of encampments that sprang up when Col. John By made it the headquarters of the Royal Engineers, who built the canal between 1826 and 1833. The canal came about because Britain's reliance on the Baltic for timber for her ships had been badly shaken by the Napoleonic Wars, which showed how easy it was to cut off this source. In addition, touchy relations with the Americans following the War of 1812 made the St. Lawrence route to the Atlantic too vulnerable to possible attack.

Right, said the Colonial Office, we will build a canal from Kingston to the Ottawa River, and to hell with the Americans. Colonel By was given the job, and he picked out a route along the series of lakes and rivers that form the Rideau system, ending on the farm of Nicholas Sparks, where the Ottawa and Rideau rivers join. A town grew up here, spurred by juicy contracts with which masons, builders, and other artisans were lured into the wilderness. Sparks, who had bought his farm for sixty pounds, was given a monopoly on flour milling and sawmilling, and he owned the only licensed tavern in the place. He sold lots under the extraordinary proviso that only those who bought land from him or his agent were entitled to vote in town elections. When he sold out his interests a few years later, he netted $2 million.

One of the greatest pine forests in the world stood to the north and west of this burgeoning centre, and soon Bytown was awash with lumberjacks, as well as canal-diggers. Most of the lumberjacks were French Canadians (then called, simply, Canadians), while most of the canal-diggers were Irish immigrants who had been brought over to New York State to dig the recently completed Erie Canal from Buffalo to Albany.

They had a fearsome reputation for brawling and lawlessness, but these Irish navvies represented an instant, trained workforce, and By offered them generous pay to cross the border. When the Canadian lumberjacks and shillelagh-toting navvies met in Bytown's bars and brothels, the air soon rang with the noise of brawling.

Every parade, horse race, or fair ended in a riot. The Irish, known as Cork-towners, fought with the Orangemen; with the "grangers," or farmers; and of course, with the "pea-soupers."

The only forces of law available were volunteer constables, and the only jail available was at Perth, eighty kilometres away. The volunteers, and such non-volunteers as were occasionally pressed into service by beleaguered magistrates, soon learned to steer clear of the riots entirely and let them roll on undisturbed. In the rare event that volunteers could be found to try to serve an arrest warrant by a magistrate, the villain had only to slip across the river to Hull, in Lower Canada, to escape the jurisdiction.

The Irish developed a new weapon, the so-called Limerick whip, which consisted of a drilling chisel fastened to a long, limber willow withe; it could be used to remove a horseman from his saddle with a single swipe. Muggings, robbery, arson, and theft, followed by retaliatory raids from the other side, became commonplace.

After the canal was finished in 1833, things got much worse, as the unemployed Irishmen tried to take over the rafting trade, then wholly in the hands of the French, with predictable results. First, the Irish moved into the heavy, dangerous work of oak cutting, which was not as well paid as cutting the red and white pine that formed the bulk of the timber trade, but which was, for that very reason, available for them. The Canadians called them, contemptuously, *cheneurs,* or oak-cutters, which was soon turned into the English word "Shiners."

Peter Aylen, who had already made a fortune in the lumber business, took up the cause of the Shiners, and promised them jobs, entertainment, and the franchise in local elections in return for their support. He had one mansion in Bytown and another across the river, in Aylmer; both were open to the Shiners, with free grog and grub in return for muscle.

Aylen aimed to control the entire Ottawa Valley, then Canada's richest sector, by simply taking it over with brute force. His first lieutenant, Jimmy the Wren, was reputed to have killed a number of enemies by throwing rocks with deadly accuracy. Among Aylen's other followers were the seven Slaven brothers, who once produced a riot as a family undertaking, and Bobby Boyle, who was almost certainly insane, and who liked to burn down the houses of those Aylen, now dubbed King of the Shiners, chose to dislike.

Aylen proposed to the lumber barons that they agree to hire only Shiners as raftsmen, and when they refused — the thought of putting a crew of wild, inexperienced Irishmen in charge of the delivery of valuable cargoes of timber to Quebec did not appeal to them, somehow — he launched a campaign of terror to get his way.

When the rafts, which were often made up upstream at Pembroke or Renfrew, arrived in Bytown, Shiners in the bars and brothels beat and robbed the crews, and then took their places on the Quebec-bound rafts.

To make good on his promise to reward the thugs who worked for him, Aylen invaded the meeting of the Bytown council on January 2, 1837, with fifty followers and demanded that the Shiners be given the franchise immediately — which would have put them in control of all town business. The demand was refused, so Aylen declared war on the council. His opening shot was a calculated insult. The Shiners set up a picture of St. Patrick on a sleigh and forced all passers-by to remove their hats in homage; those who were slow to do so were beaten. Soon after, the Shiners invaded the funeral procession of one of the men they looked upon as an enemy, drove away the mourners, dumped the casket, and left the body in a ditch by the roadside.

Bytown was in the grip of a reign of terror, but when a petition was sent to the governor for troops to intervene it was refused, as was a request that

Aylen's timber licence be withdrawn. The entire community was outraged when the Shiner King imported a new group of harlots to serve the lumber-jacks, got them hopelessly drunk, and then laid out one of the girls, completely naked, on a slab of marble, with candles at her head and feet, for a mock burial service. The service was moved out of Aylen's mansion down onto the sidewalk for all to see, and a populace that had put up with, or shrugged off, previous outrages was up in arms.

The King Was Too Powerful to Be Curbed

But there was nothing to be done; Aylen was too powerful to be curbed by the magistrates of Bytown. In one telling incident, a band of Shiners cornered James Johnston, Bytown's auctioneer, on a bridge over the Rideau Canal. Johnston's sin was that the Shiners blamed him for a futile attempt to arrest Aylen in March 1837. Aylen simply slipped over to Hull, but he apparently felt that his honour had been impugned and sent his goons after Johnston.

The auctioneer jumped into the canal and escaped, but he was able to identify two of his attackers. They were arrested and confessed that they had been hired by Aylen to assassinate Johnston. The two men were marched to jail at Perth by an armed escort, but as soon as the escort departed, Aylen arrived with a gang of his followers and the prisoners "escaped." When three magistrates later entered Aylen's mansion with a search warrant to look for the escapees, they were spirited away to Hull; the attempted invasion set off a riot that lasted all night.

What brought peace at last was not any sense of moral outrage, but two factors that had nothing to do with such high-flown sentiments. The first was a fear that the lawlessness in Bytown might persuade Britain to repeal the then hefty duties on Baltic timber, dooming the local trade. The lumber barons, affrighted, promoted the establishment of the Bytown Association for the Preservation of Public Peace, with 200 citizens sworn in as special constables. A local magistrate was at last given the authority to call out troops, if necessary, and to draw arms from the armoury to deal with rioters.

The second factor was that the Canadians, who had been slow to react, finally decided to strike back at the Shiners where they were most vulnerable

— on the rafts. While the Irish could, and did, take over Quebec-bound rafts at Bytown, they were now reboarded at Long Sault or Carillon on the St. Lawrence, and all the interlopers removed by force.

By mid-1837, after four months of riots, killings, and anarchy, the Shiner riots petered out. No one knows how many people died in the fighting; the best estimates suggest at least fifty. What is known is that no one was ever punished. Aylen moved over to Aylmer, to escape prosecution, and in 1847, he tacked up the proclamation of the incorporation of the town of Aylmer; he became an assessor, a sturdy citizen, and one of the founders of the Aylen Academy, from which all six of his sons graduated. He died in 1868, full of riches and honour.

Bytown was incorporated in 1850, renamed for the river in 1855, chosen as the capital of the united Province of Canada in 1857, and as capital of the Dominion of Canada in 1867. Every Canadian schoolchild knows, or would know if he or she took history, that Queen Victoria chose our national capital, but actually she didn't. She chose Ottawa, from a group that included Kingston, Montreal, and Toronto, to be the capital of the Province of Canada, that is, Upper and Lower Canada alone; it became the capital of the Dominion because it was the capital of Canada.

It was chosen in part because it was considered humdrum, down-at-the-heels, not likely ever to come to anything much. "With the exception of Ottawa," wrote Sir Edmund Head, governor-in-chief of Canada, in July 1857, "every one of the cities proposed is an object of jealousy to each of the others."

I'll bet Victoria would never have picked Ottawa if she had known about Peter Aylen and the Bytown Riots. She would not have been amused.

The Last Laird of McNab

When we leave the national capital, thinking kind thoughts of Victoria, we head up the Ottawa Valley, through a stretch of country that rings with the memories of heroes and scalawags. One of the most interesting of the latter was Archibald McNab (for whom our Scotch terrier was named), a Scottish clan chieftain who tried to set up a feudal estate here in the 1820s. He treated the families brought out to settle 15,000 acres near Arnprior as if they were his vassals, and it took them more than twenty years to bring him to book. Among other things, he collected quit-rents from them to which he had no right, and when they balked at accepting any of his outrageous orders he told them they were guilty of treason.

Finally, an official investigation found that he had cheated his settlers, and the land was removed from his control. He left Canada and moved to France, where he died in 1860, in the company of not one, but two, mistresses.

Arnprior has raised no plaques to McNab, although McNab Township is still on the local maps. This is lovely country, but tame these days, possibly because of the presence of the Canadian forces base at Petawawa. After ducking past Chalk River, where Canada's nuclear industry was born (with heavy water netted during a wartime raid on a Nazi facility in Norway), we skip North Bay — another pretty town, but in trouble these days with the withdrawal of most of the military payroll that kept it prosperous for decades — and head for Sudbury, where one of this country's — this world's, this galaxy's — most intriguing scientific experiments is under way.

In a Mine, in a Mine, Where a Trillion Neutrinos Shine

Sudbury, and I phrase this very carefully, is not the most prepossessing city in Canada. (I once, many years ago, wrote a magazine article pointing out that Sudbury was used to train astronauts because the local landscape had been turned, by abuse and neglect, into something that looked like the far side of the moon. This resulted in the receipt of bundles of letters from Sudbury schoolchildren, egged on by their teachers, that began: "Dear Mr. Stewart: My name is Ellen, and I am only seven years old. Why do you hate me?")

It is a tough town, and the outskirts, thanks to the regular effusions of the nickel mines that underpin the economy, still have that lunar look. But in recent years, the city has turned itself inside out to improve its environment, its tourist attractions, and with its bustling Laurentian University its intellectual outlook. The centrepiece of this new approach is Science North, the snowflake-shaped building on Ramsey Lake, in the heart of the city, devoted to promoting scientific exploration.

I walk in through a door that looks as if it is ushering me into a university environment — corridors leading everywhere, young folks bustling about — traverse a tunnel, and find myself staring up at the skeleton of a fin whale. Not that I identify it at first. I assume the curving tower of bones that soars up several storeys is a dinosaur, because it is so big, but the plaque tells me instead that this is one of Jonah's pals, from Anticosti Island. A spiral walkway follows the vertical boneyard upward, and there are scientific displays and experiments on every level. Youngsters dominate, of course. On one level, a gaggle of boys are putting together a solar-powered car, which will run on a track not far from a large exhibit of the interior of the sun. There are gyro rides and electronics experiments, a Humanosphere zone that tells me more than I want to know about my own innards, and of course, a Cyberzone, jammed with computers for work and play.

On another level, there is a giant piano keyboard where you can dance on the keys and make your own music; but with my tin ear and flat feet I resist the temptation. I haven't time, anyway; I am headed for the SNO — for Sudbury Neutrino Observatory — exhibit, which has its own set of displays and a small theatre.

I am met by a slender young woman in glasses and a white smock who offers to show me around. I assume at first that she is a high-school student, helping out, but in fact Teresa Kneller is in charge of this area. A graduate of the University of Alberta, she is not only a trained astronomer, but also a skilled explainer, and what she has to tell me leaves me agog. Briefly, it is this:

In the bowels of Inco's nearby Creighton Mine, at the 2,000-metre level, an international team of scientists has suspended a huge, spherical, acrylic vessel in a ten-storey-deep container, which is twenty-two metres wide. Think of a round-bottomed, long-necked bottle and multiply by several hundred thousand. Inside this bottle lie one thousand tonnes of heavy water, borrowed from Atomic Energy of Canada Limited for the duration of this experiment. Outside the bottle, surrounded by another vessel containing ordinary water, is a geodesic sphere on which are mounted 9,500 photomultiplier tubes, or PMTs — energy detectors. And outside this is a cavity lined with concrete on which has been laid a thick layer of polyurethane, impermeable to water and radon from the surrounding rock.

The whole affair is arranged to detect neutrinos, tiny subatomic particles from the sun. They are so tiny that if you hold up your finger, about a trillion of them will pass through before you can put it down again; so numerous that two hundred trillion trillion trillion neutrinos are created at the core of the sun every second. I don't know how many zeroes that comes to. A heck of a lot of neutrinos. They are one of the building blocks of the universe. But the question we have to ask ourselves, Mr. Bones, is: Do they have any mass? If you gather a few gazillion of them together, do they have heft? Or are they pure energy, ethereal, evanescent, and airy as a politician's promise?

This is not an idle question, because the answer determines what kind of universe we inhabit and when it will ever end. If neutrinos do, in fact, have mass, no matter how small that mass, there are so many of them that in the end, gravity will act on them. And if that is the case, the universe, which is now said to have been created with one hell of a bang — it is called the big bang theory — will eventually collapse in on itself. Not tomorrow, but someday. It has to.

We are probing, here, the fundamental stuff of the universe. Well, of course, everybody wants to know the answers to the Big Questions: Was Marilyn Monroe a real blonde? Did Faint Hope finish in the money at Greenwood? How will the universe end anyway? And other nations have neutrino experiments going as well, have done for years. At the moment, from Japan to Germany, there are twenty gangs of scientists probing this very same issue.

Deep Thoughts about Heavy Water

But where we have the edge on them, and why the SNO experiment is so important, is the heavy water. Remember the heavy water? Heavy water is the same old stuff we drink, but each atom of heavy water contains an extra neutron — thus making it heavier. This makes the heavy-water atoms a better bumper. There are three kinds of neutrinos (at least, three kinds have been detected so far), and these are called majoron, muon, and tau — think of Larry, Moe, and Curly. The heavy-water detector at SNO is the only one that can detect all three.

It is as if we wanted to find out how many cars travelled down a particular stretch of highway, but the detectors we rigged up could recognize only Fords.

Not good. SNO — thanks to $300 million worth of liquid borrowed from AECL, who don't have much use for it these days, with nuclear generation in the doghouse — is conducting one of the most important scientific experiments in the world. SNO can measure the number of neutrinos reaching the earth from the sun, as well as the total numbers of all neutrino types in the same energy range, and with that information it can be determined whether or not neutrinos produced in the heart of the sun change to another type on their way through the universe.

Briefly, if they have any mass at all, they will change, and if not, not. The answer to one of the key questions of existence is at our fingertips — or rather, hanging in a bottle at Sudbury.

The reason the experiment is fixed in the bowels of the deepest mineshaft in North America is to block out everything but neutrinos. These little rascals can whiz right through the earth and out the other side in a nanosecond, but the rock, cement, and all the other layers surrounding the experiment will filter out anything not quite so slippery. As the neutrinos stream through the heavy water, every now and then, once in several trillion trillion trillion chances, one of them will collide with a heavy-water atom, in what is called an event.

There are about twenty events every twenty-four hours at SNO, and when one happens, producing a tiny, brief smidgen of light, the computers go crazy trying to milk it for every possible shred of information. The shape of the flash, for instance, can tell the scientists which direction the neutrino was travelling in, and therefore where it probably originated (in the sun, at the heart of a quasar, wherever).

By the time I have absorbed all this, it is time for lunch; if the universe is coming to an end, better eat first. So we adjourn to the Snowflake Restaurant to lunch with Teresa, Dr. Doug Hallman of Laurentian University, a physicist and the director of communications for SNO, and the Driver. Hallman, a long, slender man with glasses and greying hair, is one of those scientists so enraptured with his own work as to make you wonder whether, if the folks in charge cut off his salary, he wouldn't keep turning up anyway, since there is nothing else he'd rather do.

He explains the incredible amount of work and co-operation between business, government, and university establishments that had to take place for over a decade before the last of the more than one million pieces of the SNO experiment was put into place on April 30, 1999, and the experiment could begin. The project cost $75 million to mount — let us call it half the take from a world tour by one of the louder rock-music groups — and costs about $3 million a year to keep running, with the money contributed by the various partners, including eleven universities. "We have used local companies when-ever possible to produce materials and parts," Hallman explains. "We have asked them to do things they have never done before, and they have come through with flying colours."

The fact that SNO began to pick up the predicted signals almost at once made the entire team heave a collective sigh of relief, but it will be a couple of years, at least, before the hypothesis behind the experiment — that neutrinos do have mass, and that, therefore, the future of the universe is finite — can be tested with any authority. In the meantime, Hallman says, "We have the satisfaction of knowing that we are part of an international team working on a hugely important experiment, and moreover we have shown how this kind of project can be mounted and kept going in a world where it is harder and harder to find money for pure science."

He has no idea what other knowledge will come of this, but the stream of data now pouring out of SNO will take years to analyze, and is bound to have repercussions all over the world — if not around the universe. "Over the next decade, we will be contributing information in areas we haven't even begun to touch yet," says Hallman.

We emerge from the Snowflake Restaurant, sated with salad and satisfac-tion. Joan says, "By golly, it makes you proud to think that Canadians are not only involved in this, but also leading it." Yes.

Do Martyrs Matter?

Instead of driving west from Sudbury, we turn back south, down the other arm of the other official Trans-Canada, the one that runs south through Gravenhurst before turning east across Lindsay and Peterborough, back to Ottawa. We are not going that far; at Waubaushene, we veer west again, for

Icebergs in the backyard are common off Plum Point, on the Gulf of St. Lawrence, in Newfoundland.

This sign on Water Street in downtown St. John's proclaims Mile 0 of the Trans-Canada Highway.

Downtown Halifax, once a dreary place, has been transformed by the Historic Properties Development.

Tourists flock to Peggy's Cove, on Nova Scotia's South Shore, because it's so damn pretty.

Confederation Bridge, the new mainland link, is a blessing and a curse to PEI. More blessing than curse.

The Passamaquoddy Tidal Power Project, near Annapolis Royal, looks weird, but proves that tidal power works.

Our male heroes get forts and museums; Marie La Tour gets a few logs near the Saint John waterfront.

At Kings Landing, near Fredericton, the visitor steps smack dab back into the eighteenth century.

This is Big Momma, the largest of the wind generators near Matane, Quebec. Do not trifle with her.

Watch the recoil, kid. We are looking at the Château Frontenac in Quebec City, from Dufferin Terrace.

Whalebones climb the levels at Science North, where scientists probe the building blocks of the universe.

At Kakabeka Falls, near Thunder Bay, a princess plunged to save the village. What else is there to do?

The Forks, in downtown Winnipeg, where rivers — and diners — come merrily together.

The world as seen from inside the Brandon Agricultural Research Station. No farmers need apply.

The Kings of the Prairies are a vanishing breed. This one, near North Battleford, is now a museum piece.

Calgary has built its winter-proof walkway, Plus Fifteen, above the street. It has everything — even hookers.

Fort Macleod, Alberta, carries a tale of bold Mounties, brave First Nations people, and white betrayal.

At Kamloops, in the B.C. Interior, where desert thrusts up from the south, the hills look like elephant hide.

Our minivan, with the Driver in place, sits outside the
Palace Grand Theatre in Dawson City, Yukon.

Never know where
you will find flowers
along the Stewart-Cassiar
Highway, in northern
British Columbia.

We thought the ferry ride up the Inside Passage to Prince Rupert would be a bore, but it was a delight.

This bold soul took a motorcycle up the Dempster Highway, a route as known for its beauty as its bumps.

Five artists of three cultures carved this striking sculpture at Inuvik to mark the creation of Nunavut.

Inuvik's main street, looking towards the Igloo Church. The town is no beauty, but it is much improved.

Midland and the reconstructed village called Sainte-Marie-Among-the-Hurons, where we learn how right the aboriginals were to do rude things to the Jesuit fathers, although that is not, perhaps, the message intended.

The first Jesuit to come here, Father Jean de Brébeuf, spent three years among the Huron, from 1626 to 1629, without making any conversions, and then he returned to Quebec City, determined to mount a new and stronger mission. In 1634, he was back, with two other priests, and the Natives at Ihonatira (which he renamed St-Joseph) built a house and a chapel for the visitors. Brébeuf, a stern priest but an intelligent and determined one, learned the Huron tongue and did a number of translations, as well as writing, in Huron and French, the famous "Huron Carol." However, the transmission of information was nearly all a one-way street. Brébeuf dismissed the Native dances, so important to the local culture, in a single sentence: "Truly, here is nonsense enough, but I greatly fear there is something more dark and sinister in it."

Far more important was the ritual the Natives thought to be nonsense, if not something more dark and sinister, by which the white men dabbed water over the faces of infants and declared them to be Christians, saved from the iniquity of continuing as poor, benighted heathen. In *Jesuit Relations,* the series of reports written by Jesuit priests in New France and published in France every year from 1632 to 1673, one of the Jesuits wrote about one of these ceremonies:

> *Father Pijart baptized a dying child without being seen by the parents, who would not give their consent. He pretended to make the child drink a little sugared water and at the same time dipped a finger in it. As the father called out to him not to baptize it, he gave the spoon to a woman and said, "Give it to him yourself." She found the child asleep. Father Pijart, under the pretence of seeing if he really was asleep, touched his face with his wet finger and baptized him. At the end of forty-eight hours, he went to Heaven.*

Or to put it another way, while a child lay dying, almost certainly from a disease brought in by the Europeans, and his parents begged the priest not to bother him with any of the foreign religion that they rejected for themselves, he did it anyway, salvation by stealth, without giving a second's thought as to how he might feel if a band of heavily armed Natives were to arrive at his home in France and perform a healing dance around one of his dying kin.

The Jesuits put themselves in a peculiar and dangerous position. They kept telling the Huron that if only they would accept the Christian God, they would be assured of health and prosperity in this world and endless joy in the next; but as far as the Natives could see, all the black robes brought with them were disease and death. In the meantime, the Iroquois were closing in on the Huron, and on the prosperous villages they had built up on the basis of agriculture (squash, beans, and corn, planted together in hills, an almost-perfect diet).

The Jesuits could do nothing about the invaders, who had thrown them out of their own territory. Not surprisingly, the Huron wondered why, if the priests were so powerful and their God so invincible, things were getting worse and worse as time went by.

It was not until 1637 that the first adult in good health was converted willingly to Christianity, and the priests made a great celebration. But that same year, the Huron held a council to charge that the whites had brought them nothing but plagues — first influenza, later smallpox — and to demand that they be put to death. In return, the Jesuits made a vow of nine masses to the Virgin Mary and gave themselves a farewell feast, in the Huron custom, to greet death. At this solemn event, Father Brébeuf delivered an impassioned speech defending the mission, and the Natives backed off, impressed by the courage of these stubborn, solitary men.

In 1639, one of the priests, Father Jerôme Lalemant, wrote in his journal that no priest had yet been put to death, and it was a received maxim that "the blood of martyrs was the seed of the church." He would get his wish.

It was decided, that same year, to consolidate all the rapidly expanding missions into a single, fortified, central station, which would be a residence, fort, trading post, powder magazine, and convent. This log-built village soon went up on the east bank of the Wye River, about a mile from its mouth on Lake Huron. It was called Sainte-Marie, and the present construction is a careful recreation from the Jesuit journals of this establishment.

At the peak, there were eighteen priests, four lay brothers, seven hired men, twenty-three volunteers who served without pay, four boys, and eight soldiers. Eleven outlying missions were served from here, and in a few years, more converts were made, usually in return for food and lodging. When famine struck in 1647 and 1648, 3,000 Huron from the surrounding territory were given food and lodging, with the proviso that "no heathens could stay overnight," a proviso that did much to help along the conversion rate. (It is not fair to compare these actions with modern times, perhaps, but wouldn't today's equivalent be offering some of the refugees of Kosovo protection only if they undertook to forswear their silly allegiance to Islam?)

The Iroquois mounted a new offensive in 1648, took St-Joseph, twenty-five kilometres from Sainte-Marie, murdered Father Daniel, the priest there, torched the town, and marched off with 700 prisoners.

On March 17, 1649, they struck again, capturing two more outlying towns, St-Louis and St-Ignace, where they took Father Brébeuf and Father Lalemant prisoner. The priests were savagely beaten, tortured, and then slain. Father Lalemant had his martyrdom. The Huron abandoned their villages and fled. The Jesuits removed anything worth saving from Sainte-Marie, and to keep the invaders from gaining either the satisfaction of conquest or any trinkets they burned it to the ground. They retreated to nearby Christian Island, but abandoned that as well, a year later, and went back to Quebec, taking about 300 converted Huron with them.

They Skedaddled Back to Quebec

As I wander about the rebuilt Sainte-Marie on a lovely, sunny afternoon, it is hard to believe that it was the site of so much tragedy, death, and — pardon me — foolishness. Here are the carpentry shop, the smithy, the cookhouse, and the chapel, exactly as they would have existed three and a half centuries ago but untouched by the events of those days. I step out of the sun into the cool shade of the Church of Saint-Joseph, where the wooden walls and bare dirt floor before a crudely decorated altar speak of an earlier time. I ask the young woman in seventeenth-century costume who is stationed here whether she thinks the holy fathers were "rather arrogant."

"Oh, definitely," she replies. "They assumed that they had the right answers, and no one else was worth listening to. I have read a great many of the entries in *Jesuit Relations,* and they utterly dismiss the very complex social and spiritual — and, yes, religious — systems that were in place here when they arrived. They don't argue about them or debate them, they simply brush them off as not worthy of discussion."

She thinks she may have been too outspoken, and recollects her duty as guide, leading me across to a cordoned-off area at the rear of the church. "This is where Jean de Brébeuf and Gabriel Lalemant were buried in a single grave," she explains. "People often come to worship at this site; it is very moving."

"They are still there then, are they?"

"Well, not really." She looks up at me anxiously. "It is rather gruesome," she says. And when I promise not to faint, she says, "They dug up the bodies and boiled all the flesh off the bones." She rolls her eyes. "The bones became religious relics and were sent all over the world. After the martyrs were canonized in 1930, they were sent to the Martyrs' Shrine, just across the highway from here."

In the Christian longhouse, a reconstruction of the building where visiting Christian Natives were housed overnight, an earnest young man, a university student of history, is in the midst of a fascinating explanation of all of the objects along one of the sloping walls when I ask him abruptly, "Was the mission here a success, do you think?"

"Oh my, no," he replies. "They came up here, trampled on everybody's rights, brought in disease and death, and then told the Huron it was their fault for not converting to Christianity. And then, when the Iroquois attacked, they pulled up stakes, skedaddled back to Quebec, and before they went they burned everything, so no one else could ever benefit from all the work that was done here, by Huron as well as Jesuits. What was Christian about that? I wouldn't describe that as success."

It strikes me that if the authorities want to keep this place as a shrine for the Jesuits, they are going to have to hire a dumber class of guide. The first time I came here, many years ago, it was a kind of litany of praise to the bravery and self-sacrifice of the martyrs; I would think that now only a narrow and self-satisfied minority could take that impression away. We drive across the highway to the lovely church atop a hill, the Martyrs' Shrine, which was built to mark the canonization of eight of the Jesuits, including five slain here and three who were killed in New York State. Among the altars and souvenir shops on this side of the road, there are no doubts, hesitations, or serious history, only praise for the undoubted bravery of these men.

Laura Secord and Molly Brant

Odd how history selects its heroes, as if bravery were all that mattered. Take two Canadian women, one of whom has been granted near sainthood and the other of whom has just about disappeared. I refer to Laura Secord and Molly Brant. Laura Secord was born Laura Ingersoll, in 1775, in Massachusetts. She came to Upper Canada as a young child with her Loyalist parents, and married John Secord, of Queenston, near Niagara. When the Americans invaded the Niagara Peninsula in 1813, John was away serving with the militia, and the Secord home was taken over as a billet for the invading troops. Here, one night, Laura heard the soldiers discussing a plan for a surprise attack on Beaver Dams (near present St. Catharines).

Laura decided that she must get this news to the British, and took off across country towing a cow — cover for her enterprise — and her sister-in-law. The cow and the sister-in-law dropped out, but Laura made it through enemy lines after a long and arduous trip of nearly thirty kilometres through brutal bush. She was picked up by some First Nations allies, who escorted her to Lt. James Fitzgibbon. A true gentleman, Fitzgibbon did not tell her that he had already heard of the coming raid from other sources, and Laura went away happily thinking — along with generations yet unborn — that her brave trek through the wilderness was what led to the surrounding and capture of the American invaders at Beaver Dams. Many years later, the Prince of Wales, on a visit to Upper Canada, heard her story and arranged for her to be given a modest pension.

The Secord home is now a museum, and the heroine got a chocolate company named for her — what higher honour can there be? — even if, inevitably, the chocolate company is now the property of an American conglomerate, which may, for all we know, start cranking out Betsy Ross confections instead.

Not to take anything away from Laura, a brave and persevering lass, but she is not in the same class as Molly Brant, who has nothing named after her — although her brother Joseph lives on in Brantford and Brant County. Molly was a Mohawk, granddaughter to one of the most powerful of the tribal chiefs, Sagayeanquarashtow, whose name became translated into Chief Brant among the whites of upper New York State, his stomping grounds.

His granddaughter Degonwadonti was in turn called Mary, at least until she moved in with Sir William Johnson, superintendent of Indians and probably the most influential white man in eastern North America in the late eighteenth century. (His son, Sir John Johnson, would become the first governor of Upper Canada after the Revolutionary War.) Mary Brant became Johnson's mistress in 1756 (there was probably a marriage by Indian custom, according to the *Oxford Companion to Canadian History and Literature,* but I have never found a trace of it), three years after the death of his first wife, Catherine. Mary ruled as the chatelaine of Johnson Hall, near Johnstown, New York. For reasons of his own, Johnson called her Molly, and that is what she became.

She was handsome, shrewd, energetic, and a politician to her fingertips. Among First Nations at this time — as opposed to among the more advanced and civilized white folks — it was not thought a fatal disability to be female, and Molly was a power in the council of the Iroquois Nations and a pivotal figure in keeping these tribes neutral during the Seven Years' War. She bore Johnson eight children, and was accepted by many of his friends and allies as his wife, although she never got along well with John, Sir William's oldest son, born to his Catherine. She ensured that her younger brother, Thayendanegea — Joseph Brant — received a white man's education, as well as a Native education in the arts of war. Some gauge of her importance is contained in a letter written by Daniel Claus, one of the prominent Native agents: "One word from Mary Brant is more taken notice of by the Five Nations than a thousand from the white man without exception."

After Sir William's death in 1774, Molly moved to Fort Johnson, his original home, and set up a spy network that operated throughout the American Revolutionary War, and that often brought information which Joseph, now a Mohawk raider, used for his own purposes. Molly warned other Loyalists, but not Sir John, who had taken over Johnson Hall, when the Patriots were poised to pounce on the fort in January 1776. Sir John managed to duck out, but his wife, servants, slaves, and son were captured.

When the war was lost, Molly moved to Niagara, where she again played a key role, as head of the Society of Six Nations Matrons, persuading the Mohawks to acknowledge themselves as subjects of the Crown, and to accept the peace treaty.

It was a very bad treaty for the Mohawks, since it gave to the Americans millions of acres of land belonging to Natives who had fought and died on behalf of the king, but the Brants argued that there was little they could do about this betrayal, except to try to get some kind of settlement from the whites in payment for their sacrifice. What they got were two blocks of land, one along the Grand River, which came to be called Brant's Ford, and another on the Bay of Quinte, near Cataraqui, now Kingston. Joseph settled at the former, Molly at the latter. Joseph was awarded retirement half pay as an army captain, and Molly received a pension of one hundred pounds a year — enough to live on comfortably — for her wartime services.

Molly settled in Kingston to be near her family and her Anglican minister, John Stuart. She visited Brant's Ford but never lived there. On her last visit, in 1794, she stayed too long, and found that the only ship available to return her home had been commandeered by the new governor, John Graves Simcoe, to move his family from Newark (Niagara-on-the-Lake), then capital of the new province, to Kingston. She went to Mrs. Simcoe, who was happy to have her as a guest, and found her to be "a very sensible old woman." She seemed surprised that Molly spoke English so well, although she had been speaking it longer than Mrs. Simcoe had been alive.

Most of the First Nations people, with their land stolen and their way of life gone, sank swiftly into poverty, but Molly did well for herself in business, and at the time of her death in 1796 she was engaged in suing a local merchant who, she claimed, had cheated her in a deal.

I am unable to explain, since we accept that Canadians are not racists, why

Laura Ingersoll Secord is accorded five stars in the Canadian pantheon of heroes and Molly simply doesn't exist. (In the *Dictionary of Canadian Biography*, Laura is there and Joseph Brant is there, but Molly is not.) Maybe it will be a good thing when the Americans take over our history and culture completely; Walt Disney will make a movie about Molly, starring Julia Roberts.

Spitting Lessons

We do not regret at all retracing our route back up to Sudbury, past MacTier, Parry Sound, Pointe au Baril, and French River. This is the highland of Ontario vacation country, and while there are rather more chip wagons and hamburger stands than the countryside really needs, most of the drive is through a landscape bathed in more colours of green than can be described, with masses of wildflowers by the roadside and the punctuation of a hundred lovely little lakes and streams. Oh, yes, and highway gangs. There used to be a sign up on the highway on the way into Winnipeg that read:

This City Enjoys Four Seasons
Winter, Winter, Winter
and Road Under Construction.

The Trans-Canada traveller soon discovers that the same applies across this broad land; road crews and the chaos they bring may be the only common bond that covers us all. We want the roads to be in first-class shape at all times; we just don't want anyone working on them when we wish to pass. Along this stretch, we notice that the usual ratio of work to supervision prevails; for every man — or woman (there are more and more of them on road gangs now, and not always just holding up the Stop sign) — actually engaged in labour, there are, on average, four consultants leaning on shovels, smoking, or spitting.

Spitting is apparently as key to gaining employment in highway work as it is in baseball, and we see neat spitters, sloppy spitters, side spitters, through-the-teeth spitters, and the one-finger-on-the-nose-turn-sideways-and-honk specimen, the worst of all. We do not mind stopping so much when there is visible work in progress, but stopping to watch spitters is not as much fun, so it is just as well the countryside is lovely enough to restore our good humour.

We are headed for Elliot Lake, about one and a half hours west of Sudbury, half an hour north of the Trans-Canada, where another experiment — not so spectacular but almost as interesting as SNO — is unrolling. When the word began to seep out in the late 1970s that nuclear reactors were not, perhaps, the answer to all our energy problems after all, there came a drastic and irreversible drop in demand for uranium, the reactor fuel. Elliot Lake, a company town erected among five lovely lakes in the middle of nowhere to provide housing for workers in the mines that produced most of the mineral, was in danger of becoming a ghost town, like so many mining towns strewn across the landscape, and history, of North America.

Then Claire Dimock, an executive with Denison Mines in that company's housing department, came up with a bright idea. (She was awarded the Order of Ontario in 1998 for it, and well-deserved, too.) Instead of bulldozing the houses the mining company owned to save on upkeep, she suggested, why not turn them over to the town instead, to serve as the basis of a retirement city?

The company went along; it was not willing to take on the job itself, but it agreed to allow the town to have the houses for a very little money, and thus in 1987 was born Elliot Lake Retirement Living, a non-profit housing corporation that now owns 1,500 dwelling units — 400 houses and 1,100 apartments — which it rents out for low rates to retirees. The province contributed $7 million to the purchase and renovation of the housing, but the funding today comes from the corporation's activities.

In Elliot Lake, you can rent a modern, equipped three-bedroom apartment in a first-class building in a beautiful neighbourhood for $408 a month. A three-bedroom detached home will cost up to $600 a month, semi-detached about $550, but all the outside chores — snow-shovelling, lawn-cutting, and maintenance — are thrown in. These rates apply only if you are retired. Chris MacDonell, the vivacious young woman who tours us through Elliot Lake, explains, "The whole idea was to bring in retirees, people who would come here and spend money, not come here and compete for the few jobs that were then available.

"So if you are not retired, expect to pay about $100 a month more. We will still rent to you," she says with a smile, "but we aren't quite as glad to see you as if you were retired." Non-retired renters appear on the corporation's book as "others."

At the end of a couple of hours of her bubbling enthusiasm about the town, the Driver and I damn near decide to chuck work and move. Elliot Lake appears to have everything a normal couple could require (and perhaps a tad more of a couple of things, such as mosquitoes and blackflies in the summer and snow in the winter, than most of us might think absolutely necessary).

We start the tour at the hotel where we are staying, for which we pay zero dollars a night. That is for the first night. For the second night, if you wish to stay — and they beg you to do so — there is a charge of thirty dollars for a double room. We did stay two nights, but we felt that it would be cheating to stiff the town when we had no intention of renting anything, so we spent one night in a lakeside motel. Fifty-seven dollars.

We see the three other hotels, the bowling alley, the sixty-bed hospital (there are fifteen general practitioners and one surgeon — specialists are flown in on rotation), the theatre, the museum (where there is a model about two metres long of "Mother Mosquito and Young"), the eleven restaurants, the five banks, and scores of small boutiques.

We visit the two large lakeside parks, with their splendid beaches, as well as the schools, churches, recreational centre, and golf course. We watch a gaggle of the non-young cavorting in the Olympic Swimming Pool (where there is a special sort of elevator-cum-harness to carry anyone who needs it into or out of the water), and they are certainly having a wonderful wet.

We had assumed that a retirement community would be stiff with senior citizens staggering around on canes, but far from it. The population of 15,000 — it dropped to about half this before retirement living began to lure people here, and is now growing every year — is divided roughly 30 percent children, 40 percent retirees, and 40 percent "working adults."

This is about the same mix as most Canadian cities, but in Elliot Lake the seniors tend to be more involved in all kinds of projects. Many of them are taking adult-education courses at one of the high schools, and the arrival of so many grandfatherly- and grandmotherly-looking people in the halls has reportedly led to a revolution in clothing and manners among the teenagers.

One old gent who has always wanted to study French and art took an art course in French last year and did very well. There are hiking clubs and bridge clubs and walking clubs and reading clubs that mix up all the ages, and clubs for just about anything else you can think of.

One couple from Windsor cross-examines our guide about the number of people who come to Elliot Lake in the summer; love the views, the activities, the general atmosphere; and then, in the middle of February, decide that they have made a terrible mistake stranding themselves up here, six hours from Toronto.

"The number of people who changed their minds or dropped out last year was about 8 percent," Chris tells them.

"That would include . . ." — the old boy hesitates, uncertain how to put this — "a certain rate of attrition?"

"Yes," says our guide, straight-faced.

A few minutes later, we drive past a cemetery, and I am able to point out that this is where the attrited people stay. The man from Windsor spent most of his working life in the auto plants, but before that he was stationed here, during construction of the town. He says, "By golly, it was a rough place then. We lived in a camp up the hill over there, and we fed in a big hall. Good food, too, as I recall, and lots of it. We worked hard, were well paid, and played hard. There was only one saloon in town in those days — I'm talking about, oh, it must have been the early 1950s — and boy was she crowded. You had to buy your seat. You would see somebody who looked as if he was ready to leave and offer him ten dollars, and he would get up and give you the seat. It was the only way you could get a drink. They wouldn't serve you standing up."

After spending the morning on a general tour, we pretend in the afternoon to be a couple sufficiently decayed to be clients for a house or an apartment, and join a tour of seniors — not fakes like us, but genuine possible future citizens — with Laurie Lortie, another of the corporation's attractive guides.

She takes us through large, airy apartments and houses, answers all our dumbest questions, and introduces us to about a hundred citizens of all ages. Everybody seems to know her, and I tell her she should run for office. "Well," she says, "I am up and down these streets every single day. It is my job to find out if anything is wrong before it gets to be a problem."

Because of the presence of retirement living, other housing is also very cheap. You can buy a condo-townhouse for less than $25,000, and the most expensive free-standing bungalow was going for $72,500; typical prices are in the thirties and forties.

While we are standing in front of one of the corporation's large apartment buildings, the city bus pulls up and a file of retirees about twenty strong boards. The driver seems to know them all by name; they certainly know him, and a great deal of good-natured chaff goes on before everybody is seated and settled down.

"Hold on to your hats, folks," the driver cries, and he roars away at about ten kilometres an hour.

Elliot Lake, so far at least, is an astonishing success story. The influx of newcomers has sparked the growth of many small local industries — everything from tourism to a call centre and a small manufacturing plant — and jobs are plentiful once more. The non-profit corporation, which is controlled by a board of directors that includes representatives from the tenants and the town, ploughs every cent it makes back into improvements.

Last year, all the refrigerators in one of the apartment buildings we visited were replaced by new models; next year, the tenants all get new stoves. What is perhaps most satisfying about this experiment is that it shows how a little ingenuity, and a lot of co-operation from business, government, and the public, can turn a potential disaster into a golden opportunity.

The Secret of the Seaway

After two nights in Elliot Lake, we are ready to move west again, through the long, mostly level stretch of TCH that borders the North Channel of Lake Huron, past Blind River, Thessalon, and Bruce Mines, up to where Lakes Huron and Superior meet, in Sault Ste. Marie.

On an earlier visit here, while working on a series about the St. Lawrence Seaway, I discovered that when this international waterway was being designed in the early 1950s, a shadow seaway was laid out on the Canadian side so that, if necessary, we could, at any time, have an entirely Canadian inland waterway. In the years leading up to this longest, liftingest waterway in the world (it carries ships up and down more than 183 metres over its 3,700-kilometre length), the Americans engaged in what Lester Pearson, then Canada's external affairs minister, called "the biggest and longest dragging of feet I have known in my entire career."

The American president, Dwight Eisenhower, favoured the project, but a number of congressmen saw the new route as a danger to traffic then moving through their areas, and they blocked the necessary legislation. The seaway had first been proposed in 1897; decades later, it was still a distant dream. Canada therefore threatened to go ahead on its own, with all the facilities and all the traffic on Canadian soil. The Americans finally gave way, and an international agreement was signed in 1956.

Still, we didn't entirely trust the Americans not to pull out at the last minute, or worse, to decide to block the waterway in some trade dispute. Although we shouldered most of the cost of the project, the Americans could cut it off any time they chose simply by blocking access to the facilities on their side. Accordingly, we designed, and partly built, alternative channels to get around this. At the Soo, this meant that when the new international bridge went up, it was lifted on the Canadian side to 120 feet, which just happens to be seaway clearance.

At the same time, the contractor was instructed to shatter the stone around all the bridge piers on our side, so that a twenty-seven-foot channel — another seaway standard — could be quickly installed if the need ever arose. The Americans were outraged when they found out. The U.S. engineering chief spluttered, "That's a hell of a way to do things." I thought it was rather clever — if sneaky — of us.

Lots of Trees Up Here

Beyond the Soo is a leap of nearly 700 kilometres to Thunder Bay, the North of Superior route. Lots of trees up here. Trees and rocks. Lovely views, certainly — many of them, hundreds of them. When we first drove this route, it was an endurance test, long stretches of gravel interspersed with occasional spasms of decent road, and whenever there was a chance to make up time there would be a humongous truck, a camper, or an RV chugging along at about half the legal limit, filling the horizon with its back end.

Now there are frequent passing lanes — not frequent enough for the Driver, but frequent — the road is well graded and finely finished (except where the construction gangs are at work), and the trip is a pleasure, not a torture. As we whiz along, we compare this route with the American interstates.

To go from, say, Toronto to Vancouver, the interstates are faster and about 200 kilometres shorter, depending on which of many U.S. possibilities you follow, and there are more (and cheaper) motels and restaurants along highways that are much wider, better built, with wider shoulders and better-designed exits and entrances.

However, there is no stretch on any of the east-west interstates to match the splendour of the run from Sault Ste. Marie to Wawa, 240 kilometres north, through Lake Superior Provincial Park. We are not seeing this at its best, for that is in the autumn, when the leaves turn; still, it is enough to be getting on with. Every time you turn a corner, there is another vista of lake and forest, presided over by a moose if you are lucky.

We have not left the Soo far behind when, in the middle of nowhere, near Chippewa Falls, we come across a small park with a large plaque marking the halfway point of the Trans-Canada Highway. During our first trip here, this was a matter of great controversy. The geniuses who laid out the highway picked this as the halfway mark, but the residents of Heyden, a hamlet closer to the Soo, objected. What was the point in placing a marker in the middle of nothing? they argued. With all the changes and multiple routes of the TCH, the mid-point could be almost anywhere within an hour's drive — why not make it in Heyden, where they sell stuff?

When Ottawa remained adamant, the protesters stuck up their own marker, but it is long gone now, and yesterday's spent passion is gone with it. The stone marker here is a reminder of how huge a province Ontario is; we are halfway across the nation and still hundreds of kilometres from the western edge of Ontario. We haven't even come, yet, to where the two Trans-Canadas join, at Nipigon, the former fur-trading post at the mouth of the Nipigon River.

Take a Gander at Wawa's Goose

Wawa, which we pass soon after this, is marked by a giant goose on the outskirts, part of the fetish to make giant objects that has plunked down everything from a giant moose in Deer Lake, Newfoundland, to a giant pinto bean in Bow Island, Alberta. Gladstone, Manitoba, is a happier town, apparently, because it boasts a huge fake rock painted with a jolly smile, just as Vegreville, Alberta, would be bereft without its big painted egg, or St-Tharcisius, Quebec, without the crude rendering of a mammoth coureur de bois. Perhaps what Toronto needs to make it less ill-tempered is a ten-storey model of a loonie or a stock share, so we all know where we are.

You would never know, as you zip along the asphalt, what the road-builders went through to ease your way. More than 2,000 highway workers withstood the torments of blackflies, deer flies, and mosquitoes to sweat the road across turbulent streams, deep ravines, granite ridges, and muskeg thirty metres deep. One day in 1964, when the gangs came back to view their work of the day before, they found it had disappeared entirely, sucked into the muskeg without a trace. Today, the tourist is whisked in comfort across this lovely, brutal land, and yet complains about the campers. With the opening of the Trans-Canada, this entire area opened up — both ways.

Not only was it easier to get people, supplies, and products in and out but the wilderness became part of the province in a way that it had never been before. The isolation was broken, for good and ill, and the silence of eons was shattered by the rumble of transcontinental trucks. Now the locals can play hockey against each other, and join together to bitch about Toronto and Ottawa, instead of merely about each other.

Between Wawa — the name is said to stand for the Ojibwa word for "goose" — and Marathon, the road leaves the water and plunges back into the forest primeval again. After driving through what seems to be a continent of wilderness, we come across a sign reading "Canadian Wilderness, Three Miles," which we presume refers to a camp.

Winnie-the-Pooh's Mum Was Plugged Here

One of the interesting towns up here is White River, famous for its brutal winter temperatures (reflected, of course, in a giant thermometer) and teddy bears. Well, one teddy bear. This is where, during the First World War, an army veterinarian, Capt. Harry Colebourn, who was waiting for a train to take him east to war, bought a female black bear cub from the hunter who had just shot its mother. He named the bear Winnipeg, after his hometown. Colebourn was allowed to take the critter overseas with him — must have been a lenient army in those days — and it slept beneath his bunk in barracks.

When he was ordered to the front, he turned it over to the London zoo, which is where A. A. Milne, the poet, and his son, Christopher Robin, saw it. Milne converted Winnipeg into Winnie, changed its sex to male, and began writing stories about it, which were first published in 1926. Winnie-the-Pooh launched a little industry of his own. He became a yellow teddy bear with an inordinate passion for honey, and eventually appeared in translation in more than a dozen languages.

White River has stuck up a statue of Winnie at the town entrance, which I guess is okay, until you reflect that the town's main contribution to the tale was the fact that one of its citizens slaughtered the cub's parent. (The local version is that the cub just wandered in out of the woods one day; perhaps Momma ran off with a travelling salesman.)

We are now moving through the land of paper mills and gold mines, neither of them doing particularly well these days, and there is a reflection for our times: to own a gold mine in a global economy may mean you are headed for receivership. It is intriguing to wonder what the prospectors who spent their days scrambling through this wilderness a century ago would think of that.

At Thunder Bay, an hour past Nipigon, we stop briefly at the Terry Fox monument, just off the highway, where the one-legged runner was forced to end his Marathon of Hope, on September 1, 1980. This stretch of road is known as the Terry Fox Courage Highway, and it lets us know that sometimes, at least, we get our heroes right.

Thunder Bay used to be the Lakehead, and used also to be Fort William and Port Arthur, until they were amalgamated in 1970 into what is a more or less shapeless blob. One of the world's largest grain-handling ports, it now owes most of its employment to pulp mills, which do not smell any prettier here than anywhere else. One of its oddities, discovered on this trip, is that it holds the largest Finnish population in the world, outside Finland itself.

In the evening, just outside our motel on Highway 62 — the road to Duluth, Minnesota — a swarm of teenagers congregates for class pictures. Rigged out in all their finery but carrying the essence of sweatshirts, jeans, and sneakers with them, they are heart-breakingly beautiful, appallingly gauche, and vibrate back and forth between the soigné and the simple-minded.

"Robinson, take the goddam gum outta yer mouth and get your ass over here!" This from a tall, slender young goddess in a plum-coloured dress that she has to keep hitching up in front to keep Robinson's eyes from popping like champagne corks.

Starting out again the next morning, we call in at Kakabeka Falls, just north of Thunder Bay. We remember this from our first trip along this road, thirty-five years ago, mainly because we thought John de Visser, the photographer with us for that ramble, was going to fall into the water, after leaning over to get the best picture of the cascade, and wind up in the hydro turbines downstream.

Another Falls, Another Princess

Now there are fences all about, to curb the over-enthusiasts, and to make up for this, the authorities have set out, in a series of panels, the dramatic story of Greenmantle, the Ojibwa princess who — wait for it — led Sioux warriors over the falls in order to save her village. An elderly gent from Wisconsin, with an expensive-looking camera, is taking pictures of the panels that set forth this dramatic, and familiar, tale.

When he sees me, he looks up. "I believe it," he says. Then he adds, "Of course, I believed the tobacco companies when they said smoking couldn't cause cancer, too."

Beyond Kakabeka Falls, the way leads north and west through Ignace, another mill town, where I insist on stopping to identify the riot of wildflowers along the roadside. The Driver, who is trying to make up time, waits by the roadside, gunning the engine only occasionally, while I poke, prod, and sniff.

"What kind of flowers are they?" she asks.

I reply, "So far, I have been able to identify your yellow ones, your white ones, your pink ones, orange ones — lots of orange ones — daisies, what looks like wild poppies, and blue ones."

"Thank God for science," says the Driver.

Skipping lightly past Kenora — where I was once sued by a local lawyer because I described the town as "racist," which he seemed to take personally — we push on to Dryden, where we eat an excellent steak in a small steakhouse off the main drag. We are served by a young woman with an accent that is pure Brooklyn.

"How did you end up here?" asks the Driver.

She thinks about it for quite a while. "Damned if I know," she replies.

The Real Scoop on Mary's Lamb

The next morning, we call in at Egli's Sheep Farm, much heralded in the tourist literature, at Minnitaki, just west of Dryden. This is Canada's largest specialty shop for wool and sheepskin products. It was started by Robert and Margarit Egli after they emigrated from Switzerland in 1952 and recognized this as wonderful country for foraging.

Today, there is a working family farm, a retail shop, and a thriving catalogue business, through which they sell lamb, wool, and just about anything that can be made of wool or leather. The Driver is much taken up with all of this, while I slope off to have a look at the sheep themselves. There is a small herd of them in a pen not far from the wool shop, and an American family, from Chicago, are oohing and aahing at them, as if they were an exotic and rare breed. The sheep stare right back.

A boy of about ten sticks his hand into the pen — ignoring all signs — and tries to pat one of the ewes, which promptly nips him.

"Holy shit!" yelps the kid. "The damn sheep bit me!"

"Roger, really," says his mother. "A sheep wouldn't bite you."

"Tell the damn sheep that," rebuts the youngster, and stomps off.

I decide that it is too dangerous for me out here among the fauna, and so I go back inside, where I come across one of those little gems of information that make travel the uplifting experience it always turns out to be. This is a clipping from an old magazine, pinned to a post above a display of woollen goods, which lays bare the stark tale behind that poem known to us all, sometimes in its clean version, "Mary Had a Little Lamb."

There really was a Mary, it seems: Mary Sawyer, who lived in Sterling, Massachusetts, in the early part of the nineteenth century. She adopted a sickly lamb, which she named Snow, from her farmer father's flock. One day in 1814, her brother Nathaniel left the gate open and the lamb followed Mary to school, where the kids were allowed to play with it before the teacher locked it in a shed. John Raulstone, a boy of thirteen and a budding poet, was one of Mary's classmates, and he managed to turn the incident into the well-loved poem.

The class teacher, Polly Kimball, sent the poem to *Today's Magazine for Ladies* in 1830, and in that simple era it went over like something out of the lungs of Céline Dion in our more jaded time. Mary's mother made two pair of stockings out of the lamb's wool before it became just another Sunday joint. Not exactly *War and Peace*, I admit, but I feel richer for knowing that there really was a Mary, and a lamb.

Can Manitoba top this?

7

Manitoba

FROM BUNS TO BRANDON

On the smooth ribbon of Highway 1 east of Winnipeg, where trees shrink down the steady incline from woodland to wheat, a 65-foot Mack truck thundered past. The rumble of her diesel engine and the whine-slap of her tires had begun in Toronto, 40 hours and 1,200 miles southeast. Between her flanks, shimmering in the prairie sun, she carried 25 tons of freight: 84 boxes of stationery, 26 cartons of shoes, 2 drums of castor oil, 7 cases of heating registers, 24 bottles of root beer syrup, cans of paint, a barrel of sandpaper, baseball bats, brake fluid, rubber matting, trouser guards, pipe fittings, electrical appliances — it was as if a department store had been tipped on its side and the contents poured into the heaving monster puffing across the plain.

— STAR WEEKLY, APRIL 17, 1965

We make two stops in the 205-kilometre hop from Kenora to Winnipeg, one more successful than the other. The first is a pause at a motel near Falcon

Lake for a hot cinnamon bun. From Ontario on east, even though there are just as many doughnut shops as in the West — one about every fifty metres, at a guess — you do not see the really impressive cinnamon bun, only pale imitations. I do not know why this is; something in the water, no doubt.

The buns we get on this occasion are not really large by Western standards — no bigger than a man's head — but, drenched with butter and steaming warm, they serve to stave off hunger for the nonce. At our second stop, to get gas, I wander off to test the facilities and manage to lock myself in the john. Well, you know how it goes. You don't want to draw attention to yourself, especially since it is going to turn out that all you had to do was give the handle a twist *that* way — not this way, sir, that is how you locked yourself in; the other way, see? — so I rattle the door a couple of times, quietly.

Then I rattle it a few more times, not so quietly.

Then I begin to bang on the door, and then I am banging and shouting and kicking until the door suddenly flies out and a flustered fellow customer, a beardless youth of about sixteen summers, gives me a very odd look, and my freedom.

"Locked myself in somehow," I explain.

"You did, eh?" He doesn't believe a word of it. He shows me, by closing the door, locking it, and opening it again, that there is nothing whatever wrong with the mechanism.

"It stuck," I insist.

"Sure," says the kid. "Sure."

I depart and find the Driver full of lively curiosity. "Where were you?"

"In the garage place. In there."

"No, you weren't. I looked."

"Farther in. You probably couldn't see me. I was interviewing the mechanic."

"No, you weren't. *I* was talking to the mechanic."

"Locked myself in."

"You locked . . . You mean that gawdawful racket, screaming and banging, that was *you*?"

"Well, I had to get help. You know."

"Of course I know. Perfectly understandable." She begins to sing a chorus of "Oh, dear, what can the matter be? / Two old ladies locked in the lavat'ry." She keeps it up for about fifty kilometres. I am sunk in thought.

The Prairies Are Waiting to Greet You

As you get farther west from the western border of Ontario along the Trans-Canada, the trees begin to shrink. You may think this is an optical illusion, but it is not. The prairies are waiting to greet you, and they announce their presence by lining up the forests in order of shrinkage, from east to west, so that by the time you are in sight of Winnipeg, there are no trees; they have shrunk away into the grass, save for timid little copses that the farmers have planted around their homes to keep from being blown to Baltimore. In this nude landscape, you can see Winnipeg, as you can see most prairie cities, about thirty kilometres off. That little handful of sticky-up bits over there, beyond the fields, those are skyscrapers, or will be in a few minutes.

The best trip we ever had to Winnipeg was in 1972, when a blizzard had shut down the airport and the railway and, for most people, the highway, but the Driver, undeterred, brought us through drift and storm and deposited us at the Fort Garry Hotel, near Main and Broadway. There might have been other guests there, but we never saw any. For a couple of days, we seemed to have the place to ourselves, with the result that the staff, bored out of their trees with nothing else to do, treated us like misplaced royalty and spoiled us forever for the Holiday Inn.

It was on that trip that Joan, looking out the window, saw a bundle of Ukrainian ladies, clad in mufflers and long black stockings, ploughing down the middle of Donald Street on their way to Eaton's. "By golly, if they can go out in this weather, I can too," she said, and disappeared into the swirl. She reappeared about ten minutes later, bright blue and covered in snow.

"Where did you get to?" I asked.

"Dunno. Maybe Brandon. Certainly not Eaton's."

It gave her a solid respect for the hardihood of the Ukrainians who, fuelled mainly by perogies, conquered this part of the country. And conquer it they did. I once ran into a truck driver who told me he came from a quiet little town in Manitoba where he felt completely at home. "No foreigners there," he explained. "Only Ukrainians."

A Lord, a Louse, and a Louis

On this trip, we meet nothing but sunshine and balmy breezes, so I totter off to a new commercial development called the Forks (because it is built on and around the forks of the Assiniboine and Red rivers, where they meet behind the railway station in mid-Winnipeg). The Forks is aptly named not only on riverine grounds, but also because it is a place where the populace seems to be plying forks all the time. Strung out over this national historic site, there are more than a score of restaurants serving everything from southern barbecue to fine French cuisine.

However, it is history, not food, that brings me here, for Winnipeg presents another of those many places in Canada where it is interesting to ask the eternal question: What makes a hero, anyway? In this neighbourhood, we had Lord Selkirk, Louis Riel, and Sir George Simpson, all within a short time span. History has made Simpson a hero, Riel a nutcase, and Selkirk an also-ran, but an argument can be made that history, as usual, has it wrong. The real story is found in John Morgan Gray's *Lord Selkirk of Red River*.

Thomas Douglas, fifth earl of Selkirk, was born at St. Mary's Isle in Scotland in 1771 and educated at Edinburgh University, where he joined a club for the discussion of social and political questions (Sir Walter Scott was another member). Here, he formed views about the ordering of society that were not proper to his station — we would call him a leftist today — but that didn't matter, since he was, after all, the seventh son, and not likely to succeed to the title.

But succeed he did; all of his brothers perished, one way or another, and by the time he was twenty-eight Thomas Douglas had become the earl and was fired with a mission. He meant to do something to relieve the misery of the thousands of crofters who had been shoved off their lands in Scotland to make way for more profitable things, like sheep. In 1803, he established, at Orwell Bay, in Prince Edward Island, a small colony of Highlanders, which slowly, and with much struggle and many setbacks, succeeded. A second small colony near Lake St. Clair in Upper Canada, at Baldoon (named for his father's estate), was a disastrous flop. After a crop failure, when heavy rains wiped out the low-lying fields the Highlanders had planted, malaria struck, and Selkirk ordered the settlement closed and the survivors moved to higher ground along the Thames River. With the lessons of these events behind him, Selkirk resolved to establish a much larger settlement in the Red River valley, with its incredible fertility, details of which he had apparently come across sometime in 1801 or 1802.

This time, he moved cautiously. Because the whole Canadian West had been effectively turned over to the Hudson's Bay Company, Selkirk bought shares in that company, which was in difficult financial trouble for the first time in its history. War in Europe and aggressive competition from the new, Montreal-based North West Company had driven the shares down from one hundred pounds to sixty pounds by 1809, and Selkirk was able to take effective control of the firm.

Thus when he proposed to establish a colony in the midst of a tiny settlement of Canadians and Métis, the company was happy to cede a tract of 25 million acres to him. Selkirk sent out two groups of settlers — the first colonists in the entire Northwest — in 1811 and 1812. In Selkirk's honour, they established a colony at a place named Fort Douglas, on the Red River, just north of the forks of the Assiniboine.

The Nor'Westers, the inheritors of the French fur trade in the West, hotly disputed the Hudson's Bay Company's right to dispose of land in the Red River country, and they set out to break up the settlement by force. They conducted raids on the Selkirk settlers, stole their food, destroyed their homes, subjected them to constant harassment for years. In return, Selkirk ordered Fort Douglas strengthened, and he appointed Robert Semple, a businessman and adventurer, as agent-in-chief for the Hudson's Bay Company in North America.

In March 1816, a group of Highlanders, acting against Semple's orders, attacked and destroyed the lightly defended Nor'Wester outpost, Fort Gibraltar, south of Fort Douglas. In retaliation, on June 19, a large force of Nor'Westers and Métis trapped Semple and a group of his followers at Seven

Oaks, near Fort Douglas, and killed twenty-one of them, including Semple.

Selkirk was on his way with a force of disbanded soldiers to guard the settlement when this news reached him. As soon as his ships reached the lake-head, he seized the North West Company headquarters at Fort William and sent a number of the officers back to Canada to face trial for the massacre at Seven Oaks. He then pushed on to the Red River, restored order, and brought the colonists, who had fled, back to their lands again. Then the whole battle was transferred to the courts in Montreal, where the Nor'Westers had power-ful political allies. With one exception, all the murder charges levelled against them were quashed, and Selkirk was instead singled out for prosecution by the Colonial Office.

After years of suits and countersuits, and despite an official inquiry that condemned the North West Company in harsh terms, Selkirk was forced to pay heavy damages for "false imprisonment," among other things. While the criminal trials were still going on, a dozen key figures, both prisoners and witnesses, had been quietly released and disappeared. At the end of the trials, a grand dinner party was given in the jail by the Nor'Westers to celebrate the fact that "the North West Company could appear to be beyond justice."

While bench warrants were sought for the re-arrest of the escapees, Dr. John Allen, Selkirk's physician and ally, noted glumly, "It is in my humble opinion, needless to send any warrants into the interior. For what purpose give these vagabonds another party of pleasure in Montreal to be again set at liberty?"

Selkirk's personal fortune was wiped out and his health broken; he died in 1820, deeply in debt.

However, the corporate battle that had led to so much tragedy ended, as so many corporate battles do, in a merger of the companies involved, in 1821. One of the traders who helped bring about the union was a new employee who had been sent out to Canada in 1820, George Simpson. The Little Emperor ruled as governor of the Hudson's Bay Company, and therefore of more than one-quarter of North America, for forty years.

He ran his empire with brisk efficiency, swooping back and forth across the continent in swift-travelling canoe convoys on inspection tours. He was always preceded into camp by a Highland piper in full fig who made the pines ring with his squalls, and who must have set the First Nations people to pondering fiercely the music of the white man.

Simpson was successful, but he was not nice. He described the Canadian voyageurs, on whom so much depended in getting the furs to market, as "mongrel half-gentry and half Northwest renegade. . . . The very dross and outcast of human specie . . . but a useful people if kept at a respectful distance."

Of the Natives who trapped the furs in the first place, he wrote, "A little rum, you know, operates like a charm on the Indians. They cannot resist the temptation and if the affair is properly managed, every skin may be had from them." (This and other quotes on this subject are taken from the *Report from the Select Committee on the Hudson's Bay Company,* British Parliament, 1857, Appendix No. 16. The report produced no reforms.)

He entered into a number of liaisons with First Nations or mixed-race women, and scattered illegitimate offspring across the West. When one of his mistresses became pregnant, Simpson, then off on a trip, instructed the post factor:

Pray keep an Eye on the Commodity, and if she bring forth anything in the proper time and of the right colour let them be taken care of, but if anything be amiss let the whole be bundled about their business.

Simpson set up a system of oppression that lasted until well into the twentieth century. The company plied the Natives with rum, cheated them in trade, beat them, starved them, and even, on occasion, murdered them. A select committee of the British House of Commons, inquiring into the operations of the Hudson's Bay Company in 1857, took the testimony of one John McLaughlin, who said that he had seen a Native hanged by the company at Pembina. He was asked if he did not know that this was illegal, and he replied that he did:

Q: *How is it that the Colonists resident upon the spot did not remonstrate against this execution?*

A: It is impossible for them to remonstrate there; they are too much under the control of the Company; the Company would stop supplies.

Hudson's Bay under Simpson ran a rigid monopoly, and if a First Nations man sold furs to a settler — instead of accepting the company's price — the company would seize the furs and imprison the Native. Those who ran afoul of any of the corporate regulations were cut off from supplies, and often died as a consequence. A Saulteaux chief testified before the select committee that

> the Traders have never done anything but rob us and make us poor. . . .
> We have many things to complain of against the Hudson's Bay Company.
> They pay us little for our furs, and when we are old we are left to shift for
> ourselves. We could name many old men who have starved to death in
> sight of many of the company's principal forts.

A surgeon who had worked for the company for three years testified that when two starving Natives came aboard a company boat to beg for food, "the Governor took an oar and beat them most unmercifully, saying, 'I'll teach you to go aboard without my leave.'"

First Nations people were forbidden to trade with each other; the object was to "prevent the Indians learning that there was another pursuit whereby they would become independent of the Company, and cease to be its hunters," according to a witness before the committee. In case these little tricks did not return sufficient profit, the company, under Simpson's rule, routinely short-weighted the Native traders.

The *Macmillan Dictionary of Canadian Biography* entry on Simpson sums all this up rather neatly, and in a single phrase: "His administration of the affairs of the company was marked by great firmness." Well, I guess. Hanging the defenceless can be called "firm," among other things. Simpson's rule was also marked, in due course, by a knighthood and a rich and happy retirement at Lachine, Quebec, where he died in 1860, surrounded by loved ones. His official biography notes that he had one son and three daughters by his white wife, Frances Ramsey; no doubt space considerations prevented the listing of his other children.

Louis Riel, Hero-in-Waiting

Louis Riel was a teacher, born at St. Boniface, educated at the seminary in Montreal, who then returned to the West, just in time to be caught up in the unrest — the inevitable unrest — that flowed from the Canadian government's decision to establish the new province of Manitoba in 1870 without any consideration of the rights of the Métis who formed the bulk of the population. Manitoba was to be ruled by an appointed lieutenant-governor and a council; the locals would have no say.

When land surveyors began to swarm over the countryside, and made it clear to the scattered inhabitants that they had no rights whatever in the land their people had held for years, Riel was persuaded to take a leading role in the protests. He set up a provisional government for an independent Métis nation at Fort Garry (the old Fort Douglas, renamed), and took a number of white prisoners during a raid on Dr. J. C. Schultz's store. Schultz was the leader of the Canada Party, which had campaigned aggressively for the takeover of the Red River area on behalf of whites only, and the store was guarded by an armed band of his followers.

One of those who escaped when the Métis attacked was Thomas Scott, a road-builder who had earlier been found guilty of assault. Scott was one of a party that had also been involved in an incident in which a young Métis prisoner was beaten to death. In February 1870, Scott and other Canada Party supporters set out from Portage la Prairie to release the prisoners at Fort Garry and capture Riel, but they were instead captured themselves, and after a "court martial" at the fort, Scott was convicted of treason against Riel's new government and shot on March 4, 1870.

This was the incident that led to the dispatch of Canadian troops to the West to restore order; meanwhile, Riel retreated to Montana. In 1871, he was back in Manitoba, for a meeting at which it was proposed that the Métis should support an invasion of the province by Fenians from the United States. Riel not only rejected this idea, but also assembled his people in arms to prevent such an invasion.

For this action, the lieutenant-governor publicly thanked Riel (though carefully avoiding any mention of his name, since he was, technically, still an outlaw). Twice elected to the House of Commons, he was very nearly arrested when he attempted to take his seat, and eventually he fled to the United States once more. Finally, it was arranged that he could return to Canada legally after a period of banishment that was to last five years. However, he suffered a mental breakdown, was confined in the asylum at Longue Pointe, Quebec, under the name Louis R. David, and on his release, went once more to Montana, where he became a U.S. citizen in 1883. He was teaching in the St. Peter's Jesuit mission there when a delegation of settlers and Métis, both French and English, came and asked him to lead them in an attempt to redress their many grievances against the government of Canada.

The buffalo had been slaughtered; the surveyors, land-grabbers, and other attendants of the CPR's invasion of their lands threatened these people with eviction, starvation, and death; and John A. Macdonald's government simply turned a deaf ear to all their pleas. Riel once more crossed the border and set up a provisional government, in March 1885. When the North West Mounted Police marched on Riel, they were routed by the Métis under Gabriel Dumont, at Duck Lake, on the Saskatchewan-Manitoba border.

But now there was a railway to the West, and within a very short time 8,000 troops were on their way out to deal with this second Riel rebellion. Riel, sensibly, surrendered at Regina, while Dumont conducted brilliant defensive campaigns at Fish Creek and Batoche, before fleeing to Montana. (He returned under a general amnesty years later.) Riel was tried for treason and, while his defence lawyers insisted on pleading him insane, protested that he was perfectly sane, and even justified in the actions he had taken.

He was convicted, and was hanged on November 16, 1885. Prime Minister John A. Macdonald, pressed to extend clemency in this case, replied, "He shall hang though every dog in Quebec shall bark in his favour," and his death left a rift in Canadian politics that was to last for decades.

In one fallout from the controversy, Honoré Mercier was swept to power in Quebec on the basis of anti-English feeling; in another, the government of Manitoba passed a law to ban the practice of teaching in French in the province, a law that remained in place well into the twentieth century. But Riel is being viewed in a new and more sympathetic light these days, and sand-blasted into the shell housing his statue on the legislative grounds are these words: "I know that through the grace of God, I am the founder of Manitoba — Louis Riel."

Mark him down as a near-hero, or a hero-to-be, in the Canadian cavalcade.

A Canadian Capacity to Build Livable Cities

Hard to believe, amid the sunshine, laughter, and cascade of languages that surround me now in the Forks, that this was once such dark and bloody ground. Easier to believe that Canada has somehow developed a capacity, possibly by learning from its own mistakes, to build large and livable cities. Winnipeg represents more than half the population of this entire province, and by rights should be subject to overcrowding and urban blight, but it is, instead, a city of neighbourhoods and, despite the long winters, a wonderful place to live in or visit.

This is also a great walking town — not many hills — and a visitor can do worse than take one of the many walking tours that begin at the Forks and ramble out in every direction, including a riverwalk that takes you along the Red River to the Manitoba legislature and beyond. I choose the walk that takes me across Hudson Bay Flats, where a couple of centuries ago Buffalo grass grew to more than two metres in height, and where, later, the Red River cart brigades assembled for the annual buffalo hunts.

Then I cut down to Portage and Main, where the drama of the Winnipeg General Strike — Canada's largest labour upheaval — took place in 1919.

The Winnipeg General Strike

It began when Winnipeg workers discovered that while their living costs had gone up by 75 percent in seven years, their wages had gone up by only 13 percent; they were being squeezed into poverty and even starvation. A series of organizing attempts and strikes during 1918 had been blocked or broken by the use of professional strike-breakers, hired goons, damage suits against labour leaders, and *ex parte* injunctions (through which employers, after refusing to recognize a union, could then go into court and have the subsequent labour stoppage declared illegal, without the union's representatives even being allowed to appear).

The Winnipeg Trades Council called a general strike for 11 a.m. on Thursday, May 15, and at that time, 22,000 workers — including city policemen — in 94 unions walked out in concert. Firemen left their stations; telephone service was shut down; commercial establishments of every sort, from businesses to restaurants, ceased to operate.

And up at city hall, over at the legislative assembly, and back in Ottawa, the folks in charge were certain that this was it, that Bolshevism had taken over the nation, and Chaos and One Night were just around the corner. The Winnipeg Trades Council became "the St. James Street Soviet" and the labour leaders "outside agitators," "foreigners," and "undesirable aliens." Arthur Meighen, the minister of the interior, arrived from Ottawa to take charge, and he immediately threw out the rule of law.

There was no attempt to bargain; instead, workers were ordered back to work, and if they proved reluctant they were simply discharged. Striking police officers were ordered to sign a pledge denouncing the trades council, and when they refused, 240 of them were fired — almost the entire force. Their places were taken by "special police," students and anti-strike war veterans who were paid six dollars a day — more than the regular police officers made. They had no notion how to do their work, and brawls and beatings became normal behaviour as the strike wound on through June.

The federal government rammed through an amendment to the Immigration Act to make it legal to deport anyone the government chose to consider "an enemy alien," and since the term was never defined the authorities were allowed a certain scope in the application of the law.

On June 17, several strike leaders were arrested under this legislation and rushed straight to Stony Mountain Penitentiary, without any sort of trial. Meighen, a lawyer, wanted them all deported, but as many of them — including A. A. Heaps, a member of Parliament — were Canadian citizens, he was persuaded that this was going too far. They were finally released on bail.

The strike committee announced a giant protest demonstration for Saturday, June 21, in downtown Winnipeg. The mayor immediately warned that all demonstrators would be arrested, and the North West Mounted Police and the militia were brought in to back up his quite illegal threat. On Saturday afternoon, just before 2:30 p.m., strikers began to mass on Main Street, near the city hall. When a streetcar containing two strike-breakers came down the tracks, the crowd took that as a deliberate provocation and attacked it.

At this, the waiting Mounties poured into the streets, with thirty-six men in trucks and fifty-four on horses, and charged into the crowd, firing their pistols and killing one protester. The police later claimed that they fired only in response to gunshots from the crowd, but there was none, as a subsequent inquiry determined. The crowd panicked, and hundreds of strikers began to run down side streets, where they were met by cordons of six-dollar-a-day special police armed with guns and clubs. Then the militia arrived, with cavalry and machine-gunners mounted in trucks, and dispersed the remaining strikers.

The Winnipeg General Strike was over, although it was not formally called off until four days later. Eight strike leaders were put on trial under a section of the Criminal Code that was hastily shoved into place for the occasion, and under which the onus of proof in a criminal case shifted from the Crown to the accused. All but one were convicted, on charges of "conspiring to bring into hatred and contempt the governments of the Dominion of Canada and the Province of Manitoba and to introduce a Soviet system of government."

In addition, J. S. Woodsworth, who was just becoming famous as a minister turned social worker and political activist, was charged with "speaking seditious words." In specifying the seditious words he had spoken, the charges cited one quotation from the Bible and another from the Rt. Hon. Arthur Henderson, a British MP and, later, Cabinet minister. Woodsworth was dying to go to trial, but the embarrassed Crown attorneys stayed the proceedings, a stay that lasted the rest of his life; he could, in theory, have been brought to trial after he was an MP and the leader of the Co-operative Commonwealth Federation.

The Winnipeg General Strike was lost, but the labour movement was re-energized by the patent illegality of the actions taken, and many of the most prominent strike leaders — including Heaps, Woodsworth, John Queen, William Ivens, and George Armstrong — were elected to the House of

Commons or the provincial legislature within the year. Ivens and Armstrong literally walked from their jail cells to the legislature at the end of their one-year jail terms.

What strikes me — pardon the pun — as I roam the streets where all this excitement took place is that it could never happen again. Whatever the faults and failings of our politicians, they cannot make up new laws as they go along and jail opponents simply because they disagree; they cannot order in the military because employers refuse to bargain with their workers; and they cannot, if they wish to remain in office, simply ignore the rule of law whenever it suits them. Winnipeg, and Canada, have come a long way.

A Plague on Both Your Formals

We are, accordingly, in a state of grace when we drive through silent downtown streets early the next morning and head for Altona, down near the U.S. border, to have a look at one of the most unusual business enterprises in the province, one that has no union whatever. We follow the Pembina Highway, the one that leads south to Grand Falls, North Dakota, and Fargo, but stop before we run out of coffee houses and doughnut shops to have breakfast at a twenty-four-hour chain feedbin called the Perkins Family Restaurant. This is a large restaurant, and there are, even at 6 a.m., quite a few young people in the squadron of booths along one wall. They are dressed in formal wear — the boys in dark suits, some tuxes, the girls in long dresses, with attendant gardenias and orchids.

"There must be some kind of plague," I tell the Driver. "Look at them."

She looks. Most of the youngsters are slumped over their plates, communing with cornflakes or pancakes from table level. One young woman, however, has gone the other way; she is leaning back, holding up the restaurant wall, and her mouth is open, oh, about a metre. From this issues a soft and sibilant sound, like the noise that might emerge from a large beehive or a small foundry. She is snoring.

"Graduation party?" Joan asks the waitress.

"Yep," says the waitress. "They came in about an hour ago, after an all-nighter, and I thought they were going to be trouble. Heck, they're no trouble."

I deplore the frailty of modern youth, which collapses after a mere twelve or so hours of revelry, but Joan says not to worry, by this evening they will have turned this breakfast in their own minds into something that might have been staged by the Borgias when they were going strong.

Pulling out of Winnipeg after breakfast — and after striving, in vain, to wake some of the dreamers for a chat — we note once more the abruptness of Western Canadian cities; one minute you are rolling along between Tim Hortons and funeral parlours and the next, open prairie. There is no tapering off; city and country collide within a few yards. Now we are driving past a vast field of canola — there is nothing in the world as yellow as a field of canola — and overhead a flock of snow geese wheel and bank in the sky, climbing by spiral, disappearing where their whiteness is blanketed in a cloud, then reappearing again in a patch of blue. Rather nice. Pretty soon, we notice hastily thrown-up dykes around some of the farmhouses; although it is nearly July, most of the fields in this corner of the province are sodden, and some are veritable lakes.

The farmers have been clobbered by nature once again, and they cannot get their crops into the ground. Some have managed, however; as we turn west along Highway 14, a biplane suddenly bops up over the bushes beside us, then settles down to place a vast blanket of spray over the land. Although we heartily disapprove of this kind of crop-dusting, it is impossible not to be impressed by the pilot's skill as he flips the aircraft onto its wing, spins about, and makes another run the other way. He could do a U-turn on the highway.

A Plant That Makes a Good Impression

We turn south on Highway 30, pass a large sign advertising the Manitoba Sunflower Festival, due in a couple of weeks, and pull up at a large factory with a sign that says Friesens. Wrong factory. We drive on another kilometre, down the town's main street, and spot an even larger factory that says Friesens. Wrong again. We are finally directed to the right one of the five Friesen establishments, this one distinguished by a neat lawn, a statue of two bears, and no sign whatever.

"I guess the locals know where it is," I say.

In fact, much of the world is now becoming aware of where Friesens is, at least that part of it connected with book publishing. This is the largest independent book-manufacturing firm in Canada, with sales of close to $100 million annually and offices across Canada — as well as two in the United States, at San Francisco and Louisville, Kentucky. This one 150,000-square-foot facility turns out about one thousand titles a year for every major Canadian publisher and, increasingly, American ones as well.

Frank Friesen, the marketing director, notes that "about 30 percent of our work now is done for people like Harper's, firms like that, in the U.S." He also notes that he is not a member of the major shareholding family. "Friesen is a very common name hereabouts."

While other Canadian printing companies have been faltering and failing, Friesens has gone on expanding, especially in the book-printing business, which was an unintended sideline. David Friesen — and yes, he is of the family — the chairman and chief executive officer, explains, "We started as a small confectionery store in 1907, then bought a bookstore. And it just sort of grew." He is the third David Friesen to head the business started by David W. Friesen, a young Mennonite farmer who moved to town in 1907 to set up a general store, which soon became the post office and an agency for the telephone system as well. His three sons expanded into school supplies and office supplies.

Then they bought a printing press in 1933, along with a Linotype typesetting machine. After a while, it seemed only natural to start a newspaper to use the equipment, and the *Altona Echo*, a weekly, was born in 1941. Soon, stationery, binding, calendars, yearbooks, and then trade books became part of the firm, and the company kept having to build new plants and hire more people. The growing business was incorporated as D. W. Friesen & Sons Ltd. in 1951.

"We are very much a part of this community," David Friesen tells me, "and we see no reason why, with modern technology, we can't do everything we need to do to expand right here."

Printing is one of the most high-risk industries in the country. By the time you have your last piece of up-to-date equipment paid for, it is no longer up to date; the trick is to be small enough to be flexible while remaining large enough to achieve economies of scale. There is no easy way to do this, and three generations of Friesens have pulled it off by nothing more magical than hard work and constant application.

Today, Friesens has separate divisions for trade books — fiction and non-fiction, cookbooks, and coffee-table books turned out for almost every Canadian publisher, including the publisher of this book; yearbooks — a very lucrative offshoot of educational publishing; wholesale — the division that handles office supplies and stationery; and fastprint — which makes all kinds of cartons, packaging, and boxes.

There is also a retail division that owns a large bookstore downtown, and — the pride of the firm — Friesens College. This is not an ivy-covered outfit with dormitories and quads; rather, the company, in conjunction with Red River Community College in Winnipeg, offers a nine-month diploma course in printing and graphics to youngsters entering its own establishment.

David Friesen says that the strength of the company lies in its staff — well, what is he going to say? — but this time, there may be something in it. Many of the 500 employees here come from the Ukrainian Mennonite community around, and they are hard-working, conscientious people. More important, they are all shareholders in the firm. You cannot own Friesen shares unless you work here, although you can work here without owning shares if you sell the ones that come to you each year. Wages start at seven dollars an hour and rise to more than twenty dollars an hour, with health and other benefits on top of that, which is not only substantially above minimum wage, but also, in this low-cost environment, pretty good money indeed.

In addition, the shares in the company have never failed to pay dividends. "When we make a profit, and touch wood we have always made a profit for the last forty years," says David Friesen, "it is not just the family that benefits. Everybody benefits."

Profit-sharing firms are not popular with unions, for a number of practical and theoretical reasons, but I come away from Friesens with the notion that they may be onto something. "I've never been in a place where everybody seemed to be working so hard, so cheerfully," I tell the Driver.

"Good," she replies. "Work hard cheerfully and find us a place for lunch."

After lunch, we skitter across the bottom of Manitoba, past farm after farm where what should be vast stands of wheat are vast stands of water instead. And where there are crops, they are as likely to be canola, sunflower, or flax as wheat. Moreover, a countryside that used to be dotted with grain elevators is now very nearly bereft. This is a revolution.

The Vanishing Elevators

When Joan and I first began to drive across the Prairies, the elevators were their most important feature. You saw the cluster of brightly painted buildings from miles away. It marked your trek across the land; it centred the towns, gave them gravity and purpose. The Driver and I used to make bets as to how far we were from the next town as soon as we spotted the elevators lined up on the horizon like a welcoming committee from the chamber of commerce. I would peer at them for a minute or so, calculate their height, allow for wind drift, and pronounce, "Six miles." (This was pre-metric.)

"Nine miles," Joan would say, and she would always be right. I lost eleven bets in a row until I finally noticed that along many of these roads, it was a practice to stick up a notice on the back side of the town sign telling you how far it was to the next town — that is, if you were driving east, entering, say, Herbert, the sign would say "Welcome to Herbert," but on the back side, where it could be read by the westbound traveller, it would say "Rush Lake, twelve miles." These signs are all gone now, but in the 1960s and 1970s, they meant that each town was giving you the distance to the next one. I, the lynx-eyed observer, never spotted this, but Joan, the shameless hussy, would engage the bet after she already knew the answer. Cheating, in other words.

This was no small matter, since our bets do not involve the exchange of cash. Joan first climbed behind the wheel about the time Barney Oldfield was reaching his peak of fame as a race-car driver, and she modelled herself on him. In Joan's world, the object of driving is not to arrive, but to set new speed records with each arrival. The idea of stopping along the way because someone else, as it might be her husband, needs to visit the biffy receives no consideration whatever. Like many of her sex, she has no bladder but some kind of giant storage tank, so missing a wayside stop is no hardship.

My way around this was to negotiate the prizes for bets. If Joan wins, she gets a double martini; if I win, a free stop on my command. You can see the difficulties that arise when I lose eleven bets in a row, and when I discovered that I was enduring agonies of suspense due to chicanery, I took it like a man — sulked for three days and refused to play.

I mention all this to indicate why it has always been the elevators that commanded the prairie landscape, in both the spiritual and plumbing sense, and now they are disappearing. Some are abandoned, more pulled down — the grain-polished wood with which they are lined is valuable — and the Prairies will never be the same. In their place are gigantic concrete structures called inland grain terminals, and I propose to go through one of these when we reach Saskatchewan, but in the meantime I want to know what is behind this phenomenon. This needs looking into, I tell the Driver, and we turn back north to the Trans-Canada Highway, then west again to Brandon, about 200 kilometres west of Winnipeg. Time to check out the Canadian Agricultural Research Station there.

Thank God I'm (Not) a Country Boy

Our entry is grand, up a long, curving drive flanked by eighteen-metre spruce trees and neatly trimmed lawns. We come to the top of the hill and pull around a circular drive in front of the main research building, which looks like a cross between an insurance firm's headquarters and a huge test tube turned on its side. This is not, needless to say, the original building for this famous centre. If James Bond's Dr. No were to come back for another try at world domination and choose the agricultural route, he might stick up something like this.

This is not the Brandon Experimental Farm of song and story, the outfit responsible for the development of hundreds of new and improved farming techniques, and crops, over the years. That one was launched with four other experimental stations by the Experimental Farm Station Act in 1886. It performed important pioneer work with honey bees, purebred cattle, horses, poultry, swine, sheep, and almost every variety of grain. (There was even an experiment with yaks, in 1909, which concluded, "The yak did not prove useful as a meat animal for conditions on the prairies.")

However, over the years, the research centres seem to have moved more and more away from what I might call the dung-and-dig approach to become the handmaidens of agri-business. They no longer carry the old-fashioned name of farms, and as suggested they don't seem to a stranger like the kind of place where a farmer would be found. Who would wear a straw hat and blue jeans into something called a research station?

Inside, the test-tube effect continues. After passing a number of notices that tell me what to do — especially, to wipe my feet — I come into an atrium where a set of stairs climbs through three storeys of open space, with little office cubicles, mostly glass-fronted, crammed against the sides and catwalks slung across the middle. From these catwalks, I imagine you can see just about anything that goes on anywhere in here. Scratch your butt, and Brandon knows.

The effect is about the same as that of an interior view of a modern penitentiary or, come to think of it, the CBC's main building in downtown Toronto, known to many of its denizens as the Lockup. This is open-concept planning with a vengeance, and perhaps it is necessary. God knows what devilment civil servants maddened by reading reports on effective breeding might get up to if left unsupervised. The overall effect is not exactly welcoming, and I cannot imagine any working farmer I know wandering past all the warning signs and actually dropping in for a chat.

Still, when I present myself at a glass-and-metal barrier mounted near the foot of the stairs, I am greeted warmly, though with a certain wariness. They don't get many unannounced callers, and while I did telephone ahead, that was only an hour or so ago, not enough time either to lay on someone to deal with me or to hoist the quarantine flag and keep me out entirely.

I am invited to wander around while an official is run to earth.

"Why not go up to the library?" suggests the receptionist. "It's on the third floor."

So I do that, checking out gangs of initials as I go, for this centre does not merely house research facilities — it is also the local hub for the PFRA (Prairie Farm Rehabilitation Administration), as well as three other agri-initial groups that mean nothing to me. When I arrive at the library, which stretches about two-thirds of the length of the building and has hundreds of shelves, I cannot find a book. There is no librarian to help me — he/she is either off or non-existent — so I wander about, seeking in vain for something book-like, and finally find a small collection right up at the desk, past which I wandered moments before.

There are a couple of dictionaries, an encyclopedia, and half a dozen other reference works. The rest of the library consists of rack upon rack of bulletins of various sorts, from manufacturers, agri-business bodies, and the research stations. They cover everything from how to squeeze more protein out of a grain of wheat to how to keep bugs out of stored feeds. (Briefly, what you do is hermetically seal the entire storage area and zap the buggers with dry ice. I spent quite a lot of time on farms as a kid, and I never met any dry ice. But then, the times they are a-changin'.)

For as long as I can remember, there has been talk of the Agricultural Revolution, or the Green Revolution, which every decade or so was said to be shaking up the farm economy and making it leaner and meaner and more productive. In fact, it has always been, still is, the same process, the process of making a given acre (now, hectare) of land produce more edible product than it did the year before.

Productivity, the watchword of the manufacturing sector, has been a part of the farming community since before we had factories. When farmers were shoved off British lands to make room for sheep, that was a blow struck on behalf of productivity, although it had the unavoidable side-effect of destroying a few hundred thousand lives. As a civilization, we have been at it ever since.

The problem that I see, as an ignorant outsider, is that the farmer doesn't ever seem to get anything much out of it. In 1917, Canadian wheat was sold for just about two dollars a bushel, or, in today's money, about fourteen times that — call it twenty-seven dollars in current funds. Today, that same quantity of wheat brings the farmer about three dollars but costs, on average, about four dollars to produce. We get much cheaper bread than would otherwise be the case — even though the price of wheat has only a distant relationship to the final price of the marketed product, given all its middlemen — but the people who produce the grain get much less.

I once wrote a profile of a wheat farmer who had grown up on a quarter section — 160 acres — on which he supported himself, his parents, and five brothers. Now he and his wife, with a couple of hundred thousand dollars of machinery purchased on credit, were farming 940 acres. But their four children were long gone from the farm, which could not possibly support them all. One son was in jail, one living on welfare, and the others worked in the city. Wheat was still cheap, though, so we have to be thankful for that.

Here at Brandon, I have all this reduced to a single paragraph by Sharon Ramsay, the sturdy young woman who finally catches up to me in the research library: "Why are they taking down the elevators? Because with the price of wheat what it is, you cannot move the stuff to market in such inefficient ways. You shut down the Crow rate and the farmer has to bear the entire cost of moving the grain to market, whether it is via Vancouver or the Lakehead or wherever. It's very expensive. So you have to lower the cost. You may not like it much, but it is just a fact of life."

The Crow rate was a subsidy paid to the railways to move grain to market. Based originally on costs to transport by rail through the Crow's Nest Pass, the Western Grain Transportation Act, the proper title of the legislation that produced the money, was seen as an interference with the efficient operation of the market economy — which, of course, it was. It attempted to redress some of the unfairness of a system that put control of prices almost entirely in the hands of a few giant firms. It was abolished in 1995, and about $1 billion a year in extra costs was handed to Western Canadian farmers.

An inland grain terminal can store, on average, about ten times as much grain — wheat, canola, flax, soya beans, peas, whatever — as one of the wooden elevators. It is thus more efficient to operate. This efficiency can be increased by making the farmer truck his crops farther and farther to a few huge terminals, rather than allowing him to drive a few kilometres down the road to a local elevator, where he probably wastes time chatting with the operator or even, God forbid, drinking a cup of coffee.

Of course, the cost to the farmer for trucking goes up, and so does the cost of road maintenance, in direct proportion to the reduction in costs for the elevator firms and the railways, but these are not matters that concern the people who make these decisions. They fix their minds on the need to produce a metric tonne of grain more cheaply than their competitors on the world market — especially the Americans.

Since the Americans always carry larger subsidies on their products than we do, while carefully denying that they pay any subsidies whatever, this is bound to be a losing proposition. But we are a game bunch, and as long as the costs are borne mainly by the farmers, a less and less significant proportion of the voting population with every passing year, this is not an important consideration.

The same phenomenon that is wiping the elevators off the face of the prairie is observable in every sector of the agricultural economy. And that is why the library in this research centre is chockablock with pamphlets instructing our rural population on how to increase productivity or fast-freeze bugs, not because they will thereby gain wealth — what a thought! — but because their descent into permanent and irreversible poverty may be at least somewhat retarded.

The research station, at a glance, is simply a pawn of agri-business, indeed is selling the same products: lower costs, narrower margins, and higher profits. The profits do not come here, of course, where they would be wasted, but end up in the cities where the firms that control marketing dwell.

Fewer and fewer farms, with larger and larger facilities, keep pouring out more and more food. We cannot eat, cannot sell, cannot even give away all we produce, but we have to continue down this endless spiral because otherwise the market, the one true god of globalism, will be displeased.

I emerge from the Brandon Centre looking grumpy, and the Driver asks, "Well, what did you find out?"

"I found out that they don't keep books in the library," I reply, "and that they have to knock down the grain elevators to make the farmers rich."

"The farmers will never be rich," she says.

8

Saskatchewan

GOING AGAINST THE GRAIN

Out here, waist-high wheat nods to passing traffic, then turns to flow across stretching fields and wash ashore on grain elevators standing in multi-coloured clumps. A telephone pole is an event on the landscape, and overhead the sky is a blue dome arching to meet the horizon all around; you feel like a piece of Cheddar under some celestial cheese bell.

— STAR WEEKLY, APRIL 17, 1965

Saskatchewan is another province — like Nova Scotia and Ontario — where we once lived. I taught for a time at the University of Regina, so in order to gain that touristy feeling, we tack back and forth across the map, trying to feel like strangers. We start driving west from Brandon about five o'clock one morning, cross the Saskatchewan border about an hour and a half later, and stop for breakfast at a highway gas station west of Moosomin. It has been our experience that Saskatchewan gas stations serve a toothsome breakfast, with or without cinnamon buns.

Our arrival brings a momentary hush to the restaurant, where, ranged over a dozen booths and as many tables, are gathered the tribal elders of the farm district. In Newfoundland, we reflect, this would not matter, and we would be joined into the club, offered cod tongues or toutons, but this is Saskatchewan, and the elders are a little tetchy of their dignity. They are dressed in the local uniform — high overalls, plaid shirt, heavy boots at one end and a base-ball-style cap at the other. One elderly gent, spotting Joan, shifts the rim of his cap uneasily, a sort of vestigial doffing that goes no further. All other caps remain in place, advertising John Deere tractors, Quaker State Oil, and other cultural icons.

After a couple of minutes, the exchange of spirit and soul we interrupted by our entrance recommences, with Larry, in one corner of the restaurant, asking Mel, in the diagonally opposite corner, how the work is going. This sets off a rumble of guffaws, raising the possibility that Mel is not known as a hard worker, although he is sporting a Saskatchewan Wheat Pool cap.

In turn, he asks Charlie, in a third corner — for it is a rule of these social interchanges that the men who want to talk to each other sit as far apart as possible, thus opening the conversation to the entire ensemble — how that lame horse of his is coming along, and has he decided to put the poor beast out of his misery yet? "Not till you get rid of that lame tractor," Charlie ripostes.

The walls are covered with photos of local sports heroes — mostly hockey greats-to-be, a reminder that we are the sort of country that breeds Bobby and Brett Hulls, Gordie Howes, and others of that ilk. There is a good deal of chaffing about a local game — probably, but not necessarily, baseball — which the locals lost to another town last Saturday, mainly, it would appear, because of "bum calls."

The waitress — there is only one, a woman well past the springtime of life, but still game — plies the floor, helped quite a lot by the customers, who rise from time to time to pour and renew coffee for all comers, even strangers like ourselves. The waitress knows everybody, knows what they want for breakfast — "Oh, Lord, here comes Billy; put on some more ham, Wendell" — and rules with a firm hand.

"I'm trying to decide how I want my eggs, Millie," says an old boy with a bright green hat that says Prestone on the bill. "Whaddyathink?"

"Order them any way you like, Les," says the waitress. "They all come out the same."

She treats us with great seriousness, writing down our commands for two poached eggs on whole-wheat toast very carefully on her clipboard before bringing us fried over easy, like everybody else.

By the time we have disposed of these, the room is aroar with customary clatter, about ten different conversations bouncing off the walls. Then the door bangs open and brings another pause.

"Oh, oh, it's Helmut. Close the door," shouts one of the elders.

"Too late — he's already in," groans another. This is regarded as a witty sally, and everybody laughs, including Helmut, who stamps in, pours himself a cup of coffee, laces it with a long pour of sugar, a longer of cream, blows on it, and sits down. At this, another of the elders rises, hitches his hat forward and back — hail and farewell, I guess — and announces, "Well, I can't sit around all day like you boys. I'm not a farmer. I got work to do." He drops money on the table and exits, to jeers and catcalls.

"What is this, a lodge meeting?" asks the Driver.

Cannington Manor: Pratfall on the Prairie

We turn south at Wapella and head across back roads — in very poor condition — for one of the province's little-visited tourist sites, Cannington Manor, southeast of Moose Mountain. This was where, in the early 1880s, a small herd of dreamers, drifters, scoundrels, and second sons migrated, hoping to recreate the genteel life of an English manor on the bald-headed prairie. They had heard that there was good land to be had for nothing — no one mentioned that it was as dry as the morning-after mouth of a desert — and, no doubt, servants could be found at cheap Canadian prices. These were remittance men, mostly, chaps of good family who failed to inherit the titles, owing to being born too late, and so were shuffled off to the outposts of the empire to live on letters of credit or bank drafts from back home.

They were led by Capt. Edward Mitchell Pierce, a stout, red-faced ex-army officer who had never been near a prairie before, never been to Canada, come to that, but who brimmed with that buoyant self-confidence, or lunacy, that inspired so many British venturers to bring the benefits of civilization to other and lesser races.

Captain Pierce, known to intimates as the Skipper, was a man of impeccable antecedents but somewhat peccable finances, having just gone through a bankruptcy, but he had a personal letter of introduction to Sir John A. Macdonald when he arrived in Ottawa in 1882, and Sir John was happy to hand him off a large parcel of the land that his government had recently taken over from the Hudson's Bay Company. The Canadian Pacific Railway had not reached this far yet, and settlers were pouring into the West, all right, but mainly heading for the Dakotas, so the administration was happy to support any venture that promised settlement north of the border and didn't cost anything. Pierce named his acreage after a place in Somerset that he admired.

There were other settlers in the district, but the good captain appointed himself their leader and spokesman, writing to Ottawa that "it is the universal desire, as soon as the districts are incorporated, that I shall represent the people at Ottawa." This would save the fuss of an election.

His notions of leadership did not, needless to say, involve actually sowing seeds, weeding, and digging; he saw himself more in an executive capacity: "There is a pile of work to be done here of which I am more fitted to undertake, than grubbing up of the land around me for grain growing, etc."

To give him his due, he did set to work writing letters to the English newspapers to stimulate immigration (he told prospective settlers that they could "live like princes on the money required in England just for taxes"); founding an agricultural college (that is what he called it; others called it "the pup ranch"); and establishing, with three other partners, the Moose Mountain Trading Company, which was to be the heart, and cash box, of the colony. Among its activities were two cheese factories and a hog-packing plant, which promised "the Choicest Bacon and Hams, Like English Wiltshire."

Cannington Manor was a company town, with a carpenter's shop, school, land-titles office, flour mill, "teacherage," and the principal houses all built and owned by the company, which also provided post office facilities, building materials, implements, seed grain, cattle, freighting services, marriage licences, mortgages, and even insurance, to all comers, for a price.

The community was instantly divided into three classes: the "English group," the homesteaders and tradesmen, and the bachelors. While the homesteaders and tradesmen buckled down to work, and the bachelors to play, the English group went about being, well, English. They brought their maids, their monocles, their tennis racquets, and their riding habits with them. They bowled and sipped tea, rode to hounds (there were foxes in the area around Moose Mountain), attended cockfights and horse races, played cricket, and looked down their noses at the Ukrainians and other odd persons who kept "grubbing up the land for grain growing, etc."

The English referred to all people who actually worked as "Canadians," although they were much more likely to be Ukrainians, Hebrideans, or even English. The word was meant to describe their class, rather than their nationality. Sadly, there is no record of what the First Nations people, who had front-row seats for all this, thought when the Cannington Manor hunt headed off in its pinks to chivvy a fox, or the ladies walloped a croquet ball past the astonished gaze of a line of gophers.

Only one of the gentry families had much in the way of real cash; the Beckton brothers arrived at Cannington as agricultural students in Captain Pierce's college, but the death of a wealthy grandfather over 'ome changed all that, and they and their wives soon constituted the "sportin' set" so necessary to English manor life, if not exactly *de rigueur* in Southern Saskatchewan. The Becktons held an annual hunt club ball, at which evening dress was required. Among the foreign visitors to the place were Lloyd George, a future British prime minister, and Bertram Tennyson, nephew of the poet laureate, who settled down nearby and had his own verse published in the *Moosomin Spectator*.

The manor was doomed, alas, though not so much by the time wasted chivvying foxes, hunting balls, and building mansions as by the more usual prairie advents — early frosts, drought, and drooping wheat prices. In 1888, Captain Pierce died of a stroke, and the CPR decided to build the branch line that would have brought easy access to market through Carlyle, sixteen kilometres south, instead of through Cannington.

The manor could not compete with the farmland around it, and it sank into oblivion. The homesteaders who struggled through the 1890s were rewarded with an improvement in the economy in the early years of the twentieth century, but by that time the village was deserted, its businesses failed, and its residents gone.

The Triumph of British Boneheadedness

It is an eerie place today as we wander about listening for distant echoes of "Well played, sir," or "Tallyho!" and catch nothing but the endless moaning of the endless prairie wind and the rattle of rain on the score of empty buildings that still stand here, waiting for someone to move in again. I think there is much to be learned from experiments like Cannington, because we so often read about the plucky pioneers who upped stakes in the Old Country and came out to Canada, where, after much travail, they succeeded, learning how to play hockey, spit, and say "eh?" There were a great many attempts that failed, and a great many attempts that were doomed to failure before they began, like this one. But what made the British such successful colonizers, in the long run, was their incredible stubbornness, an obstinacy that either refused to see or brushed aside anything in the way of local difficulties, such as a lack of transportation, suitable soil, markets, or money. They were not always bright, but they were nearly always bold.

This is now a provincial park, but there is no one around to talk to or ask questions of. Instead, as is increasingly the practice across Canada, a nation that cannot afford its own history, visitors are asked to stick money in an envelope and shove it into a box that has been made burglar-proof except, I would guess, to any ten-year-old with a screwdriver.

We pay our money and admire a wonderful display of old photographs in the deserted visitors' centre, then try in vain to get into the one facility still in use — the All Saints Anglican Church, now the property of the Diocese of Qu'Appelle. Because Joan's late uncle, Fred Jackson, was the archbishop of Qu'Appelle, she has been here for services. She reports that the church, built in 1884 with funds solicited in England on land donated by Captain Pierce (he is buried here), is "a gem," but all I can see are locked doors, shuttered windows, and a tombstone that reads "Gone But Not Forgotten."

I grumble, "The trouble is that this place is both gone and forgotten."

Murdered by Mounties

When we leave Cannington Manor, we drive south on a dirt road that hits Highway 13, the southern east-west highway, and soon run into the little markers showing a North West Mounted Police officer in a cap — we are on the Red Coat Trail. This is the route the police followed when they came out West to Fort Whoop-Up, now Lethbridge, and we will catch up to it again. First, however, we turn south once more to visit the ugliest corner of the province, around Bienfait and Estevan, where the Mounties, to put it bluntly, disgraced themselves in 1931.

That year, the coal miners in this region had reached the nadir of despair, and they foolishly went on strike. Their wages had been driven down by the Depression to $1.60 a day, their working conditions were unsafe, and their living conditions appalling. The sixteen-year-old daughter of a Bienfait miner later described her home to the Wylie Commission, which investigated this little patch of history:

> One bedroom, two beds in there, dining room, no beds in there, kitchen, one bed, and eleven in the family. I think we need a bigger place than that. When it is raining the rain comes in the kitchen. There is only one ply of paper, cardboard paper nailed to about two-inch wood board [on the walls]. . . . When the weather is frosty, when you wake up in the morning, you cannot walk on the floor because it is all full of snow.

This house belonged to the mining company; some of the privately owned shacks were worse. An inspection after the strike showed that of 113 miners' houses and shacks, 53 had inadequate heat, 43 were leaky, 52 were dirty, and 25 were overcrowded. Almost all needed repairs.

The miners had to trade at company stores that charged exorbitant prices, so they were going further and further into debt while working harder and harder. When they tried to organize, they were met by the cry of "foreign agitators," a richly humorous cry in that almost all the miners were foreigners, too. A union organizer did come to town, and was kidnapped and threatened if he would not clear out. The seven men responsible were tried and acquitted; they included a corporal in the Saskatchewan Provincial Police.

In those days, there was no attempt on the part of the police to pretend that they were either impartial or non-political. Maj.-Gen. James O'Brien, the commissioner, made a speech in Toronto in 1932 in which he made it clear who was to blame for the Depression: "foreign agitators."

Finally, the miners organized themselves without any outside help, and they then applied for membership in the radical Mine Workers' Union of Canada. An organizer from that body arrived and signed up members, but the companies refused to recognize the union, which was, they said, connected with the "Red Internationale of Soviet Russia," although they did not explain how this came about. In response, a strike was set for September 7, 1931.

This brought in a dozen members of the RCMP — as the NWMP had become in 1920 — who joined a force of thirteen special constables in the direct pay of the Saskatchewan Coal Operators' Association. Farm workers were brought in to dig the coal, but a mass meeting of strikers descended on the mines and the farmers cleared off.

As the strike continued, the workers announced a protest meeting in Estevan for September 29; this would be addressed by Annie Buller, of the Workers' Unity League, an undoubted communist. The affair was to start with a parade, but the Estevan town council, meeting hastily, passed a bylaw banning any sort of demonstration. A letter was dispatched to the strikers to inform them that if they went ahead, they would be met by police force; but the letter did not arrive until several days too late.

The postmark showed that it had been mailed at 10 p.m. on September 29, seven hours after the protest meeting began. The workers had heard by word of mouth that the council had met, but they thought that what had been banned at the meeting — which was closed, of course — was a parade, so they changed their protest to a motorcade instead, and thought themselves very clever. (This remained a secret in most of Canada until Stuart Jamieson's *Times of Trouble* was published in 1968; it was commissioned by the federal government to probe national labour unrest.)

Accordingly, when a caravan of 400 miners and their families arrived on the outskirts of Estevan in the early afternoon of September 29, to be met by a cordon of police, they were outraged and decided to push on, regardless. A bloody battle broke out at Fourth Street and Eleventh Avenue, with the strikers using clubs and stones and the police wielding guns and riot sticks. The RCMP were equipped with 30 rifles, 48 revolvers, 48 riding crops, and 4 machine guns. Police reinforcements soon arrived, and the battle turned into a rout.

After about three hours of fighting, the streets were cleared, leaving two miners dead and one fatally injured. He died after the local hospital refused to treat him. (Knowing there was likely to be trouble, the hospital director issued orders that no wounded strikers were to be admitted unless they could pay a week in advance; however, anyone in uniform was to be admitted because "the government pays." The miners had been making weekly payments to the hospital for years, of course, as a form of insurance.)

In addition, 8 miners, 4 bystanders, and one Mountie were shot, and 8 police officers received injuries. Since the strikers had no firearms, the Mountie must have been hit by one of his own (nearly all the policemen involved were raw recruits, with little training and no experience). The strike was broken and the union smashed, and 22 workers were convicted of various offences in connection with the affray.

No police officers were ever charged or even reprimanded for killing and wounding miners and bystanders. One of those jailed was Annie Buller, although no evidence was ever adduced to show that she had participated in the riot. About all that remains to record what happened here is a monument in the cemetery at Bienfait; it names the three dead miners and adds: "Murdered in Estevan, September 29, 1931." The original inscription added the words "By RCMP," but the phrase was removed by order of the Bienfait authorities.

Oddly enough, the countryside hereabouts remains much as it must have been back then, which is to say downright ugly. The province, for its own reasons, does not ever seem to have required the mining companies to restore the devastated landscape of the Souris valley, and the result is a wilderness of bumpy little grass-covered mounds that runs from Estevan clear down to the U.S. border. Coal mining is still a major industry, and massive earth-moving draglines — a dragline is a sort of steam shovel on steroids — tower over the open-pit mines. (These new operations will be cleaned up and restored in time.)

The city of Estevan (pop. 11,081) was christened by combining the names of the CPR's first two railway presidents, George Stephen (este) and William C. van (van) Horne, into a singularly unattractive whole. The Energy Tour, which visitors can take to check out the coal mines and power plants in the area, does not mention the 1931 riot.

The Driver wants to know why we have come here. "Do you just want to make me feel bad by pointing out everything nasty?"

"No, I want to make myself feel good by seeing how much we have improved." I add, "Never mind. To cheer you up, we will go up to Regina and blow the wad at the casino."

Two Solitudes, with a Side Order of Gripes

Regina, a two-hour run north from Estevan, is an attractive city with wide streets, spacious parks, and all the amenities, including one of the finest, friendliest, and best-managed public libraries in the country. When we lived here, in 1987 and 1988, we were so taken by its combination of open friendliness and sophisticated arts and culture that we began to grumble about Easterners, and centralists, and the blockheads in Ottawa who never give the West a fair deal.

This is a strain that runs deep in the West, not just in Alberta, where it receives its most strident expression, and one possible explanation is that there is something in the charge. On our first evening in town, I have a chat with a senior civil servant in the Saskatchewan government who is directly concerned with the devastation dealt the area by the floods that prevented the planting of wheat across most of the southern part of the province this spring.

"It's the same old thing," he complains. "If there was a disaster like this in Quebec, the federal government would be all over it, but when it hits the West, well, you're on your own, boys."

I point out that Ottawa has offered $1.5 billion in extra aid, money that can be used to top up a farmer's income when it falls below 70 percent of the average that same farm made over the previous three years. The kicker is, of course, that farm receipts have been so low for so many years that many farmers will not be able to qualify for this help unless they are in virtual bankruptcy.

Moreover, the proffered package does nothing to meet the fact that with grain prices so low, most farmers cannot cover their costs, which is why more and more of them are giving up and selling out to the agri-businesses that only make matters worse. These vertically integrated companies are happy to keep commodity prices low, and to take off their profits when the products are processed and sold.

"It isn't about this year's problems," my friend tells me. "It is about the historical attitude that discriminates against the West and always will. Take the dairy industry. Quebec has about one-third of all milk quotas. Why? Because it has a very effective lobby, and because if it's Quebec they have to be given what they want. Always have, always will. When you see this from inside government, day after day, year after year, you realize that it is a pattern, a permanent pattern, not just an occasional grievance."

The most obvious pattern an outsider can see, actually, is that Quebec musters seventy-five members of Parliament, who tend to vote as a bloc on many matters, while the combined Prairie provinces bring forth fifty-six MPs, who are all over the map on almost every issue. It is not surprising that the federal Cabinet, whatever its political stripe, and the Prime Minister's Office, which now runs the nation, are more receptive to Quebec's demands than Saskatchewan's.

Not that Quebec sees it that way, of course; what Quebec sees is that every time a contract or concession comes its way, there is a howl of protest from the Western provinces. The two solitudes have not become closer over the years; they have just become sufficiently bored with the argument to promote bouts of truce between the shouting matches.

Two Solitudes Be Damned

The light shining into our hotel room at 5 a.m. the next morning beckons me to the window, where I sit entranced to watch the sun's capture of the prairie. From my vantage point, I can see the unlovely railway yards in the foreground, but beyond them the city's trees and streets give way to the golden glow of fields, many of them planted with canola, marching off to the horizon. A farm tractor — or it may be a truck, I cannot tell — is kicking up a plume of dust in the distance. Looks as if the farmer has been at it all night. The work may not pay, but you have to get at it early anyway.

Descending to the lobby shortly after six, I run into a little gaggle of elderly ladies, all dressed alike in dark jackets, giving the night clerk a hard time. One of them tells him he is *pas gentil*, and he rolls his eyes. What in tunket do they mean? They speak not a word of English, he not a word of French, but gestures, apparently, have not carried them past their mutual incomprehension.

They, it turns out, are from a convent in a town in Quebec whose name I cannot catch, and the problem is that last night they asked the clerk — not this one, but another, who had some French — when they were to catch their bus for the airport. He thought they were asking when buses start to run, and told them six o'clock, so they assembled in good order.

And then it occurred to them that six o'clock was rather early to catch a bus for a flight that didn't leave until ten, so they went to the night clerk to straighten it all out. In the torrent of French that poured over the desk, the only word he recognized was *aéroport*, so he called them a taxi, whose driver left when the ladies indignantly refused to go with him. He didn't speak French either.

It is surely one of the great advantages of being Canadian that with a miserable mumble of words in the other language, you can get to feel like St. George after an outing with the dragon. I tell the ladies that they can catch a bus at 8:30, after a nice breakfast in the dining room here, and I tell the clerk why they were confused, and we all feel as if we have pulled off some great diplomatic coup, with smiles all around. I earn a long blast of what I assume is praise from the oldest of the ladies, along with a handshake; they turn for the elevators to grab another hour of rest, I guess, and I stride out into the sunshine, fit for any fate. Two solitudes be damned.

Life Is a Gamble, but Is Gambling a Life?

Across Saskatchewan Drive from the hotel, where there was once a busy, bustling railway station, there now lurks instead a huge casino, which is already open when we finish breakfast, and is sponging down the suckers at a rapid rate of knots. Casino spending, which now runs at more than $10 billion annually in Canada, turns up in economic measurements as part of the gross domestic product, just like teachers' salaries or hospital construction.

This means that all across Canada, poor saps are having their pockets turned inside out, not to pay taxes to governments, for that would be iniquitous and a waste, but to make rich people richer still. And it all comes out as positive economic activity. Time was when governments considered gambling illegal, which didn't stop it but did keep it under some sort of control; now our governments themselves have turned into bookies and croupiers, hooking in customers with the kind of pitch that used to give snake-oil salesmen and carnival touts a bad name.

The provincially run lotteries, united as they are in such nation-building exercises as Lotto 6/49, which you have approximately the same chance of winning as you do of being struck twice by lightning, are promoted by advertising campaigns that make it look as if all we have to do is plunk down our dough and retire. At least the casinos, as they sprout from coast to coast like some sort of mushroom growth, provide us with something to look at. The Regina Casino, like the Halifax Casino, and Casino Rama, near Orillia, Ontario, and the Royal Diamond Casino in downtown Vancouver, and every other of its ilk, is a thing of flashing lights, cheery noises, and glum customers.

I wander through acres of video terminals, where the players crouch on high stools and lean forward to feed buckets of tokens into the maws of the machines. The more athletic customers stuff their contributions into terminals where you are required to pull a handle down to make the machine eat your money. But there is no need to do this; you can just push a button, watch the pretty colours whirl by, and kiss the rent money farewell. Even the winners don't seem to be elated; a win brings a crash-tinkle of tokens into the bin below the flashing lights, and the player just scoops them up, dumps them into a bucket, and begins feeding the machine again.

However, as I penetrate the building, I see a large table display that looks more promising. It is called Royal Ascot, and it at least provides some entertainment for your money. In the middle is a green-baize racetrack, about one and a half metres long and one wide, backed by a bank of lights. There are six plastic horses, with jockeys, that race each other, finishing in an order determined by the random programming of a computer. There is a horseshoe-shaped bank of betting posts around the track, where the punters sit, and another bank of posts in front and slightly above the display.

Every punter has a terminal in front of him or her, and this is where the odds on each horse for each race are displayed. There is even a breakdown of the past performance of the beast in plastic-land. You pick your horse or combination, dump in your money, and with a grand flourish of trumpets, they're off. The plastic ponies jog around the track while, on two large TV monitors above, cartoon replicas race to the rhythm of a caller who couldn't be more in earnest if he were in the middle of the Ascot scene in *My Fair Lady*.

I decant a few loonies before deciding that the real fun is watching, not wagering, so I step back, out of the view of the multitudinous security guards — who like the clientele to gamble, not just gawk — and observe. I am drawn in particular by one young woman, about thirty, who seems to be consulting a little notebook before every race, and who writes down the results after. A system, no doubt about that.

She is winning — she keeps saying "Yes!" and banging herself on the thigh, so there may be something to her system — or maybe she knows some of the jockeys. A couple of seats down from her is a man who might just as well have "Farmer" stamped on his cap, rather than "Texaco," a horny-handed, large-bellied, middle-aged man in overalls, galluses, and glasses who would look far more at home on a combine than squeezed into one of these plastic chairs. You can't tell whether he is winning or losing.

He is whistling soundlessly, and at the end of every race he gives the edge of the plastic surround in front of him a little tap, but his facial expression never changes from a benign, interested stare. He probably looks the same when the rain goes around his section and leaves it dry.

I can take it no more, and when the seat next to him becomes vacant I slip in beside him to ask how it's going. He gives me a what-the-hell-is-it-to-you look, and then grins. "I've lost $120 so far," he says. "At home, I've probably lost five times that today."

Visions of his wife, no doubt an apple-cheeked homemaker, flash through my mind, and I ask him if he thinks she'll be upset if he comes home broke.

"Oh, Emily," he says. "Last I saw her, she was over there somewhere, looking for a game of blackjack."

I think this is what they meant by the agricultural revolution.

An Elevating Experience

The next day, we drive up to Saskatoon, 250 kilometres north and west, stopping for breakfast in Davidson, one of our favourite Saskatchewan towns. This is not only because it is pretty and the restaurant in the Esso station knows how to deal with an egg, but also because our favourite farm lies along this road, marked by a huge sign on the barn roof that puts the farmer's lot into three words: "Scratch and Hope."

This is where the Driver had her first trip up in a grain elevator. Grain elevators are not complicated. What you have is a place where the trucks dump the crop through a metal grate into holding bins beneath; two or three "elevating legs" that carry the grain up to be dumped into the appropriate storage bin — essentially, running scoops on a belt; and a spout to direct the stored grain from one of the storage bins into the railway car that has been pulled up at the other side of the elevator. To one side, there is the engine room, which provides the lifting power, and a large belt that carries the harnessed power.

Right beside the dumping grate, there is a scale where the incoming crop is weighed, with a little table for the farmer to bang as he tells the operator that his wheat is not shriven, has not been touched by frost, and deserves a better price than whatever it is he has been offered. And then there is the man-lift. Not person-lift, or man-or-woman lift, but man-lift. This usually runs right beside one of the legs that carry the grain to the top of the terminal, and it consists of a tiny platform that is operated by weights and is balanced to carry the elevator manager, and no one else, to the top.

Joan, on a tour of the Davidson terminal one day some years ago, jumped on the lift and went soaring aloft — nearly went right through the roof, in fact, since she lacked the heft of the operator for whom it was rigged. She had a lovely look at the countryside then stepped onto the platform to descend.

Nothing happened. She gave a small tap with her toe, which was supposed to release the brake. Nothing happened. She called down — a modest-seeming girl, she can, if required, call the cattle home across the sands of Dee — and explained her dilemma to the operator.

"Jump on it," he shouted to her.

Joan declined. If she was to jump on that tiny little bit of wood, it would probably plunge her down a couple of hundred feet.

"Oh, all right," bellowed the operator. "I guess I'll have to climb up."

There is a set of steps, smaller than the rungs of a ladder, beside the man-lift for just such an emergency, but the thought of the operator, a man well-stricken in years, climbing a couple of hundred of these rungs to her rescue conjured visions of heart attacks, and Joan, with a cry of "Here I come!" leapt onto the man-lift and floated floorwards like the down of a thistle. It forms a bond, and we will always visit Davidson until they tear down the elevator and make it into packing cases.

Tales of the Flog

From here, we head through Saskatoon, possibly Canada's most livable city, which I recall fondly as the place where I once enjoyed myself on a book flog, not a common experience. To describe what happened, I must lift the curtain that keeps book publishing concealed in a decent secrecy, and let you in on the inside.

Every spring and every fall, it happens again. The great flocks begin to gather, herded together by the shrill cries of their leaders and an instinct as old as time itself. Individual members of the flock become agitated — they begin to preen themselves, to make short dashes to and fro, disturbing and exciting other members. The cries become more strident, more insistent, and then, suddenly, one of the flock is airborne, followed by a second, a third, a fourth, until the very sky seems darkened by their passage.

The Great Semi-Annual Book Flog is on.

When swallows, salmon, and caribou migrate, they do so for sensible reasons — sex and food. Authors have no such excuse. We are simply trying to sell more books, on the notion that any given writer, if he or she appears on enough TV talk shows, butters up enough reviewers, signs enough autographs, and survives enough open-line radio shows, will somehow become a best-seller, and his or her monumental work, *Periodontis and I,* will climb up there with *Alias Grace.* Sometimes it works. Besides, the publisher, with some help from the Canada Council, is paying the shot. And as one publisher said to me many, many years ago, "You get to see the country."

Fat chance. What you get to see comes in this order:

1. The insides of the cars of publishers' representatives.
2. The insides of radio stations.
3. The ditto of television studios.
4. The ditto of hotel rooms.
5. Other authors.

I have left out the insides of overcrowded airplanes, which is what most authors get to see most of all. Thanks to the Driver, I avoid this, and we do in fact see the country. This once led to a story in a newspaper reporting that I was afraid of flying, which I did nothing to discourage because it gave me a touch of oddness, instead of being so dreadfully normal.

The publishers' reps look harried, the other authors bewildered, and everything else looks dingy. At the end of a book flog, I have only the vaguest recollection of what happened; all that is left is a blur of klieg lights, microphones, blank faces, and a voice, my own, saying, "I'm glad you asked that question. Er, would you mind repeating the question?"

The memories an author carries away from book flogging are mostly embarrassing. This is as it should be. It is one thing to write a book, another to flog it. The talents required are not the same. McClelland & Stewart once produced a book by two gifted academics who seemed to have a talent for conveying difficult ideas in a clear way, so they decided to send them on the flog. But they didn't want to send both of them — that would cost too much — only one, and M&S left the choice up to the authors. Not long afterwards, the chosen chap turned up with briefcase, a copy of the Book, grim determination, and one of the worst stutters in recorded history. The flog was cancelled.

Al Purdy, a great poet but an in-and-out flogger, once arrived for a live radio talk in Montreal, a show for which he had prepared by reinforcing himself in the bar downstairs, and by air time he was unable to pronounce anything, including his name, much less read a poem. It made for an interesting ten minutes.

The burden of the flog is borne by the publisher's rep, who must bone up on the book, put up with the author, suck up to the media, and stick up for the publisher — no mean task. The job requires the tact of a diplomat and the stamina of a mule.

It is the rep's job to convince the producer of the show that his viewers or listeners will love the "lively, controversial" author of *Whither the Kumquat? An Overview,* and, when the bid is rejected, to con the author into believing that he or she is being saved for another program, when there will be more time.

The fact that all the gang are out beating the bushes at the same time makes the task doubly difficult. I once walked into the city room of the *Winnipeg Free Press* to see the books editor, who had already processed three authors that morning, make a wild dash for the elevator. The rep and I tried to corner him in the hall, but he escaped, laughing wildly, down a stairway that we had foolishly left uncovered. The rep said he had probably forgotten our appointment.

Winnipeg has never been one of my great flog towns. I like Winnipeg, all right, but the sentiment is not returned. I once walked into the studio presided over — ruled over — by Peter Warren, one of the great radio talk-show hosts. He greeted me kindly, offered me a cup of coffee, exchanged small talk, and then, when the red light went on, indicating lift-off, leaned into his microphone and growled: "My guest this morning is Walter Stewart, who last Sunday on national radio called me a yahoo!"

"Oh," I said brightly, "you're *that* Peter Warren." We spent the next hour hearing from listeners who wanted to know who that eastern yob thought he was, anyway.

The Poet and the, Um, Lady

I once interviewed John Newlove, the poet, to check out a story I'd heard that while flogging in Nanaimo, he had been beaten up by a prostitute. He instantly denied it:

She didn't beat me up — I beat her up. I was in a hotel bar, uh, prepar-
ing for a poetry reading, when a hooker sat down beside me and said,
"What's in the folder?" I said, "Poems." She said, "No, I mean, really,
what's in the folder?" I said, "Really, poems." So she picked up the folder
and it was really poems, and she dumped them on the floor, so I dumped
her on the floor. After that, it got kind of confused.

Part of flogging, the part most authors hate worst, is book signing. Book
signing is great if you happen to be Hillary Clinton or the Duchess of York,
not so great if you are merely one of the mob trying to make a living, and are
well aware of the fact that you yourself wouldn't walk across the street to pick
up a book you didn't want just because it was signed by an author you had
never heard of.

Fond memory shines the light on one of these sessions in Regina, in the
book department of the Hudson's Bay Company, where I bought three books
and sold one in a one-hour session. The publisher's rep and the book manager
kept explaining that people were probably not buying because it was such a
sunny day. This is one of those reversible explanations; if it had been raining,
that would have explained it. While I was not selling books, just across the way
a noted cook-celebrity was selling microwaves like, well, hotcakes.

Never mind — I have had two grand moments on the flog, one in
Vancouver and one, as I started to say a while ago, in Saskatoon. In Vancouver,
a comely publisher's rep, closely followed by a CBC camera crew, burst into
my hotel room at seven-striking-a.m. in the morning and ran full tilt into the
Driver, who is not at her best before coffee.

"Oh, Mrs. Stewart," the darling thing trilled. "It must be such a thrill,
travelling across the country with a famous author."

Joan eyed her levelly. "It may look like a thrill to you, sweetie," she said, "but
it's a pain in the ass to me."

In Saskatoon, I was booked for an hour and a half — or in metric, ninety
whole minutes — on an open-line radio show. When I sat down in the
visitor's chair and put on the earphones, I noted with delight that the host had
apparently read the book, and had made copious notes on a long, yellow legal
pad he had nestled in front of him.

In the normal course of events, not one interviewer in ten has read the book — how could they, when about a hundred tomes are poured into the station in a three-week period? — which is not necessarily a disadvantage. It is nice to be able to say, when confronted by a particularly asinine passage from one of your own works, "You obviously haven't read the book, or you would see that, in context, it makes perfect sense," and watch the interviewer's face go blank.

Still, it is nice to think someone took the trouble, and I was prepared to preen myself when the interview began:

Q: *Now, this fellow Tom Thomson, he was a rather strange fellow, wasn't he?*

A: Yes. Eccentric, to say the least.

Q: *Wasn't there something odd about his death?*

A: Yes, he drowned, and some people think he had stood up in his canoe to take a leak, slipped, knocked his head on the gunwale, and drowned. Why are you asking me questions about Tom Thomson?

Q: *Didn't you just write a book about him?*

A: No, that was Harold Town; he's one day behind me. You probably have him booked for tomorrow.

Q: *Oh, God, what do we do now?*

A: I have you in my power. Now, my book, *Strike* . . .

Ninety minutes later, he had to admit that it sounded like an interesting book, and he hoped everyone would rush out to buy it. For some odd reason, I have never been booked on that radio station since.

A Terminal Illness?

Today, there is no question of flogging; we are here to visit an inland grain terminal. Check that, not merely an inland grain terminal, but the largest inland grain terminal extant, a concrete battlement off Highway 7 that bestrides the flatland like Colossus and makes us wonder why the whole province doesn't sag hereabouts. We can see it from kilometres away, can even read the huge sign that tells us that this place is owned and operated by AgPro Grain, a combination of the Saskatchewan and Alberta wheat pools.

As we pull into the visitors' parking lot, a middle-aged, middle-sized, bearded man comes up to the van, looking friendly but a little anxious.

"Did they tell you about the hat and boots?" he asks.

This is Leonard "Call Me Lenny" Blais, who runs this facility, and who has been told by the Saskatchewan Wheat Pool central office, which I contacted some time ago, to show me through the place and, if possible, not let me kill myself in the process. Nobody said anything about hats and boots.

"Never mind," says Lenny. "You can probably get into Ray's." He looks anxious again as he peers through the open window at Joan.

"I'm not coming," she says.

"You're more than welcome," says Lenny. Then adds, "The tour takes quite a while."

"I've got a book," says Joan, and adds, "I spend most of my life waiting."

"Ah," says Lenny.

We take the tour, first calling in on a bewildered Ray to borrow his protective gear. We climb over things and under things, we go through tunnels and along corridors, we visit the weighing room and the lab and the place where they de-bug the grain — rather disgusting, but fascinating — and the storage bins and the cleaning floor, and the railway yards and the offices. And the computer room, of course, where everything is controlled and documented, and where the farmer can, in fact, still bring his complaint that he was yizzled on the grading of his crop, although he will have a rather tougher task proving his case against the science arrayed here, where samples of his delivery can be tested against standards.

We take the elevator — no man-lift here — to the seventh level and look down into the tops of the 300 bins where various crops are stored, everything from wheat and barley to mustard, flax, canola, lentils, and even peas. From the outside, it looks as if the terminal consists of a set of silos stacked up against each other, with the grain stored in the circular towers, but in fact the triangles between the silos are used, too, and the whole facility holds more than 3 million bushels of combined crops.

Up here, there is a fine layer of dust over the floor, and Lenny points to this.

"Somebody left a window open, and a while back some kids climbed up the fire escape on the outside and got in. They had a lovely time jumping into the grain from the top. The only way we found out was that one of the fellows spotted the bare footprints in the dust."

"Did they do any harm?"

"Not in wheat, no. But if they'd jumped into flax, it wouldn't have held them; they'd have gone right down and suffocated." He shivers.

This is not a new facility, Lenny explains; it was actually built in 1914 to form a giant storage facility during the First World War, and later was expanded and modified to meet modern requirements. But it is, in essence, just like every other grain elevator I have seen, raised to the tenth power. There is the dumping pit — well, nine dumping pits that hold forty-six tonnes at a whack — the legs, the bins, the scales, and the spouts.

While we roam about the place, a gang of loaders are filling railway cars outside with wheat. In eight hours, they will load one hundred cars, all bound for mills in Eastern Canada. However, the process is essentially the same, except for its size and its cleaning capacity. This terminal can clean more grain faster and better than just about anything else in the country — and then can reclean it so the company can sell not only the screenings, but also the dust itself — which pig farmers use as a food additive.

As we dive under a conveyor belt, sprint between two cleaning machines, check out the way the various spouts can be switched and mixed to produce exactly the grade of grain ordered by the mill — much the way distillers produce blended Scotch by mixing various years and qualities — Lenny is stopped and asked questions by everyone we meet. He gives his instructions with a cheerful smile and says thanks.

"Like your job, do you?" I ask.

"Oh, I love my job," says Lenny. Then he adds, "Though, come to think of it, I have loved every job I ever had." He laughs.

Lenny does not regard himself as a businessman trying to get what he can out of the farmer. His company is, essentially, farmer-owned, and he has every sympathy for the agriculturists who are so cruelly pinched by modern conditions.

"This is not a favourable time to be in the agriculture industry," he says. "I have worked for the pool for twenty-two years, and I have heard a lot of griping from farmers — it is one of the things they do — but I have never seen things as bad as they are right now."

As far as he is concerned, the inland terminals are simply the only way to get down the cost of handling and moving the crops. "The railways have been allowed to cut back, and if you've got an elevator in Delisle but the railway no longer goes to Delisle, tough bananas. The people who can grease the right wheels are always going to win this sort of battle, so you've got to be in a position to compete."

Eighty percent of the grain in North America is being processed today by a handful of firms owned in the United States, and "we have to be able to go head to head with them, which means squeezing every possible economy out of the system."

Sadly enough, that means the elevators will continue to disappear. "You may not like it, but you can't stop it. When I started in this business, there were 1,200 elevators open in this province; today, there are about 300. Five years from now, who knows?"

When I emerge from the front door ninety minutes later, de-booted, de-hatted, and dazed by an outpouring of facts and figures, the Driver asks, "What about the elevators?"

"Doomed," I reply. "Too bad, but they're doomed."

"Nonsense," says the Driver.

The Cypress Hills

If you are in Saskatoon and are headed for the West Coast, and if you have any sense, you will pick up the Yellowhead Highway, which runs from just east of Portage la Prairie, Manitoba, to Prince Rupert, on the coast of British Columbia, through Saskatoon, Edmonton, and the Peace River country. It is an even prettier drive than the Trans-Canada (it is officially a second Trans-Canada, but no one ever calls it anything but the Yellowhead), more varied and less crowded.

However, we are going the long away around, and instead cut down Highway 3, which drops through Saskatchewan like a plumb bob and carries us to Swift Current, where we turn west and south again to visit the Cypress Hills. It is one of the libels on Canada's prairie country that it is all the same, all flat and featureless. In fact, Saskatchewan is a place of infinite variety, which just happens to be presided over by a lot of sky. The views are varied and endless, from the broad sweep of grain fields, as in the cliché, to the vast whiteness of the patch along the Trans-Canada near Chaplin, where potash deposits turn the land to a winterscape, even with the thermometer blowing its top. It is in the Cypress Hills that the standard view of the prairies falls utterly apart.

This is a section of lodgepole pine–forested highlands, formed millions of years ago by sea and river sediments, which escaped the grinding of the glaciers during the ice ages. There are hills and valleys, forests and streams that would do credit to Algonquin Park, and as we wander through the cool pine woods, scramble along the paths, peer at the exotic wildlife — there are more than 200 species of birds in the interprovincial park that straddles the Saskatchewan-Alberta border, along with eighteen species of orchids, to say nothing of elk, moose, coyotes, beavers, and an endless supply of red squirrels — we remember that this country looks exactly as it did a hundred thousand years ago, if you don't count a tourist lodge or two.

Fossils that date back 40 million years have been found in these hills, although all I find is a Coke can, which probably dates back a week.

This is where Sitting Bull came to hang out, along with 5,000 refugee Sioux, after the unpleasantness at Little Bighorn in 1876. They stayed around Fort Walsh, where there is a reconstruction of the North West Mounted Police fort, and shouted rude things back down towards the U.S. border until 1881, when they all went home again under an amnesty. Maple Creek, the town nearest the Saskatchewan park entrance, is an attractive town studded with historic reconstructions, including Saskatchewan's oldest, the Old Timer's Museum.

Eastend, nearby, is where the late Wallace Stegner, who won the Pulitzer Prize for literature, lived for a number of years, eventually making it the setting for his novel *Wolf Willow.* Sharon Butala, who is at least as interesting an author, lives on a ranch just outside town.

"What I can't get over," says the Driver, as we stand on a towering hill in the middle of the park and gaze off across a sea of meadows a couple of thousand feet below us, where a giant hawk spins and searches above the meadow grass and a soft wind soughs through the trees, "is how anyone could get the notion that there is anything dull about Saskatchewan."

9

Alberta

OIL BE SEEING YOU

From the eastern edge of the province, the road scats through rich wheat-land, lifts into the knobby hills and scrub brush of the oil and cattle country around Calgary, then sweeps in climbing curves into the awesome majesty of the Rockies at Banff. Into this 300-mile stretch are packed flatland, semi-desert, sand cliffs, rangy hills and towering mountains. In a single day we saw antelopes, purebred cattle, prairie dogs and moose, cliff swallows and ducks.

— STAR WEEKLY, APRIL 17, 1965

From the Cypress Hills, it is only a short drive back to the Trans-Canada, and a slightly longer one to the Alberta border, where the highway, which has become slimmed down to two lanes — perfectly adequate, so far as I can see — broadens out again to four. We are in a fast-moving province now. We go into the tourist information centre at the border and learn that in Klein country, just as there is no free lunch, there are no free maps. Or anything else.

I buy a road map, for two dollars, no sales tax, from the cheery young woman and ask her for information on the CanWest Heritage Park on the Cochrane Ranche (so-called because the original owner thought it sounded tonier than plain, old "ranch"), near Calgary. She produces a brochure, but the only thing she knows about the CanWest Heritage Park is that they sell great ice cream there.

"At the Heritage Park?"

"Not there, in town. There's a little store; it has always been famous for its ice cream."

I also ask for information about Head-Smashed-In Buffalo Jump, near Fort Macleod.

Never heard of it.

No, no, I say. You must have heard of it; it's a big deal, a UNESCO World Heritage Site.

She thinks I am making the whole thing up, but nevertheless checks through all the literature on hand. "I guess they didn't send us anything," she says.

"You mean you wait for tourist attractions to provide you with information, and if they don't you don't know anything about them?"

"Well, of course."

I clump back to the minivan, and we roar away westward. While the road to hell is paved with good intentions, that to Calgary, Edmonton, and other Alberta points is paved with finest asphalt and posted with signs that invite the Driver to skim along at 110 kilometres an hour, which she naturally interprets as permission to go 120. We are passed, at this speed, as if we were standing still. It is part of my duties to indicate when the speed signs change to allow an increase; I have been slow to point out the 110 signs, and thus earn a rebuke.

"But you were *going* 110," I protest.

"I was going 110 because I thought the speed limit was 100. If it says 110, you can go 120 without getting a ticket."

"What if they put it up to 120?"

She doesn't answer, because she knows I know. She would go 130. We are not really in a hurry, I point out, and she gives me a look. What has that to do with anything? We hum right along to Medicine Hat, a mere fifty-seven kilometres from the border, where we buy gas for ten cents a litre less than we paid in Saskatchewan.

Malls Multiply like Zebra Mussels

Medicine Hat is surrounded by the same encrustation of malls, which multiply, like zebra mussels, wherever there is an odd lump of rock to cling to, anywhere in North America. We eat lunch in a chain restaurant and cannot miss the fact that this mall is like every mall in Canada — in the United States, come to that — the same bulbous stores, the same chains, the same fast-food restaurants (about one in twenty of which is Canadian in thought, word, or deed), the same slab of concrete for a parking lot, and the same bad-tempered drivers trying to get in and out and around at the same time.

Canadians, a various and interesting people, are intensely regional in their loyalties, which may be part of the reason why we form so loose a nation. But give us a mall, and we sink to uniformity. Perhaps we would be better off if we lowered our sights and decided that we had solved the issue of Canadian identity the day we were able to overcome "You Deserve a Break Today" as our anthem and replace it with "You've Always Got Time for Tim Hortons."

At Medicine Hat, we catch Highway 3, the road that angles down through Taber — great sugar-beet country — towards Lethbridge. We come across a large herd of llamas dozing in the sun, looking stately and dignified. It is a ramp; they are not dignified, just mean, and they represent part of our nation's new passion for importing exotic breeds. They raise emus in Prince Edward Island — quite a few islanders lost their feathers trying to make money on emus — and bison in Ontario and elk in Quebec and llamas from one end of the country to the other.

All good, clean fun, and all, at another level, attempts to break out of the trap our farmers and cattle-raisers find themselves in. Why, if you can't make money on Herefords, you think you can pull it off on llamas, I do not know, but I admire the faith and enterprise it represents. At one time, large numbers of camels were imported to the Cariboo country of British Columbia, and some still survive. We nod to the llamas, but they do not deign to nod back.

On the Trail to Fort Whoop-Up

Now, as the roadside signs tell us, we are once again on the Red Coat Trail, and in fact a symbolic recreation of the original Red Coat ride is only a couple of days behind us — moderns on horseback trekking where once the Mounties trekked. A grand thing entirely.

In 1873, American wolf-hunters attacked a small band of Assiniboine Natives near Fort Whoop-Up, at the junction of the St. Mary and Oldman rivers, in the middle of what is now downtown Lethbridge. The Americans thought one of the Assiniboine had stolen a horse from them; it turned out that the critter has just wandered away, but that they discovered later on. The mistaken wolfers attacked the encampment, killing twenty people, including women and children, and took four of the women back across the border with them.

This was only the most recent in a series of outrages perpetrated by the wolfers, who came from Fort Benton, Montana, built small forts with names like Whoop-Up and Robbers' Roost, sold bad whisky, and cheated the First Nations people out of furs and horses. They behaved with a contempt for the law that was then common on their side of the border, and in Ottawa the government was already concerned that the continual incursions of Americans might lead to a claim on Canadian soil. This incident provided the goad for action.

The Macdonald government for once acted with dispatch — that is, only a little more than a year later, a cavalcade of North West Mounted Police was on its way west. The NWMP had been formed in May 1873 — just before this tragedy — and given the mandate to police the entire North-West Territories.

The force of 275 officers and men set out with banners snapping, horses prancing, red coats glowing, and brass gleaming on the morning of July 8, 1874, from Dufferin, south of Winnipeg, not far from what was then the end of rail. Their destination was Fort Whoop-Up, and if their commander, Commissioner George Arthur French, a combative Royal Artillery officer on loan to the Canadian government, had only the vaguest idea of where that was, he showed no sign of it as he led them boldly forth.

He had improved the already impressive military spectacle by dividing his force into six divisions, with each division mounted entirely on horses of the same colour — dark bay, light bay, dark brown, bright chestnut, grey, and black. The train stretched a mile and a half, and included (besides the 275 troopers) 73 wagons, 114 Red River carts (full of ammunition and other supplies), cattle for slaughter, and mowing machines to cut grass to feed the horses and cattle. There were also field kitchens, portable forges, two nine-pounder artillery pieces, and two brass mortars. A constable was paid one dollar a day, a sub-constable seventy-five cents, so I guess you needed all the glamour you could get to make up for the lousy pay. "It was a splendid sight," one of the men wrote in his diary, "destined to last but a short time."

There were a number of problems, not the least of which was the fact that most of the men had no more idea of how to go through prairie country than the commissioner himself. They were the rawest of raw recruits. Another was the fact that it was impossible to keep the cattle up to the mounted men. Pretty soon the supply wagons were lagging, too, so far behind that when the exhausted troopers stopped at the end of the day, it was to find that they had no food, no water, no shelter.

One trooper, ordered to drive the oxen, failed to reach camp until just before midnight, and when a sentry challenged him with "Who goes there?" he replied, "A famished man." The sentry let him pass. While Commissioner French could, and did, order his troops about, he could not do the same for the mosquitoes, whose presence was described this way:

> Your eyes, your nose, your ears are invaded. If you open your mouth to curse at them they troop into it. They insinuate themselves down your collar, up your sleeves, between the buttons of your shirt. . . . You can brush them off your coat in layers.

Then there were the grasshoppers, which descended in droves and ate everything they could get a mandible into, including the paint off the wagons. Oh, yes, and thunderstorms and hail the size of golf balls. Before long, there were desertions, and by the time the expedition staggered to Roche Percée, on the Souris River, 270 miles and sixteen days out of Dufferin, their path was strewn with broken carts and dead animals. French decided to split the column.

He would send the "barnyard contingent" — cattle, surplus wagons, and the weaker horses — straight on to Fort Edmonton, to the northwest, while the main body would continue to Fort Whoop-Up. By early September, when the five divisions with French reached a place just west of the Cypress Hills called Dead Horse Camp — because they left so many dead horses there — the weather had turned cold, water was running out, and morale was below sea level.

The soldiers accused a Métis guide of steering them the wrong way, although what he was actually doing was following a map provided by the soldiers themselves. They rested for four days, then pushed on west, only to discover, when they at last reached the place where they expected to find Fort Whoop-Up, that there was nothing there but three dilapidated log huts and a lot of empty prairie. French turned the whole expedition south, where his scouts told him there were grass and water to be found, if not whisky traders, and headed for Sweet Grass, Montana. A constable wrote: "This march had all the appearance of a retreat. It was well for us that the Indians did not prove hostile. None of us would have returned."

French decided to split his force again, and he sent his assistant commissioner, James Macleod, on with 150 men to find Fort Whoop-Up, if possible, while he led his remaining force back to Swan River, Manitoba, where the department of public works was building a permanent headquarters for the force. Macleod had a rather better grasp of things than his commander did, and he also had the good luck to hire a short, bow-legged, whisky-sucking Métis scout named Jimmy Potts.

Potts was paid ninety dollars a month to serve as guide and interpreter, but his interpretations tended to be terse, as was all his speech. After a Blackfoot chief orated for several minutes at Macleod one day, with grand gestures, Potts was asked to translate. "Dey damn glad you here," he said. Another day, an anxious trooper asked him what was over the next hill. "Nudder hill," said Potts. But Potts knew his business, and he soon found decent water to drink, buffalo to feed on, and the way to Fort Whoop-Up. On October 9, the NWMP force came over a hill and looked down on the fort. When artillery had been duly sited and aimed, and troops stationed, Potts and Macleod rode up, dismounted, and banged on the front door. They were greeted by a tall, bearded American who invited them to dinner. The rest of the Americans had skedaddled long since to Fort Benton, Montana.

Macleod tried to buy the fort from the American, whose name was Dave Akers, and we stop here to ask ourselves, Do you suppose that if the Americans had marched out with loaded cannon to displace a gang of Canadians who had recently murdered a score of people, they would offer to *buy* their fort from them?

Akers refused to sell, and Potts led the Mounties to a fine site on the Oldman River, forty-five kilometres to the west of Lethbridge. Here, the force built its first fort in the West — named after Macleod — and from there, this able and intrepid officer led a campaign that crushed the whisky trade; confiscated furs, booze, rifles, and revolvers; and saw the Americans paying heavy fines. They were indignant, of course, and newspapers on the U.S. side of the border bristled with angry editorials about the effrontery of the Canadians trifling with "the persons and property of American citizens."

Fort Whoop-Up is a tourist attraction now, or at least a reconstructed fort serves that function on the riverfront in Lethbridge, as does a similar facility in Fort Macleod. There is an extensive display in the Fort Macleod museum of the history of the force, which became the "Royal" North West Mounted Police in 1904 — a reward for service in the Boer War — and the Royal Canadian Mounted Police in 1920. That was the year it moved its headquarters to Ottawa and absorbed the Dominion Police.

These displays make the crucial point, I think, that the Mounties, however they might have stumbled on their grand trek west, did persevere, did get the job done, did bring peace to this part of the country without having to impose it by slaughter, as so often happened below the border.

The Tragedy of Crowfoot

As I wander around Fort Macleod, I am pleased to come upon a building that did not exist when Joan and I first came here a couple of decades ago (it was opened in 1983). Built in the form of a longhouse, it is dedicated to artifacts of the First Nations, a dazzling display that includes portraits of many of their leaders — to match the portraits of Mounties in the RCMP museum across the way — and even a little plaqué honouring one of the most remarkable of them, Crowfoot. The inscription reads:

On December 1, 1874, Chief Crowfoot of the Blackfoot Confederacy arrived at Fort Macleod to meet Assistant Commissioner Macleod. Upon their meeting hung the peace and well-being of this part of the Canadian West.

First Nations people who know their history must find this display honouring the two statesmen a source of bitter amusement. Not long after that meeting, Crowfoot's people had all been herded onto reservations, most of his own children were dead of tuberculosis, and the thought that white and First Nations leaders would meet as equals had become a sick joke.

Crowfoot was a man of astonishing qualities. Courageous, yes, of course — he was fierce in battle, and once killed a grizzly bear with a spear to save a child — intelligent, certainly; generous; honest; open — all that — but he had in addition the indefinable quality of leadership. He was a great talker, but the world is full of talkers; the point is that when Crowfoot talked, people listened. When the whites came pouring into the First Nations' lands, Crowfoot held his people in check; he was shrewd enough to see ahead, smart enough to count, and he knew that in any pitched battle, his people would simply be massacred. When the depredations of the whisky traders brought drunkenness and disease, he welcomed the Mounties.

In 1874, he could easily have wiped out Macleod's tiny band, but he knew, and Macleod knew, that the police were bringing peace and justice and a fair break for the Natives — after all, it was all written down that way. What followed was a decade of betrayal, and the rapid disintegration of the Blackfoot and other tribes that signed Treaty 7, the document that delivered their lands over to the invader. Despite this, when the North-West Rebellion broke out in 1885 and the Métis pestered Crowfoot to lead his people into joining in a great crusade to drive out the whites, he refused to budge.

He had seen the whites, seen their guns, counted their houses, watched their trains; the way to deal with that horde was to negotiate, not to fight. So he toured the prairie tribes, and even though his adopted son, Poundmaker, took up arms (it worked out about the way Crowfoot thought it would, with Poundmaker in penitentiary and most of his followers scattered or dead), even though his own life was threatened by followers who resented his blathering on about peace, Crowfoot kept his people in line, honouring the commitments made to Macleod and to Canada.

But the whites did not.

The promises given were simply forgotten, ignored, or buried. Crowfoot was soon reduced to leading an impoverished, diseased, and puny band living on government handouts. Their land was gone, their livelihood was gone, and many of their children were dead of malnutrition or white man's diseases. When Crowfoot made his last trip among his allies, the Assiniboine, women spat at him, young warriors greeted him with rude gestures, even some of the older ones jeered. He died the next year, ill, poor, and powerless; from statesman to bum in five years.

I emerge from the darkness of the longhouse into the brilliant sunshine, blinking and bothered. Would it have done any good for Crowfoot to take up arms? I cannot believe it. It might simply have justified the land grabs, the betrayals, the degradation of this proud people.

In the long run, the best weapon the First Nations have had on their side in a battle that continues to this day is the fact that anyone can see that they kept their word, and that we did not.

I Know You Can Do the Shimmy, But Can You Do the Buffalo Jump?

We need cheering up, I judge, so we turn north on Highway 2, cut across a small road marked 785, and look for Head-Smashed-In Buffalo Jump. As we climb into the foothills of the Porcupine range, the Driver is certain that despite clear markings on roadside signs, I have brought us the wrong way. Well, she is *always* certain that I have brought us the wrong way, but this time I fear she may be right. We can't see anything. This is a huge facility, but I glower up the hills and can see nothing.

"Perhaps you can get a job as an information officer with Alberta tourism," says the Driver sweetly.

And then, there it is. The reason we cannot see it until we are almost on top of it is that it has been built right into the hills, with the least possible disturbance to the surrounding countryside and the greatest possible preservation of the original site. The interpretive centre is constructed in layers, so that the visitor can look at things in any order, and I choose to go right to the top, walk out, and see where they drove the buffalo to their doom. By a stroke of luck, I get to the edge just as Kyle Blood, a guide (and a member of the Blood tribe), is explaining everything to a group of visiting Blackfoot people from across the border.

Head-Smashed-In was only one of 120 such jumps that have been found across Alberta, Kyle tells them (while my ears flap in the brisk breeze); this one was found in 1938, and is one of the largest, oldest, and best-preserved such sites in North America.

The name does not come from smashing in the heads of buffalo, a dubious proposition, given the hardness of their skulls. The story goes that one day a young warrior who was watching the animals flying off the cliff above became trapped under the piled-up carcasses, and it was *his* head that got smashed in. Well, it's a story, but as I walk over the ground, I don't see how it could happen. He might get smothered, assuming he was too stupid to get out of the way when it began raining bison. Hercule Poirot would want to know whodunnit.

According to carbon dating of the bones found in a huge pile at the foot of the low mountain — called the killing site — where we stand, this place was used as a jump 5,700 years ago — half a millennium before the first pyramids were built in Egypt or Stonehenge was erected in England. There are indications hereabouts of human encampments that date back more than 9,000 years.

While the jump itself was simple enough — 300 to 600 bison were driven over a cliff about twelve metres high — the preparations were long and arduous, and included much praying and casting of omens, backed by extensive scouting expeditions to seek out a herd of animals that could be driven to the jump.

The buffalo runners would pass near the herds; some, wearing buffalo skins, would pretend to be injured animals, while others, with wolf skins, might make a short dash against the herd or against straggling animals, thus pushing and pulling the beasts in the right direction. Gradually, after several days, the bison would be lured into V-shaped drive lanes lined with rows of stone cairns to resemble men; these would funnel them towards the cliff.

An adult buffalo can weigh more than 500 kilograms and run for long distances at fifty kilometres an hour or more, so in a day before the horse and before the rifle, this was a tricky business indeed, and failure often meant starvation for an entire tribe. The hunt was therefore pursued with endless patience.

Once the runners judged that the bison were in place, they would rush in from behind, panicking the animals into a mass plunge over the cliff. Below, other hunters waited with spears and bows to dispatch stunned or wounded animals. There was a strongly held belief that if any animal escaped, it would go and warn other buffalo of the trick that had been played, ending the hunt forever, so every animal was hunted down and slain.

A successful jump brought more food than could be eaten at once, so the meat was dried and made into pemmican, while marrow was extracted from the bones. "They used everything," Kyle emphasizes. "Everything including the horns, hides, and tails. Absolutely nothing was allowed to go to waste. Bone splinters were used as awls for sewing, bladders as bags to store fat. Everything."

Because the site has been so carefully preserved, it is easy to imagine, from our position overlooking the plunge, exactly what took place, and I decide I would not be surprised to see a herd of bison, followed at a suitable distance by a couple of skin-clad young men, appear over yonder rise.

I wander down into the display area, which contains exhibits on the hunt, and on the way of life of the hunters, spread over three floors. At one point, I find myself standing beside one of the Blackfoot visitors from Montana, and I ask her if she has ever heard of Crowfoot.

"Crowfoot!" she almost snarls. "That asshole."

Apostles of peace have a hard life, even when dead.

Why Did They Paint the Barns Red? Glad You Asked

We drive north on Highway 2, past Claresholm — once home of the finest restaurant in Western Canada, the Flying N — past a sign advertising the Williams Bee Ranch, which conjures up some strange visions. This highway parallels the Rockies, now looming larger and larger across the foothills. To our right is flatland, awash in green of a hundred different shades, punctuated by ranch buildings. To our left, the land slopes into a line of hills backed by the mountains and flecked with light and shadow. Sunshine catches the snow on the mountains. It reminds me of Omar Khayyám's line about the rising sun catching the sultan's turret in a noose of light, and makes me wax poetic.

"Nice scenery," I tell the Driver. "Really spiffy."

We duck west around Calgary, and head for Cochrane and the CanWest Heritage Centre. Alberta, in our time, has become known for oil and dinosaurs — some of them in Drumheller, where fossil collectors frolic; some in the legislature — but when it was part of the North-West Territories, it was farm and cattle country, and it remained that way right up until the big oil find at Leduc in 1947.

The cattle background is celebrated on the property once owned by Sen. Matthew Cochrane, who established a ranch on 109,000 acres here in 1881. His life's work went about the way a lot of these efforts do: he lost 8,000 head to drought and weather in the first two years, sold 67,000 acres to the Mormon Church to keep going in 1887, and was down to 665 acres by the turn of the century. Reminds me of the story of the rancher who won a huge lottery and was asked what he intended to do with his millions. "Oh, I dunno," he said. "I guess I'll just keep ranching until it's all gone."

Where Matthew Cochrane's cattle once roamed, or fell over a nearby cliff, there is now an imposing centre celebrating ranching, farming, and the rodeo. There are displays on sheep, cattle, and horses, with life-size replicas that look so real you expect them to bleat, moo, or neigh, according to taste; other replicas show how they work inside, including giving the lowdown on a cow's four-compartment stomach, from which I quickly avert a sensitive eye.

Among the famous cowboys celebrated here is John Ware, a black man, who went from slavery in South Carolina to ownership of his own large spread north of Brooks, Alberta. He was famed on both sides of the border for his skill as a horseman and roper, but he died, still a young man, when his horse stepped in a gopher hole in 1905 and tossed him on his head. Never should have come to Canada — an American cowboy would have been gunned down or strung up, not done in by a gopher.

The displays are graphic and fascinating, and feature a series of full-size set scenes of cowboy life, including one in which a bunch of the boys are sittin' around the campfire, jawin' and chewin' and singin' songs, and when you press a button, by golly, they sing the song of your choice. I opt for "Cool Water," performed by Hank Snow, and break off after the fourth playing only because a gaggle of schoolkids, nervesome brats, begin to show signs of restiveness behind me. They want a turn, and as I walk away I am followed by the strains of George Fox singing — or, rather, singin' — "Here's Hopin'." He's okay, but he's no Hank Snow.

A lot of the museum is interactive, and you press a button to answer any of the score or so posted questions you cannot solve. One of these reads, "Why are barns red?" I guess — because the farm is usually in the red, because they are easier to see, etc. — and press the button. The answer is that red was the easiest paint to make. You fill a bucket with buttermilk and iron scraps, and wait for the metal to rust and turn the whole thing red.

I wander upstairs, where all the rodeo displays reside. I am not into rodeo much — far too cruel for my liking — but there is an inherent fascination in the displays of man and mount, frozen in the midst of a buck or steer-wrestling. One large display case is given over to "The Stewart Bronzes," so I naturally have a look at those. They commemorate four rodeo performers who were killed on their way to a meet in 1979. When their aircraft went down, a lot of money was raised to help look for them, and quite a lot of it was still left when the crash site was found, so it was used to commission bronze statues of the men, both in repose and in rodeo action, by the sculptor Linda Stewart. They almost turn me into a rodeo fan.

When I finish in the museum, the Driver and I go into a large restaurant on the premises for what turns out to be a very good lunch. Joan has been otherwise occupied all this time, so I ask her, "Hey, why are barns red?"

"Because it was the easiest colour to make," she replies. "You just needed buttermilk and metal."

I hate it when she does that.

We drive down to MacKay's ice-cream store on the main drag, and the cones are as good as advertised.

The Panhandlers Knock Off at Five

Calgary, our next destination, is essentially a financial centre now, although it spends much time and paint portraying itself as a kind of hick cowtown. On the way to our hotel, we pass a restaurant that sells bull gonads, also known as prairie oysters, as an exotic dish; it is advertising a Testicle Festival. Just part of the act.

What the populace is really interested in is the spot price for oil and what is happening on the world stock markets. I go out for a walk, and have not gone far along Fourth Avenue when, at the corner of Second Street, I come upon a young couple, plus dog, begging. The woman, rather attractive despite greasy blonde hair that last saw a comb about the time Matthew Cochrane last punched a cow, holds a crude cardboard sign informing the world that they are about to be evicted from their apartment. There is a Kentucky Fried Chicken bucket on the sidewalk in front of her to receive the remedy for this impending tragedy; it has a few loonies in it.

The man, who is in his thirties, is dark, intense, and staring down at the dog, a border collie–cross of some sort, which lies at his feet. The trio takes up most of the sidewalk at this busy intersection in the shadow of oil towers, hotel complexes, corporate headquarters — one of the wealthiest spots on earth.

I ask them how things are going.

"Not so good," the man tells the dog's back.

"Lose your job?"

"Yup."

"But this province is booming, this city is bursting at the seams. Can't you find work?"

"His health isn't good," explains the girl.

The young man coughs, which causes the dog to raise its head. He pushes it down again.

"How about you?" I ask the girl.

"I got fired, and I didn't have enough days in for UI." UI is no longer UI, actually, but EI — employment insurance, not *un*employment insurance — one of those Orwellian switches that hasn't taken hold yet.

"That's tough," I say, and drop a doubloon in the bucket. At this, the young man picks up the bucket, chirrups to the dog, and they start to move off.

"Through for the day?" I ask.

"Well," the young man explains reasonably, "it *is* five o'clock."

Further along Fourth Avenue, I find myself confronted by the Harry Hays Building/Édifice Harry Hays, where the federal government hangs its Stetson hereabouts, and it sets me to wondering about Alberta politics. Harry Hays was a highly intelligent, hard-working, likeable gent who spent almost his entire adult life in politics — first as mayor of Calgary, then as a member of Parliament, then as a senator and Cabinet minister (agriculture).

And he spent almost his entire adult life attacking politics and politicians for all he was worth. I once approached him after a speech in which he confided to the crowd that he was going to tell them things that "they wouldn't understand in Ottawa." The burden of his speech, however, turned out to be that your average Conservative was a wall-eyed, knock-kneed burglar and bum; apparently, they don't understand that in Ottawa.

I asked Harry why he spent so much time attacking politics, especially when he not only loved it, but also was good at it. His explanation was, roughly, that the politics-is-crud line works. It wouldn't work in Saskatchewan, where politics is a sport, a religion, and a private passion, but it works here.

How the United Farmers Formed a Government

It has always been this way. In the early part of this century, the farmers who formed most of the population were so often bamboozled and abandoned by politicians that when the Grange movement drifted up from the United States, they embraced it. They were led in this direction mainly by Henry Wise Wood, who was born on a farm near Monroe City, Missouri, in 1860. Wood was trained as a preacher, but he worked as a farmer and became active in agricultural politics. He moved to Alberta the year it was founded, 1905, and joined the infant United Farmers of Alberta (UFA), which he ruled from 1916 until 1931.

In Missouri, he had seen the agrarian movement wrecked by venturing into party politics, so he became convinced, and convinced the UFA, that the proper approach was to discard political parties, which were financed by "interests." Instead, the voters' representatives should group themselves by occupation. Farmers should form a farmers' group in Parliament and the legislatures, and should co-operate with any other group of representatives that brought in legislation favourable to farmers.

At this time, that meant low tariffs. UFA candidates were required to sign a recall that could be employed against them if they ceased to be true "delegates" of their constituencies. (Delegates, as we are taught in Political Science 101, represent the voice and opinion of the constituency, even if they don't agree with it. Representatives, by contrast, see themselves as put in place to exercise their own judgement, which they commonly surrender to the party that elected them in the first place.)

The UFA began to gain increasing popularity, which posed a problem. What if the party got elected and lost its purity? In 1919, the annual convention passed a resolution instructing the UFA to enter politics, which Wood initially opposed but accepted once it was done. Two years later, the UFA sent eleven MPs to Ottawa and formed the government in Alberta (Herbert Greenfield became premier, not Wood).

The UFA MPs joined others of their ilk from Manitoba, under the leadership of Thomas Crerar, and the whole group formed a loose alliance with other farm-based MPs under the name Progressives. After the 1921 election, they were entitled to form the official opposition in Ottawa, but that would have made them just a party like the others, and Crerar rejected the notion firmly.

Within a very short time, the wily Mackenzie King, who needed their votes to maintain a minority government, had picked off the key members, starting with Crerar, by offering them Cabinet posts and other appointments, and the Progressives disappeared into the ashcan of history. (The remnant joined with the emerging Co-operative Commonwealth Federation in the early 1930s.)

The UFA retained power in Alberta until 1935, becoming more and more like any other political party. It was defeated by "Bible Bill" Aberhart and the Social Credit, on a platform attacking politics and political parties as the captive of "interests." The UFA should have sued for breach of copyright.

What Alberta got out of all this is that political parties are bad and ought to be avoided, and it has been gospel ever since. You can get elected in this province only by saying what a rotten thing elections are, which seems rather odd.

When the Reform Party came roaring and raging out of the West in our own time, it was based almost entirely in Alberta, and was driven by a claim that all politics is corrupt because it is based on "interests," just as in the time of Henry Wise Wood. Reform would seek purity by being a different kind of party, one with delegates, not representatives. They can't help themselves; it is in the blood.

Next door, in Saskatchewan, the argument went the other way. There, the United Farmers and Progressives were bundled together into the Farmer-Labour Party by M. J. Coldwell, who, with his friend and disciple, Tommy Douglas, led that group into the Co-operative Commonwealth Federation. This was very much a political party — though it preferred to call itself a movement — and it behaved as such when it came to power under Douglas in the Saskatchewan election of 1944.

The result was that in Saskatchewan, politics is considered a decent occupation, while right next door, in remarkably similar circumstances, it is a hissing and a byword. Another result is that Henry Wise Wood, a very interesting gent, has disappeared from sight, and when we drive past a school bearing his name with some Calgary friends they have not the vaguest idea who he might have been or what he might have done, although what he did, fundamentally, was to determine the kind of politics that runs their province.

Walking on Air

The next morning, I head out again, fifteen metres high. Every major Canadian city now has a network of walkways to protect pedestrians from the lousy weather and, not so coincidentally, offer them places to buy things as they go. Most cities stick this walkway underground, where rodents dwell, but in Calgary it is laid out along what is called the Plus 15 Elevated Walkway — because most of it is fifteen metres above the ground. Much more civilized.

Not only are the walkways much brighter, with natural light pouring in the glass walls, but you can look out and down on the peasants below, and watch life unfold in downtown Calgary. On the Plus 15, you can go almost anywhere, from the public library east of the Macleod Trail to Mount Royal College on Eighth Street, from the Calgary Tower in the south to the Shell Tower in the north. You can read a book, visit a broker, take in an art gallery, rob a bank and wind up in the clink — the courthouse and court of appeal are both along the way. You can buy anything here, including, as it turns out, sex.

I am moseying along, minding my own business, when I notice two undoubted hookers standing beside one of the exits and plying their trade. I can't help wondering where they go to, ah, complete the transaction, so I ask a clerk in the men's department of the Bay. "Oh, there's lots of hotels off the Plus 15," he explains. "Good ones, and ones where they can go as well." He says he has noticed more and more of the prostitutes on the way to work. "If they get to be a nuisance, somebody will do something about it."

My destination is not a hotel, classy or otherwise, but the Petro-Canada building, also known as Red Square, both because it was once a government operation and because the building is clad in reddish stone. Petro-Can is in a strange position in this city, primarily because it's a corporation that started under government auspices, which brought it all the dislike and disdain that accumulate here around anything governmental, plus all the dislike and disdain that attaches to Ottawa (never mind that it has always been head-quartered here).

In particular, it attracts all the venom unleashed here by the National Energy Program of the early 1980s, which convinced Western oilmen that Ottawa had concocted a plot to impoverish the province. This has apparently made the corporation inordinately shy; although everybody in Calgary knows where Red Square is, there is nothing to cry out the company's name. Inside, there is a whole Noorduyn Norseman bush aircraft hanging from the ceiling of the atrium, which gives a sort of hint that we are dealing with oil exploration, but you have to get up to the third level to see a modest Petro-Canada sign.

The man I am hoping to see is busy, so I pick up a cup of coffee from an array of cafeterias in the second-floor lobby and ask two men at a table if I can join them. They look pointedly at an empty table nearby and grunt okay.

Do they work for Petro-Can?

Yes.

Enjoy the work?

Yes. Well, you know . . .

Do they consider Petro-Can to be a publicly owned company?

No, definitely not. An oil company like any other.

Do they know anyone in their own industry who considers Petro-Can to be a company like any other? Anyone at all?

The two men get up and huff away.

Personally, I thought it was rather clever of the Canadian government to set up its own oil company in 1975, not only to get in on the action, but also to be able to exercise influence in a vital industry now totally dominated by foreign firms. Of course, this doesn't help the locals, who consider Ottawa foreign. We taxpayers own only about 18 percent of the firm now, strictly as an investment, with no thought of control. We began to privatize it in 1991, and it would be all gone now, except that there were some lean years in the oil industry and the value of our shares slipped, so we hung on. We still aren't doing too well on our investment; in 1998, admittedly a tough year for the industry, the operating return on capital was a meager 3.6 percent. When that number gets better and share prices improve, we will probably sell our stake.

But I am not here to buy (or sell) shares; rather, I'm here to look into one of the monumental developments now shaking the industry.

The Great Gas Cap Wars

Canadians have been told for the past twenty-five years that we are running out of oil, will soon be out of cheap oil, will soon be lucky to scrape along on matches. The National Energy Program was unrolled with a lot of numbers that showed the price of oil reaching seventy-seven dollars a barrel (170 litres) in 1986, and increasing by 13 percent annually thereafter. You would think that this would have made us pay more attention to, and spend more money on, alternatives such as wind, solar, and tidal power. But no.

When it turned out that the gang with the slide rules and computers had made a little boo-boo, and oil, instead of costing a dollar a mouthful, sank to ten dollars (U.S.) a barrel in 1998, the solution was to reinforce the cartel that controls prices and jack them up artificially. While all this was going on, the cost of gasoline refined from oil multiplied twelvefold, without arousing any significant complaint (because, after all, we were going to run out of the stuff — if not now, soon). This is still the way the numbers read. In 2010, according to current projections ("Oil Production in the 21st Century," *Scientific American*, March 1998), the world's oil-thirsty economies will be demanding about ten billion barrels more than the industry can produce.

However, there is more oil trapped deep underground in Western Canada than Saudi Arabia can shake a sheik at. We have all read about the stuff in the Alberta tar sands, but that is close to the surface, where water mixes with the sand and hydrocarbons to form bitumen (a generic term for mixtures of hydrocarbons, including petroleum, asphalt, and tar, which can be and this is being extracted by open-pit mining and refined to provide crude oil.

However, far below this are huge supplies, gigantic supplies, of bitumen that has lain undisturbed for eons. The most recent estimate of Alberta energy experts puts the total "initial volume in-place" reserves of "surface mineable" bitumen at 24.1 billion cubic metres — roughly 152 billion stock-tank barrels; the "in situ" (deep-down) reserves are put at 245.7 billion cubic metres, more than ten times this, although it is far from proven that all of this can or will be recovered.

The conservative figure floated before an Energy Board hearing this summer was that this in situ bitumen represents the equivalent of 300 billion barrels of oil. Put another way, there is somewhere between a 600- and 1,200-year supply for Alberta, at current levels of consumption. Put any way, a hell of a lot of bitumen, capable of being turned into oil at economic rates, is there for the taking. The tricky part is taking it.

One of the methods now being explored to get at this resource is to insert two pipes down into the sand or shale, one of which will carry steam down to the bitumen. Once it is heated, the stuff thins and forms pools under the site of injection. These liquid pools are then carried off by the second pipe. This technique, called steam-assisted gravity drainage (SAGD), can work only if there's a cap of natural gas above the oil, constantly exerting downward pressure. In effect, a pressure chamber is formed between the gas above and the Devonian layer of rock beneath. If you siphon off the gas, the pressure eases and you can't get out the oil.

Well, that's easy, you're probably saying. Don't take the gas off until the oil is removed. Not so easy. It used to be that oil and gas were considered as one resource, both subject to the regulatory authority of the Alberta Energy Conservation Board (now called the Alberta Energy and Utilities Board, or EUB). But then they were split — and the right to exploit the two resources was auctioned off separately. Oil and gas producers were pitted against each other. Gas producers wanted to get their product out as fast as possible, to realize a return on their investment. Oil producers wanted the gas left in place until the underlying oil was removed.

They indicated that if the gas went first, the whole area would be "sterilized," because it would become either impossible or uneconomic to remove the oil (I am quoting from the hearings before the board). When the same company was involved — Petro-Canada, for example, has both oil and gas subsidiaries — this was an internal corporate issue. However, when there was a head-on clash between firms producing gas alone and those in the oil business, matters became messy.

On November 12, 1996, Gulf Canada Resources Limited applied to the Alberta Energy Conservation Board to shut in gas above the bitumen deposits in a zone called the Surmont area, along the Athabasca River, where Gulf has bitumen deposits, "until oil sands development is completed." Gulf contended that if the gas goes, as much as 15 billion barrels of oil would be lost — at a huge cost not only to Gulf, but also to Alberta and Canada. "Extraction of the bitumen resource could become impossible," Gulf argued.

Petro-Canada has a bitumen lease area close by, called Chard. Scott Miller, assistant general counsel for Petro-Can, notes, "Geology and pressure [do] not recognize township boundaries." So his firm joined the Gulf application.

Miller's complex argument about the technical aspects of this case consists of two simple points. The first is that the oil resource that may be squandered is gigantic, the gas resource merely large. "We are talking about the order of billions of dollars, as opposed to millions; it's as clear as that." The second is that "if the bitumen producers are wrong in their analysis, a shut-in can be reversed. If the gas producers are wrong, a decision not to shut in the gas is irreversible."

The gas firms, in a consortium now called the Surmont Gas Producers (SGP), replied to the attempt to block their production from 183 wells by speeding up removal of the gas while the legal wrangling went on. When the EUB reported in March 1998 that "the Board accepts that associated gas production would have a detrimental effect on SAGD performance" and that "the Board believes that in some instances the effect on the ultimate bitumen recovery could be significant," you might have thought the matter was decided.

Fat chance.

The oil company sought an immediate shut-in of the gas, and the SGP immediately filed for a deferral of at least one year of the implementation of the board's findings. Then, more than two years after the process began, the SGP sought to have the whole process derailed on the grounds that the EUB had no jurisdiction over the gas. It lost that case, so it appealed, and the appeal is still under consideration.

More than three years after it became urgent (assuming the oil companies have it right) to take immediate action to conserve the oil by shutting in the gas above it, gas is still being sucked away. Soon, Gulf claims, the whole issue may be moot, because the damage will be done. The board is now mulling over the results of its hearings in Calgary, which produced more than 7,000 pages of argument and testimony and 453 exhibits. When it reports, in due course, whatever findings it makes will be appealed as well, no doubt, no matter which way it goes. And the gas will continue to be sucked away.[*]

Scott Miller says, "They have made the legal process into a classic stall; they have set up every roadblock they could. They have claimed that the board doesn't have the right to act to conserve energy, although it is was founded as the Alberta Energy Conservation Board. They have claimed that the science is

---

[*] This decision came down on April 3, 2000. The board ruled in favour of Gulf and ordered the shut in of 146 wells. As this goes to press an appeal is expected, but not yet filed.

flawed, although we are using it, they —" He throws up his hands. "Gulf even offered to make a joint deal with them. Let us take the oil out first, and we will pay you as we go along, and then you can take the gas out, and we will share in that. Nothing doing."

The oil companies may be wrong — they have been wrong before — but if they are right, a monumental waste of a vanishing resource is taking place under our very noses while a gaggle of lawyers test their mellow tones and collect their fat fees. Prudence and the public interest suggest that the brakes should go on while we discover if we are headed for a cliff.

This seems to me an issue that Canadians might want to look at.

The gas companies, naturally, want to get the gas out, want a return on their investment. They contend, as well, that the theory advanced by Gulf and Petro-Can is flawed, even though a pilot project now in place appears to show that it is true. Despite this, the SGP group says that the gas cap may not be essential to bringing out the bitumen. And even if it turns out that the gas was the key to the whole process after all, they say, that can be remedied. All the oil gang has to do is to re-inject gas — how about methane? — or even water, to provide the necessary pressure. In any event, they are entitled to get their product out because they paid for it, and nuts to anything else. This is the way this point was put by A. McLarty, the counsel for the SGP, in argument before the EUB:

> What Gulf is asking you to do is to dispossess the Surmont Producers of their property, and they ask you to do this because, they say, it's the right thing to do. Characterizing something as the right thing to do has never, and should never, become an option available to any statutory tribunal as the sole reason for achieving a public-interest objective.

Skipping lightly over the fact that this was not, in fact, the sole reason Gulf gave for achieving a public-interest objective, we are left to contemplate the real problem here — namely, that the public interest has no champion in these matters; the whole debate is taking place offstage, among a shoal of corporation lawyers with their own interests very much to the fore. McLarty is no doubt correct in arguing that doing the right thing is no business of statutory tribunals, but we are left to ask, "Then whose business is it?"

In the three years of this imbroglio, only one person who appeared before the board seemed to have as his sole concern the impact of the decision on the public weal. His name was Gord Stabb; he has long had an interest in bitumen recovery, and has worked as a consultant for Petro-Can. He contended that there was only one worthwhile issue here, the conservation of the resource:

> *Sir, a fundamental norm in our society is that the right of one entity should not supersede the right of society to thrive. It is for that very reason that the concept of conservation exists. It is for that reason that each and every person in this room is present today. Conservation is why so many have worked so tirelessly to provide decisive information. You, the members of the panel, and your staff have listened carefully to all of the relevant matters in this issue. The decision of this hearing will clearly set the precedent for the future of oil sand thermal development. Today, the responsibility is passed to you to ensure the right of this industry, of this province and of Canada to thrive. . . .*
>
> *I think of Canada's Maritime provinces, sir, and of the disappearance of the Northern Cod Fishery, and with it, the disappearance and the loss of a way of life for thousands of people for the past hundreds of years. The loss of this resource was avoidable. It was lost for want of timely and prudent regulatory intervention. Now it is too late; now the cod are gone. The Energy and Utilities Board of Alberta faces the challenge of conserving the oil sand resource. Can Alberta learn from the loss of the Atlantic fishery? I remind the Board that this conservation issue has been before it for more than three years. Bitumen continues to be wasted at Surmount and across the Athabasca with each and every day. Time is of the essence.*

What we have here is a battle among giant corporations for shares of spoils that belong not to them, but to the people of Alberta and Canada, people who are shut out of the process as effectively as if they were a choked-off gas well. The gas producers have already extracted 179 billion cubic feet of gas from this area, according to the evidence produced before the board. They have already had their money back, but they want more, and every day they can spin this out, they are getting more — about $140,000 worth every twenty-four hours. But if it is really a fact that removing the gas first will make the oil either unavailable or too costly — even if this is just a strong likelihood, as the board has already determined — surely the provincial government ought to step in and sort the whole mess out.

The obvious solution is to jam the resources back together and give the gas companies a return on the oil recovery. That way, they can earn something on their investment right away, and then give the oil companies a return on the gas. If the issue simply drags on, the gas will be gone, and the decision will have been made without making a decision.

What this requires, in fact, is a political solution, not a market one.

What am I talking about? We are in Alberta.

The Name is ffrench, Conrad ffrench

After the second-best dinner of the entire trip — at the Westin Calgary, where the hostess gave Joan a rose when we sat down, a wise investment — we are ready to move west again and depart Calgary to drop in, only briefly, at Banff, in memory of Capt. Conrad Fulke Thomond O'Brien ffrench, marquis de Castel-Thomond. One of my pals.

I came to know the captain by accident. During a visit to Banff, I was taken by a young friend of mine, late at night, to see an enormous, and locally famous, log cabin — twenty metres to a side, two storeys high, superbly crafted — which had, according to my friend, been the home of the real-life model for Ian Fleming's unlikely hero, James Bond.

I snorted politely, but the next day I went to the Banff Archives, where the director, Maryalice Stewart, unearthed old clippings from the time when Princess Margaret visited Fairholme Ranch, the place in question. She also unearthed a clipping showing that a Captain ffrench of West Vancouver had received a thousand-dollar Canada Council grant to write the memoirs of his life as a member of the North West Mounted Police and a British secret agent.

Through the Canada Council, I ran Captain ffrench to ground, and before long I was cosily ensconced in his living room, admiring the view of English

Bay, ogling the paintings and *objets d'art* that vied for wall space with long shelves of books, and listening to his story.

An impressive man, well over six feet and bearing a remarkable resemblance to David Niven, he was then eighty-one but looked sixty. With his steel-grey hair, a face lined but still extraordinarily handsome, and lithe figure, he looked like the white hunter who leads the girl astray about the third reel in one of those African adventure films.

Frankly, when he began to talk, I assumed that he was a monstrous fraud, but he punctuated his tale by bounding lightly from his chair to fish out documents, diaries, and other memorabilia. One of these was a note from Stewart Menzies, once head of MI6, the British military intelligence branch (he was known as S.M.; in his books, Fleming shortened that to M.), complaining about ffrench's expense account. He had lost a tape recorder, and Menzies wanted him to pay for it.

There were long letters back and forth about ffrench's activities, not, alas, detailing midnight trysts, but instead weaselling on about expenses, and was he sure that trip to Geneva had been necessary? There were the captain's diaries, twenty-nine of them, full of names and dates and secret meetings; any one of these, in the wrong hands at the wrong time, could have put a rope around his neck. There were photographs and books, the most interesting of which was *Invasion, 1940,* by Peter Fleming, Ian's journalist brother, about the beginnings of the Second World War. This contained a copy of the German security service's blacklist of the most wanted British war criminals, who were to be executed after a Nazi victory. Captain ffrench appeared as no. 28.

"You will notice," he told me, shooting his cuffs, "that my name appears before that of Winston Churchill."

I blurted, "But that's because it's alphabetical; Castel-Thomond, marquis de, comes before Churchill, Winston."

He gave me a hurt frown.

Conrad ffrench, I learned from all this, was born in London, England, in 1893, the son of an Irish adventurer and a beautiful Victorian socialite. The couple settled in Italy, but they came back to England when Conrad was due so he could be born British. Conrad lived back and forth between England and Italy, and by the time he was sixteen he was a bit fed up with the whole process and longing for adventure. One day during the Easter holidays in 1910, he was out walking in Kent when he met an elderly gentleman on holiday from his life as a rancher and justice of the peace in a far-off place called Buffalo Lake, Saskatchewan.

As the old man and the boy talked and walked across the Folkestone Downs, he spun wonderful takes of the opening of the Canadian West. Conrad was enraptured, and when his new friend suggested that he should come out and join the Mounties he agreed at once. The next spring, he boarded a ship for Canada and, at the age of seventeen, became an NWMP recruit.

He served in detachments all over southern Saskatchewan, chasing rustlers, busting broncos, settling barroom brawls and family disputes until mid-1912, when a letter came from his mother. She was back in England, dying of cancer. Conrad immediately purchased his discharge and went to England. After his mother's death, he joined the Royal Irish Rifles and was sent to France just in time to take part in the Battle of Mons.

There, he was severely wounded in the shoulder and chest, taken prisoner, and after he tried to escape (despite his wounds) sent to a prisoner-of-war camp well inside Germany.

He spent most of his time in a camp containing many British prisoners, some French, and a few Russians. The British were snobbish and the French full of their own cares, but "the Russians, taking things philosophically, were extremely good company." So he attached himself to the Russians, and learned to speak and read and write their language, a skill that would come in handy later on.

In England, just before the war, he had met Cathleen Mann, the pretty and talented daughter of the portrait painter Harrington Mann, and she wrote to him frequently in prison camp. Cathleen had gone to work in the War Office, and he began to send her secret messages by the childishly simple device of writing in invisible ink made from potassium iodide, which he got from a hospital orderly, ostensibly to treat his wounds. Many of the prisoners in camp were pilots who had been shot down, and who had vital information about troop movements and the state of roads and bridges. Conrad ffrench sent all this information home.

As a result, when the war finally ended and ffrench was released after his years in prison, Stewart Menzies, then second-in-command of military intelligence, offered him a job as a secret agent in Stockholm. He would be attached to the British embassy with the cover of military attaché, but his real job was to gather information from Russian refugees fleeing the aftermath of the 1917 revolution. His fluent Russian fitted him perfectly for the job, and in January 1919 he arrived in Stockholm as Agent ST36.

His most important assignment was to smuggle a Communist diplomat, Leo Krassin, through the ring of hostile countries surrounding the Soviet Union and out to England for an interview with Prime Minister Lloyd George. It was the first face-to-face conversation between the new Communist leadership and the outside world, and ffrench took a number of pictures of Krassin and himself.

The post-war depression brought cutbacks, including some to the secret service, and ffrench went back to England to chase foxes and visit friends. Then the prince of Wales (later, briefly, Edward VIII) was sent on a goodwill tour to India, and ffrench dusted off his military kit and managed to land himself a job as an aide-de-camp. In India, he took up mountain climbing and earned the nickname the Eagle for his exploits.

When the prince returned to England, ffrench joined the 16th Queen's Lancers, but he developed a circulatory disorder and retired in 1926 to recuperate and chase more foxes. There followed a time of travelling, mountaineering, and the study of painting. He had always dabbled in art, but now he took it up seriously, and spent six years studying in England, France, and Jamaica. He was now nearing forty, and the only thing he had done really well was to be a spy, so he went back to that, in a rather curious way.

In 1931, he married a Swedish beauty whom he had met in Rome. They honeymooned in England and Vienna, and while there ffrench organized a tourist business to take package tours across the Austrian ski country. It was centred on Kitzbühel, in the Tyrol district of west Austria. In June 1935, Maud ffrench announced that she wanted to go back to Stockholm to have the baby they were then expecting, and Conrad decided to go skiing in Lapland, where there was snow even in summer.

He stayed in Riksgranzen, a resort town on the rail line, and one day while he was sitting on the porch there, he noticed a great many trains, all laden with ore, passing through. With a worldwide depression on, who would be buying so much ore?

"I thought there was something fishy about those trains," ffrench told me. "So I went into the hotel, grabbed my passport, and hopped onto one of the ore cars." Well, naturally. Wouldn't you?

From the trainmen, he learned that the ore was bound for the Krupp munitions plant on the Rhine River. This was solid evidence that Germany was re-arming, in contravention of the Treaty of Versailles.

He sent off a report to Stewart Menzies, by now chief of military intelligence, and Menzies, duly grateful, invited him back to England and took him back on the payroll as a spy; he was still based in Kitzbühel, with the cover of his tour business. He stayed there, except for one long fact-finding trip across Russia to China, until March 1938, when German soldiers marched over the Austrian border to enforce the *Anschluss.*

Outwardly, ffrench throughout these years was a handsome playboy and sometime tourist agent with such interesting friends as his old boss from India days, the duke of Windsor, who often visited Kitzbühel after the 1936 abdication. He was also friendly with the Fleming brothers, Peter, then a foreign correspondent for a London newspaper, and Ian, a novelist. Conrad ffrench was not taken with the younger brother:

> That Ian was glamorous is certain; nonchalant, restless, spoiled, more cynical than funny, strong-willed and ambitious, and a first-class athlete. . . . He was a very complicated, imaginative and subtle character who lacked staying power, and yet was most intolerant of failure in others.

He was also, ffrench believed, a danger to him. Ian Fleming had worked in naval intelligence and was fascinated by spying. He introduced Maud ffrench to a German named Markwert, a suspected Gestapo agent, who took Maud out to dinner and plied her with questions about Conrad. When he asked her point-blank if her husband was a spy, Maud told him, "Not a chance. He's much too stupid to be a spy."

Fleming went back to London to work as a stockbroker and later blossomed as the author of books featuring dashing spies. Soon after this, ffrench's marriage broke up, and he spent most of his time gathering information from a network of agents he had built up, on pay that, he complained, "was less than that of a window cleaner," and getting into rows about his expenses. When he visited London, he insisted on staying at the Carlton Hotel, and "there would always be quibbles about my travel costs."

However, the money turned out to be well spent when, on March 11, 1938, he was able to get out the first word of the invasion of Austria. His method was direct and rather dull: an Austrian living on the border sent him a message, and ffrench simply popped down to the corner phone box and called Whitehall. Assuming that his cover was now broken, he bundled together all his secret papers and decamped for Switzerland by train.

In the confusion caused by the invasion, he got through without so much as having his passport stamped, although by the next day Gestapo officers were ripping the soles off travellers' shoes in their search for incriminating documents.

Since he could no longer work as a spy, ffrench decided to return to Canada, a country that held only happy memories for him, but no one would offer him a job, so he went to England to work as a translator and interpreter for the rest of the war. While in England, he married again, and he brought his new wife, Rosalie, back to Canada at war's end. The newlyweds drove to Banff, a popular honeymoon spot, and there they learned that a rare piece of freehold land was coming up for sale within the national park boundaries, eight kilometres east of town.

This was Fairholme Ranch, and they bought it on the spot. The ex-spy designed and built the huge log building that caught my eye, then settled down to a life of raising horses, teaching at the Banff School of Fine Arts, and raising a new family of two sons.

However, the second marriage didn't last either, and ffrench began to spend more and more time at 100 Mile House, in the B.C. interior, where he became absorbed in a religion-cum-philosophy called ontology (the word refers to the Greek for "discussion of being"). With the breakup of his second marriage, he moved away from Fairholme, which was sold to the Canadian government.

(The log cabin was dismantled and moved to Edmonton.) He bought a home in West Vancouver, which is where I first met him, then moved to Loveland, Colorado, the U.S. headquarters of ontology.

When the Driver and I, with our grown daughter, Sandra, visited him there, he was living like an Oriental prince. He had given most of his money to ontology in return for living quarters in a splendid cabin on a mountaintop, where *five* — no kidding — young women took turns making sure he was well fed and cared for. We lost touch with him some years ago — he was still working on the memoir the Canada Council had advanced him a thousand dollars to write — but every time we drive through Banff, the Driver says, "That Conrad ffrench, now there was a handsome man!"

10

British Columbia

WHO'S CRAZY NOW?

The tree-ringed mountains take over again near Lytton, where the Thompson River joins the Fraser and where, 150 years ago, Simon Fraser bartered with the Indians. His journal notes, "Here, I obtained, for an awl, passage to the next village, a distance of three miles through strong rapids." Here, we obtained, for a tankful of gas, passage to Vancouver, a distance of 163 miles, through strong traffic.

— STAR WEEKLY, APRIL 24, 1965

British Columbia, like Saskatchewan, is a province most Canadians think they know, but it ain't necessarily so. The vision most of us have is of a place full of mountains, meadows, salt sea, and crazy politicians. At first, the geography, at least, seems to conform to this vision. Driving the Trans-Canada westward from Banff, the traveller encounters a block of country like something out of *Heidi:* every curve brings another lofty mountain — sometimes tree-covered, sometimes bald up to the snow line — followed by a babbling brook, a placid lake, another curve, and another mountain. The vision of goatherds in lederhosen hovers over the landscape, and you expect the echo of a yodel to break the alpine stillness.

The Driver is not too keen on this section of the trip; she feels the mountains are closing in on us, and longs for a bit of roadway where she can see ahead — and, not coincidentally, where she can pass some of the campers that clog the highway's arteries from Lake Louise to Revelstoke. She thinks these recreational vehicles, and the trans-continental trucks that travel in convoys with them, lie by the side of the road until we come in sight, and then pull out ahead of us, to follow in front at a sedate fifty kilometres an hour.

I like the mountains, find them restful, even serene, and try to cheer her up with reminiscences of earlier hikes along the route. Once, entering Field, B.C., on the Alberta border, we stopped to look at statues of elk that the tourist authorities had apparently placed in front of the information kiosk, only to discover, when we stopped the car in the evening gloom to get a better look, that they were real elk. It is hard to say who was the more startled, the animals or us. Another time, we saw a fox sitting by the highway on his haunches, and he didn't even turn his head as we came up. I was sure he was waiting for the bus to Vancouver.

Then there was Cougar Creek, near Rogers Pass, the summit of the Trans-Canada. We stopped at this rushing river — creek is far too modest a name — on a hot summer day in 1964, on our first trans-Canada trip, and Craig, our son, went tearing off up the hill to sample the snow. He thought snow in July was a wondrous thing. A few minutes later, Joan and I were looking upstream when we saw John de Visser, the photographer who was with us for the trip, lean over and hook something out of the water, exactly like a bear snagging a salmon. This turned out to be Craig, who had tried to cross the stream on rocks, slipped, and was headed for somewhere south of the border when John gaffed him and brought him to land. We didn't even have time to be frightened.

On this current trip, we stop at the impressive interpretation centre at Rogers Pass — named for Maj. Albert B. Rogers, the surveyor who first explored this route for the Canadian Pacific Railway in 1882. The railway was punched through the Selkirk range of the Rockies in 1885; it was built in a series of endless loops to climb the 1,327 metres to the summit, and required more than a dozen bridges over plunging gorges. On completion, it was considered to be a significant engineering feat, which it was; unfortunately, however, it was not a usable railway line.

The massive snowfalls in the area, which average nearly seven metres annually and occasionally reach twice that, leave huge blocks of unstable snow on slopes that tower 1,800 metres above the roadbed. Frequent avalanches plunge down with a hiss and a roar, at speeds up to 320 kilometres an hour. No train was actually swept to its doom in those early years, but the piled-up snow frequently made the route impassable.

In the winter of 1885–86, the track was blocked almost as much as it was open, so the engineers threw up thirty-one snowsheds during the following summer, to divert the avalanches. They were, to put it mildly, inadequate to the task. Between 1885 and 1911, more than 200 people, nearly all of them railway employees — and many of them Chinese — were killed along this route. In 1910, when crews went out to clear the track of the massive results of one avalanche, another swept down on the workers from the other side of the valley, and wiped out sixty-two of them.

The CPR responded by boring the Connaught Tunnel, eight kilometres long, to go under the pass, and the completion of that task in 1916 ended the immediate danger to trains.

When the time came to build the Trans-Canada, the decision was made to follow the old, now abandoned, railway bed, since that route saved a 240-kilometre detour up an old logging road known as the Big Bend Highway. The Big Bend followed every twist and turn of the Columbia River, and was often closed for days at a time in the winter. The new, much shorter route would be made safe by a clever series of dodges, only some of which are visible to the traveller. As you mount the forty-kilometre ridge leading to Rogers Pass, you go through nine large concrete snowsheds, shrewdly positioned to bear the brunt of many of the avalanches that continue to plague the route.

You can also see, at intervals, where slopes above the road have been buttressed by earth dams and rubble barriers to break up the slides, by diversion trenches to steer them away, and by flat benches, some of them 300 metres long by 50 metres wide, to catch them. And you can hardly miss the large cement circles stationed at intervals beside the highway throughout Glacier National Park, the park that spans Rogers Pass.

What? Shell-Shocked Snowbanks?

These mark the emplacements where 105-millimetre howitzers are brought in and mounted, during avalanche season, to trigger off slides before they can become too dangerous. A ten-person artillery crew is stationed at the pass, ready for action when ordered in by a team of snow technicians, whose job it is to judge when the time is right. The technicians ski into the mountains to test the state of the white stuff and, from time, to time, drop explosives on "indicator slopes" to see if the snow can be persuaded to move. There is not much point in bombarding the hillside if the snow isn't ready to come down.

Once the technicians determine the time has come, the road is closed and the artillery does its stuff, lobbing shells into the whiteness to set off slides. In the blizzard conditions that often prevail, they sometimes can't tell whether they have caused a slide or not, so the technicians drive a truck out to check — and if they hear a rumble, they get the hell out of there. The roadway is closed for a few hours from fifty to sixty times every winter, but there have been no fatalities because of the avalanches since the system came into effect.

Even with all the precautions, motorists are occasionally stranded inside one of the snowsheds for a few hours, but for most of the year this pathway through the mountains is, except for the RVs, a stairway to serenity along a route where hundreds once died. One of the difficulties the park rangers have today is convincing travellers that they still have to take the danger of avalanches seriously.

Before the Trans-Canada opened, the magnificent national parks in this area were available only to a few rich Canadians. In 1961, fewer than 200 people went through on the old highway; in 1962, the number was 200,000, and within five years it topped 2 million.

Just west of the interpretation centre, at the actual summit of the highway, there is a large monumental arch marking the official opening of Rogers Pass in August 1962, by Prime Minister John Diefenbaker. An American visitor wants to know, "Who the heck is this Deefenbachia? I never heard of him."

I tell him he was a Saskatchewan boy who once said that "only dogs know what to do with polls," and for this I earn a puzzled look from the American. His attention is taken, instead, by a gopher who insists that he came here to be fed, it is time for feeding, and how about it? He appears to live somewhere within the wooden arch of the monument, and tries to exact a toll from everyone who stops.

So does the government. Some optimist has installed a machine where you are instructed to insert a doubloon, which will entitle you to park and look at the arch. We work it out that we have lingered here twenty times over the years, without paying, and we don't wish to break the habit of decades now.

We stop for lunch just down the road at a vast motel called 3 Valley Gap, to mark the fact that three river valleys come together here. This motel used to sell coffee for five cents a cup until a couple of years ago, but now it wants a whole quarter; however, the refills are free and the coffee is good, so we don't grumble too much.

A Hell of a Lot of Houseboats

At Sicamous, the country changes; instead of close-pressing mountains, we encounter wide valleys, majestic lakeland, prosperous-looking farms. Sicamous is a Shuswap word meaning "squeezed in the middle," an accurate description of the narrow pathway between the giant Shuswap and Mara lakes; either that, or it means "hell of a lot of houseboats," since this small city at the top of the Okanagan Valley boasts of being the "houseboat capital of Canada."

Why anyone would want to boast about that is a mystery, since houseboats, and I say this with no bias whatever, are well known as among the prominent banes of modern civilization, floating booze-boxes usually piloted by thumb-handed maniacs. Along the Trent-Severn Waterway in Ontario, where we live, they are called wallbangers, from their habit of colliding with the sides of locks when not actually thumping into other water traffic. Anyway, this is where they come from, and aside from hoping that they will all develop wood rot and sink we pass them by without comment.

At Chase, just past Salmon Arm, where Highway 97 slips off down the

Okanagan Valley, we run into the most dramatic change of scenery on the whole Trans-Canada. This is where the drylands begin. Reaching up between the Rockies and the Coastal Range from the southwestern United States is a blunt arrow of semi-desert aimed at the heart of interior British Columbia. It cuts the Trans-Canada in a broad swath between Chase and Spences Bridge, 200 kilometres southwest. From either side, cloudbanks thrusting for this dry belt lift over the mountains and lighten as they lift, leaving their moisture on the slopes below; by the time they hit the Trans-Canada, their brooding darkness has become fluffy whiteness, and the skies are not cloudy all day. At Ashcroft, near the centre of this arid area, annual rainfall averages about twenty centimetres. On the mountainside eighty kilometres away, ten times that amount falls every year.

Cattle are a major crop on this sandy land, where the hills are as wrinkled and grey as an elephant's hide, where tumbleweed blows and sagebrush abounds, and where the rare mountain lakes, acrid with alkali, are more precious than molten gold. Irrigation keeps the land alive. The deed of each ranch includes water rights, which are policed by a water bailiff who's hired collectively by the ranchers to dole out the precious fluid in strict rotation. If five ranches are tapping a single lake for water, each will be connected to it by a funnelling stream.

The streams are blocked off most of the time, but for a set number of hours each week the bailiff lets the water flow to each ranch in turn. He controls the amount of the flow by the size of the hole in the board he drops across the stream in use. A number of years ago, one rancher was caught cheating by letting more water flow to his ranch than he was entitled to; he lost his water rights, and the ranch became worthless.

The Elixir of Life, No Less

At Pritchard, west of Salmon Arm along the Thompson River, we spot the first ginseng farm along our route. This is clearly a part of the agricultural revolution; the generations who planted, tended, pruned, and pampered apples, peaches, and pears decided they had lost money enough, and plunged into this exotic crop. From the road, what you see is a large patch of ground, sometimes several acres, covered over with a dark green polypropylene tarp suspended on two-and-a-half-metre pylons. The ginseng growers are doing their best to recreate the shady hardwood forest gloom from which this Asian plant first sprang.

From above, when you are driving down a hill towards a ginseng "garden," as the farms are called, it looks like a giant parking lot; a farmer friend of mine swears that the tarpaulins used are stretched so taut that local kids can — and do — go rollerblading up there.

My curiosity about ginseng was aroused by an article in the *Los Angeles Times*, which described it as "the hottest crop on Canada's West Coast, arguably the most lucrative legal farm harvest in the world, and lure to a new wave of Canadian agricultural entrepreneurs." Pause briefly to note the word "legal" in this description; the most lucrative farm harvest in British Columbia is probably marijuana — unofficial estimates put the annual take in the province from this cash crop at more than $2 billion. Marijuana is also luring a new wave of agricultural pioneers, and they are only slightly more reticent about their work than the ginseng gang.

Ginseng — *Panax ginseng* to pals, or in its American form, *Panax quinque-folius* — has been cultivated in China for more than 3,000 years, and is purchased mainly by the people of Southeast Asia and the Asian Pacific Rim nations, where it is the most commonly used herbal medicine. It is called the elixir of life, and the claims for its virtues sound like the spiel we used to get from snake-oil salesmen:

> *If taken regularly, it is said to reduce stress, increase physical stamina, quiet the nerves, enhance blood flow, help in blood sugar and cholesterol levels, help regulate blood pressure, strengthen the metabolism, vitalize glandular functions, slow the degeneration of cells and increase longevity.*

This is not the pitch on the back of a bottle, but the cold-blooded prose of a brood of B.C. bureaucrats in a snappy little pamphlet on the crop. They say nothing about two other claims that appeared in the *Los Angeles Times* article: "It is reputed in Asian folklore to . . . hold off senility and revive sexual prowess." Well, I mean . . . The genus name, *Panax*, comes from a Greek word that means "to heal"; the word for a cure-all, "panacea," comes from the same root. The first commercial planting of American ginseng, cousin of the Asian herb, took place in 1982.

Since it takes a year to prepare the ground, and three to five years after that to produce a crop, not much happened for a while. And then the first crops were harvested, sold to the Hong Kong brokers who control ginseng importation to China with an iron grip, and the first cheques were cashed. Ginseng is expensive to grow — the shade cloth covering costs $9,000 an acre and the seed $50 a pound; even the cable and other hardware needed to hold up the shade cloth comes in at more than $2,500 an acre. But if all goes well, an acre will produce 3,000 pounds of dried ginseng root, which was selling, by 1990, for $55 a pound. You can't gross $165,000 growing an acre of carrots or wheat, and it is not surprising that the rush to plant the elixir was on.

Production of ginseng grew by 325 percent between 1990 and 1995; by 1996, Canada was the largest producer outside China of a crop most Canadians had never even heard of a few years earlier. Ginseng can be grown in only a few places in Canada, which is probably just as well or we would be up to our knees in it. It requires extremes of temperature, from very hot to very cold, and general climatic conditions that can be found in the area around Kamloops and in Southern Ontario, especially in Norfolk County, where tobacco farmers turned to it as a substitute for shrinking markets.

I am as anxious as anyone to reduce stress, increase blood flow, and teach the old blood sugar to take a joke, to say nothing of the little add-ons mentioned in Asian folklore, so before this trip began, I put in a series of calls to ginseng growers along the route, hoping to have a look at their operations.

Answer came there none. Time after time a cheery voice would ask me to leave a message and my call would be returned as soon as possible, and time after time I would leave a message, which I might just as well have scribbled on a bit of paper and tossed into the sea, for all the good it did me. However, when we reach Kamloops, centre of the industry in British Columbia, and I look in the Yellow Pages of our hotel room telephone book, there, under "Ginseng," is Sunmore Health Tech Ltd., with the address and phone number of the factory. I didn't even know there *was* a factory, since the *Times* article specified that the crop was all shipped offshore.

A few minutes later, we are pulling up in front of a neat, new grey-and-red brick building, with a large sign on the side that reads "Sunmore." This is repeated in a sign over the front door that adds "Fountain of Youth." I tell the Driver that if Ponce de Léon finds out that these birds are infringing his copyright, there will be hell to pay, and the Driver tells me not to be a smartass. I enter the plant.

Things I Cannot Do

Just as I come through the door, a small gaggle of people is being led into the showroom, where samples of manufactured ginseng can be seen on the shelves, and I advance boldly, notebook in hand, to join in. I am neatly cut out by a tall young woman wearing spectacles and a fierce frown who wants to know if I am a member of the group. When I explain that I am merely a wayfaring stranger who wants to learn more about the fountain of youth, she clucks disapproval, holds up her hand to tell me to wait, and disappears down the corridor. She reappears a few minutes later with a list of things I cannot do during my visit. These include:

- *taking pictures;*
- *writing anything down;*
- *asking to look at any part of the production process;*
- *asking questions about prices;*
- *asking questions about the company itself;*
- *taking pictures, again;*
- *writing things down, again.*

I point out that I have been cleared by the FBI for a pass to the White House, and get another frown. I put away my camera and notebook, and promise not to remember anything she tells me. Satisfied, the young woman leads me into the showroom.

We circle the place counter-clockwise, while the real visitors, who are here to buy, go the other way. We begin with a small cup of ginseng tea, which tastes like a weak sherry beaten together with an old rubber boot. Next, ginseng candy — "Maple sugar and ginseng," my guide explains — which tastes like maple sugar beaten together with an old rubber boot. I turn down the ginseng powder, tablets, capsules, wine, tonic, and half a dozen other products, on the theory that if the herb works as promised, I am probably young, fit, healthy, calm, and blood-enhanced, to say nothing of sexy, enough already.

My guide explains that ginseng has become popular only with the recent influx of Asians. She explains that the difference between North American ginseng and Asian ginseng is that although both contain the same key ingredient, and both have the same beneficial effects, "ours works on the principle of relaxation, theirs on the stimulation."

"You mean ours doesn't make you sexy?" I ask.

She passes this by like the idle wind, which she respecteth not, and adds, "Both help to balance the principles of energy and balance." I want to know how you balance balance, but I receive no reply.

She sees that I have brought out my notebook again, glowers, sighs, and goes on. "This is the largest, well, probably the largest, manufacturing facility for ginseng in North America."

"How large?"

No reply.

We go on to the display of ginseng in all its stages, from seeds to dried root, which is how Asians generally take it.

"Canadians are not accustomed to ginseng yet," my guide says, "so they prefer it in tea, or these other things." She gestures to the array of goodies I am not allowed to photograph. She explains that it usually takes six years for a farmer to get into production.

"Does the company help him?"

"No. We just buy the root. We buy our product from two or three farmers, and then switch to other farmers. That way, we get it at a better price."

"But what about the farmer who has just put a couple of hundred thousand dollars into growing the stuff?"

No reply.

I ask her about prices, since we are now, well, not exactly matey, but a little less stiff.

"Prices were very good a couple of years ago. Then they went down. Now they are going back up."

"From what to what?"

"I cannot tell you that."

"Because you don't know, or because you can't tell?"

"I can't tell."

She knows. Turns out, she is the company bookkeeper. "I was looking for a job as a bookkeeper, and I saw this ad in the newspaper and applied, and here I am."

"Who is Sunmore?" I ask.

"The company is owned by a Taiwanese lady," she replies.

Feeling we are now old buddies, I ask if I can take a couple of pictures of the ginseng garden outside.

"Definitely not."

"Why not?"

"It has to do with their traditions," she explains, although it is no explanation. We are not in Taiwan but in Canada, and I can walk across the road, turn around, and take pictures till my eyes bubble.

She shrugs, and I depart.

Ginseng Is a Chancy Proposition

The next day, in Vernon, an hour's drive south of Kamloops, I talk to a farmer, Jim Kicey, who has looked over the possibilities of joining the ginseng parade and opted not to.

"It is far too chancy a proposition for the grower," he says. "You are selling to people who are very close-mouthed, with a very tight grip on the market. For a while, people were making fortunes, so naturally a lot of the guys around here jumped in, with the inevitable result that prices went through the floor. Right now, it costs you about twenty-one dollars a pound to grow, if you really know what you're doing, and you get somewhere between nine and twelve dollars. Planting now, what will the price be in four years?"

He adds, "The big change came when Hong Kong joined China. When Hong Kong controlled the trade, it was a bit loose, but the Chinese soon put an end to that. The walls went up, and the price came down."

Sunmore and other firms are now selling within Canada, as well as to Asia, trying to create a larger market here in competition with two publicly traded companies, Canadian Imperial Ginseng and Chai-Na-Ta Corporation, a firm based in Langley, B.C., that describes itself as "the world's largest supplier of North American ginseng."

I tell the Driver, "I think I'll grow apples instead."

On due consideration, however, probably not. Jim Kicey, my Vernon farmer friend, has been in the apple business for decades, and he says that if someone made him a good offer — even a fair offer, even a not-so-fair offer — for his orchard he would leap at it.

"Why?"

He answers with a question of his own. "Who do you think is the world's largest apple producer?"

"The United States."

"Wrong. China. China is growing and shipping apples, putting them on the market in downtown Vernon for less than I can. What is really funny about it is that they noticed that apples carry a little sticker that says "B.C. Delicious," or whatever, and a number. Now they counterfeit the sticker, put on a little thing that just carries a number, so the consumer thinks it must be one of ours. They are killing us. Most of my crop went for five cents a pound to the juicers last year, then I walk down to the supermarket and see apples selling for $1.29 a pound. Somebody is making a killing, but it isn't the Canadian producer. . . . I am the sixty-second of 252 producers selling to the fruit co-op here, and I got my last cheque four months ago. What do you suppose is happening to the people below me?"

He scorns the notion of government help. "It has been my experience that if the government gives you a dollar, it takes back ten."

The real problem, he contends, is that "Canada is fixed on the idea of a low-cost economy in the agricultural sector. The global market decides the price, and that is fine for the consumer, but what it means is that a lot of the guys are just going out of business, just not growing any more, just pulling up their trees and burning them. . . . We used to get clobbered by Washington State in the apple business. Now we're getting flattened by China. As long as the

Chinese can land a drum of apple juice in British Columbia for much less than I can produce it for, the Canadian customer is going to be happy and the Canadian apple grower is going to be screwed."

As we drive south out of Vernon after this interview, I tell the Driver to forget about apples.

"Right," she says. "What are you going to grow?"

"Sagebrush," I say. "Now, if only I can find a market. . . ."

The Coquihalla Puts the High into Highway

For decades, the usual way to reach Vancouver from the B.C. interior was via the Trans-Canada, a pretty route through Kamloops, Cache Creek (entry to the Cariboo country), Spences Bridge, and Lytton to Hope, where the land flattens out. There is another route south of this, which uses the Crow's Nest Pass, skirting the U.S. border much of the way, but it is slower than the Trans-Canada.

However, in a burst of energy just before the opening of the 1986 world's fair in Vancouver, Expo '86, the B.C. government slung a toll highway over the mountains between Merritt, south of Kamloops, and Hope. This is the Coquihalla, named for the Coquihalla Pass, through which it, ah, passes. (It comes from a Salish word meaning "stingy," which is not at all appropriate. The B.C. government budgeted $150 million to do the job, but ended up spending more than $250 million; nothing stingy about that.)

For ten dollars, you can cut off at least an hour of driving, as well as experiencing one of the highest, wildest highways extant. Many drivers hate it — there are no service stations, towns, or stops of any sort, except for the toll booth halfway down, and the surrounding mountains are bleak and windy. Joan loves it — "You feel exactly as if you are driving on top of the world," she says — and besides, you can make much better time.

We drive south from Vernon to Westbank, outside Kelowna (Kelowna is possibly the ugliest city in a beautiful setting in all of Canada, a sprawling spawn of malls, malls, and more malls), then turn west on Highway 97C — C for "connector" — which will take us over to the Coquihalla. As we begin to climb — the date is now July 2 — we see the signs that warn us to expect

"Winter Driving Conditions." A few minutes later, we see a flashing sign that says "Slushy and Slippery Sections," and a few minutes after that a white blanket comes down, a wind-blown whirl of snow, fog, rain, hail, and sleet that reduces visibility to yards, instead of miles.

As we inch along, expecting to overtake traffic but finding none, I suggest that if we had gone the other way, maybe it would have been faster in the end, but since I was the one who suggested this route in the first place, the Driver does not deign to reply. On other trips, we have revelled in the swoop from summit to summit, overlooking the wide-swathed valleys on either side, but this time, we feel as if someone has hung a white sheet about twenty metres wide on every side of the van, and that is all we can see.

At Merritt, a neat little city at the junction of the Coldwater and Nicola rivers, and surrounded by Canada's largest ranch, the 2,200-square-kilometre Douglas Ranch, a modest sun begins to peak through the clouds; and by the time we finish the climb to the toll plaza, 55 kilometres south of Merritt, the snow has turned to streaming rain. From here, the road is literally all downhill to Hope, past more gun emplacements — for shooting down the Coquihalla avalanches — and past a series of roads called Shylock Road, Portia Road, and so forth, reflecting the love of Shakespeare that moved the original surveyor of the route to drop these names along the way.

Those Who Live in Glass Houses Should Not Throw Headlines

At Hope, a rather gloomy town overshadowed by the mountains and usually, when we visit, in the midst of a downpour, we pick up the Trans-Canada again for the run along the Fraser Canyon into Vancouver, an hour and a half of flat, green, lush land that grows magnificent crops, humdrum restaurants, and a sprinkling of small cities — Chilliwack, Abbotsford, Sardis — that are among the nation's pleasantest places to live.

We stop for lunch at Abbotsford and pick up a newspaper that contains one of those articles — the latest in a long, long succession, running back a decade or more — that endeavour to explain why British Columbia politicians are all crazy. Well, not all crazy, perhaps, but mostly crazy. The piece is amusingly written, and cites the usual suspects: Amor de Cosmos — real name, William

Smith — who changed his moniker to mean "lover of the universe" and was elected premier of the province; W. A. C. ("Wacky") Bennett, who claimed to talk to God; and Bill Vander Zalm, who raised tulips and hackles and was known for extravagant statements. Vander Zalm's malapropisms, which provided the text for a whole book, included his thoughtful remark that "If I always thought before I spoke in detail, perhaps I wouldn't say some of the things I did."

This article causes me to grumble — it always does — to the Driver that Vander Zalm's verbal hitches are scarcely to be compared with those of Robert Thompson, the Alberta Social Credit leader, who said, "The Americans are our friends, whether we like it or not," and, "You've buttered your bread, now you have to lie in it," and my favourite, "Parliament is being turned into a political arena."

If we are moving past mere foot-in-mouth to genuine nuttiness, what price William Lyon Mackenzie King, our longest-serving prime minister, a Toronto lad who talked to, among others who had shuffled off this mortal coil, Sir Wilfrid Laurier, Franklin D. Roosevelt, his mother, and his dog, Pat? Not only talked to them, but they talked back, and gave political advice, which he followed. (The ghost of FDR warned him that the next war would break out in the Far East, in 1947; King thereupon demanded that Canada withdraw its delegation from a United Nations commission in Korea.)

How about Charles Tupper, the Ram of Cumberland, the Nova Scotian politician, and, briefly, Canadian prime minister whose sexual peccadilloes make Bill Clinton look like one of the Hardy Boys? Let us not forget Sir Sam Hughes, minister of defence in Robert Borden's Cabinet, who was "compounded of one part panache and three parts paranoia."

Borden, although he kept him in his Cabinet, regarded his defence minister as close to certifiable, and wrote in his memoirs, "He was under constant illusions that enemies were working against him. I told him on one occasion that I thoroughly agreed that he was beset by two unceasing enemies. Expecting a revelation he was intensely disappointed when I told him they were his tongue and his pen."

It was Sir Sam's lunacy that forced the Ross rifle on Canadian troops during the First World War, although it had the minor drawback that it jammed almost instantly in battle, and thus resulted in the deaths of nobody knows how many Canadian troops. It was scrapped by order of the British high command, with Sir Sam screaming outraged protest. He was only forced out of office in 1916, after he concocted a plot to overthrow the government, get rid of Borden, and take his place. The voters of Victoria-Haliburton, which centred on Sam's hometown, Lindsay, Ontario, promptly voted him back into office as MP, and kept him there until his death in 1921.

There is no need to confine the argument about nuttiness to British Columbia, or more to the point, no need to confine the argument to this singular profession. The newspaper business, to come right down to it, where all these stories get their play, has produced its own plentiful crop of nutcases; it's just that they seldom get exposed to exposure, if you follow me. The *Vancouver Sun*, to take the example of the newspaper that most often runs this "aren't B.C. politicians crazy?" material, has, among its illustrious alumnae:

> Ivers Kelly, *famous for eating copy paper, including, once, a piece of copy paper with the headline for the final edition on it. He was the church editor, and wore suspenders decorated with naked women.*
> Bryce Williams, *who ate himself to death.*
> Black Nels Hamilton, *also known as the Runner in Innocent Passage, a title he bestowed on himself in explanation for cutting off a dog's tail.*
> Gar MacPherson, *a police reporter who packed his own revolver and once answered Police Chief Walter Mulligan's office telephone pretending he was the chief.*
> Bill Dennett, *a photographer who carried around a stuffed squirrel, for nature pictures.*
> Count Stephan Franz von Beriot, *a madcap Austrian nobleman who did not, in fact, exist. The night staff of the newspaper made him up to fill a column called "Names in the News." Among other things, the count was drummed out of an Austrian hunt club for shooting deer with a machine gun, arrested for pulling the emergency cord on a French express train so he could pick flowers, and wounded in a duel with an Italian butcher. Tom Ardies, given the task of writing his*

*adventures, got fed up with the count and killed him, polished him off
with cirrhosis of the liver in Milan, Italy.*

The point is that when it comes to mental fruitfulness, this is a subject that
journalists should treat with modest stillness and humility, in the first place,
and in the second, what the record shows is that B.C. politicians are no more
prone to this weakness than others of their tribe elsewhere, and probably a
good deal less prone than the ragtag and bobtail who report on them.

Don't Send Me Your Poor, Your . . .

Two hours after delivering this post-prandial diatribe in Hope, I am standing
in front of the tall, narrow, garish building that Stanley Ho, the Hong Kong
entrepreneur and multi-millionaire, has chosen to erect at the very gates of
Stanley Park in downtown Vancouver. Many Vancouverites object to the rather
vulgar display of wealth this building represents, and I guess they have a point.

All the same, as I walk around the edifice and admire the passing throng of
young, old, white, Chinese, black, brown — whatever — people thronging
into the park, I cannot help thinking what a long way Vancouver has come
from a past soured and scoured by racism.

Take the Chinese. Between 1881 and 1884, 15,000 Chinese were brought to
British Columbia to work. They were never intended as permanent settlers;
rather, they were indentured to labour in the coal mines and on the building
of the CPR. Their role was to take on those tasks — including such unsavoury
ones as getting blown up by carelessly laid dynamite charges — that
Canadians were content to leave to others. These so-called coolies were, to
all intents and purposes, slaves; they were sold under contract by Chinese
companies to white railwaymen or miners. The Report of the Royal Commission on Chinese Immigration of 1885 contained a memorable description of
their living conditions:

*The Chinese live, generally, in wretched hovels, dark, ill-ventilated, filthy
and unwholesome, and crowded together in such numbers as must*

preclude all ideas of comfort, morality or even decency. . . . I have yet never known an English or French gentleman from the old countries who would feed their [sic] dogs upon the food consumed by the ordinary Chinese labourer.

The official government attitude was laid down in the Electoral Act of 1885: "'Person' means a male person, including an Indian, and excluding a person of Mongolian or Chinese race." However, these non-persons were welcomed by one class of people — the employers. Prof. Chester H. Rowel wrote approvingly of the Chinese that "he will transform less food into more work, with less administrative friction, than any other animal."

The cheapness and docility of the Chinese worker made these immigrants ideal fodder for the workforce, but their employment was fiercely resented by whites, because they would work for a dollar a day, instead of the princely two dollars demanded by whites; they would live in hovels and feed on slop, and when labour battles arose they could be, and were, brought in as strike-breakers. The newly formed Knights of Labor took on the task of cutting back this "Mongolian competition to citizen labour," and the Nanaimo Knights of Labor submitted a brief to the 1885 royal commission that complained:

The Chinese . . . are not only able to live but [also] to grow rich on wages far below the lowest minimum on which we can possibly exist. They are thus fitted to become all-too-dangerous competitors in the labour market, while their docile servility . . . renders them doubly dangerous as the willing tools whereby grasping and tyrannical employers grind down all labour to the lowest living point.

As it happened, the grasping and tyrannical employers were the folks in charge in British Columbia at that time, so the obvious solution — raising Chinese wages to parity and providing decent living conditions — was ruled out. The Chinese problem remained and, fed by the ordinary mixture of bigotry and fear, blossomed into a full-fledged riot in 1887. A massed crowd in downtown Vancouver was apprised of its duty by strident speakers and started out, about midnight, for McDougall's Camp, on the city outskirts, where the coolies lived. The Chinese, swarming out of their tents at the sound of the approaching horde (they were singing, of all things, "John Brown's Body"), took one look and ran. They were chased and scattered, many of them forced over a cliff for a six-metre drop into frigid water. No one knows how many of them died.

The next morning, the crowd descended on Chinatown and cleared it out. One Chinese was allowed to stay in each store; the rest were removed by force. Some were tied together by their pigtails to keep them from escaping, and they were all loaded on a steamer for Victoria. No one was ever punished for his part in the riot, and the solution propounded by the 1885 royal commission turned out to be a "poll tax" of $50 to be levied on every Chinese person entering the country; this tax was eventually raised to $500, a staggering sum for those involved.

To make assurance doubly sure, British Columbia passed a law in 1900 under which every immigrant could be compelled to write an application to the provincial secretary "in a European language." Those who could not, or did not, were subject to fines, imprisonment, and deportation. Other provinces followed the B.C. lead, and then the federal government, in 1923, passed a straightforward law called the Chinese Immigration Act, which effectively banned all Chinese immigration to Canada.

Between 1923 and 1947, only forty-four Chinese entered this country legally. An odd record for a nation that prides itself on its open borders.

The Komagata Maru

Not that the Chinese were the only foreigners who were subject to racist policies; here on the peaceable outskirts of Stanley Park, I think about the *Komagata Maru* and the poor, dumb bastards who thought they could ride her into Canada.

She was a Japanese-owned passenger ship of 3,000 tons, and she sailed into Canadian waters on May 21, 1914, in a brave attempt to crack Canada's race barrier. Her passengers were Sikhs from India — 371 men, two women, and three children, all dressed in their finest clothes, slicked down, brushed up, and waving to the crowd that gathered along the shore near the immigration station at Victoria, B.C. Nobody waved back.

These Sikhs were British subjects, and thus Canadian law, so handy against the Chinese, could not be used to exclude them, but a cunning regulation had been devised in 1910 to fit the case. It said that all immigrants must arrive "by continuous journey and on through tickets" from their homeland. There was no direct service from India, so the regulation effectively barred Indians without ever having to say so. However, an unruly Sikh named Narain Singh landed in Vancouver with thirty-five countrymen, contested the regulation, and had it declared *ultra vires* by the courts. This victory caused another Sikh, Gundit Singh, who had made a fortune in Malaysia, to charter the *Komagata Maru* and head for Canada with his shipload of hopeful immigrants.

The Canadian government met this piece of impertinence by passing three new regulations, specifically barring all Asian immigration. As a result, when the *Maru* cleared Victoria harbour and sailed into Burrard Inlet, off Vancouver, on May 23, 1914, she was met by a special detachment of police and an order to anchor 200 yards offshore.

The Sikhs sat in the harbour for two months while the ship grew fouler, the passengers' tempers shorter, and their food and water scanter. No one fooled around about the reasons for their exclusion. "We must keep the country a white man's country at any cost, and a British country if possible," was the verdict of the *British Columbia Magazine.* A Vancouver cleric, thundering against the insolent Asians, was overcome by a momentary fit of Christian charity. He said, "It is our duty to explain to those men in the harbour that we do not despise them as dogs" — to which his parishioners thundered back, "But we do!"

A protest meeting was held in downtown Vancouver to demand the expulsion of the invaders, and when two men at the meeting rose to speak on behalf of the Sikhs they were dragged down by members of the audience and marched off by the police.

The law at that time required a board of inquiry to probe into cases like this, but any legal probe was bound to find that there was no reason, except prejudice, for the action taken, so the law was simply ignored. Instead, a single test case was brought to court and the ruling went against the Sikhs on dubious legal grounds. They decided not to appeal, which had been their original intention, because they were slowly forming the opinion that they were not welcome here. So they said they would stay put until the government came up with enough money to allow them to go home again, and then they would go.

We weren't having that, either. On Sunday, July 19, the tug *Sea Lion* chugged away from the Vancouver shore bearing 120 policemen and forty immigration officers. Their plan was to swarm aboard the *Maru*, quell the Sikhs, and set the Japanese crew members — who had been prevented from sailing home by the angry Sikhs — back in charge. Then they would tow the pest ship out to sea and to hell with her. A brilliant plan, with one minor flaw: the *Sea Lion*'s deck was a full four and a half metres below the *Maru*'s. Swarming was out. When the cops came puffing alongside, the Sikhs, most of whom were war veterans and all of whom were ready for battle, greeted them with salvoes of garbage, chairs, scrap metal, lumps of coal, and driftwood. The *Sea Lion* beat a hasty retreat.

Canadian dignity had been offended. HMCS *Rainbow*, a battered but serviceable cruiser, was brought around from Victoria and augmented by eighty sailors from HMCS *Niobe*, who had been rushed over from Halifax by train for the next sea battle. The *Rainbow* trained three powerful firehoses on the *Maru* and ordered her to leave. The Sikhs finally gave up, and on July 23, two months after she first sailed into Burrard Inlet, the *Maru* sailed out again, tailed by the redoubtable but leaking *Rainbow*. Another page had been turned in Canada's guest book.

Eighty-five years later, we are going through a new fuss; four boatloads of Chinese immigrants have landed, unbidden, unwashed, and unwanted, on British Columbia shores, and their arrival has raised a certain amount of stink — including one headline, in a Vancouver paper, that reads, "GO HOME!" and belongs to the *Maru*'s time, not ours. However, matters, including legal matters, are somewhat different. The invaders, this time, are landed, brought into barracks, fed, housed, provided with social services, and helped by a bevy of immigration lawyers to file for refugee status. Among those who protest are members of Vancouver's Chinese community, who argue, correctly, that the newcomers have jumped the immigration line and ought not to be rewarded for breaking the law. What the recent fuss tells us is that Canada's immigration policies are a long way from perfect, but, my word, they are immeasurably better than they used to be, and the nation is immeasurably richer for it.

Because of the inrush of immigrants, Vancouver is another of our city successes, a metropolis that somehow still works. A walk down Robson Street from the Vancouver Hotel to the edge of Stanley Park is a stroll through a dozen neighbourhoods, peopled by immigrants from a hundred lands, now stitching the Canadian mosaic together in a way that is not always smooth but is never dull.

Victoria, a Small Town with Large Pretensions

After an all-too-brief stop in Vancouver, we take the ferry to Victoria, where ladies in white gloves still drive at thirty kilometres an hour down the main drag and call the cab drivers who curse them "my good man." Here, we treat ourselves again, and to hell with the budget, camping in at the Empress, where they charge you as much for afternoon tea as our weekly food budget. My, it is grand.

Victoria is essentially a small town with large pretensions, and despite the presence of one of the nation's foremost museums — the Royal British Columbia, renowned for its aboriginal art and a full-scale replica of Capt. George Vancouver's ship, *Discovery* — and the legislature — renowned for its crown of lights and the noise of its debates — it retains the accessible feel of a small town. It is our national dowager; I love it.

I wander off to Beacon Hill Park, to have a look at the sign that says "Mile 0." This is the other bookend to the sign in St. John's; it is surrounded by a gang of Japanese tourists, festooned with cameras, who seem to think I was sent out to explain what the sign means, although they speak no more English than I do Japanese. We bow and smile a lot, and take each other's pictures, and I do my best, with gestures, to get across the idea that this is the start of a road that extends clear across Canada. I have no idea what they think I am saying, but we are very pleased with each other.

The road up the island from Victoria is, like so many of the roads we have travelled on this trip, improved beyond belief from the crowded pathway we first followed here a third of a century ago. The first part, however, the splendid, soaring drive up the Malahat towards Duncan, is still narrow and crowded, but it makes up for this with the breathtaking views of Haro Strait and the clusters of offshore islands. We stop briefly at Goldstream Provincial Park to gape at the towering, pristine stands of Douglas fir, western red cedar, oak, and arbutus trees. The park gets is name from a gold find made here in the 1850s; it is better known today for a salmon interpretive centre, which carries a sad echo of that sign we saw weeks ago and thousands of kilometres away in St. John's — "Where's the Fishies?"

At Chemainus, we see the collection of murals that causes this town of 4,000 to bill itself as "the world's largest outdoor art gallery." When the local sawmill, then the world's largest, closed in the 1980s, Chemainus was as devastated as Elliot Lake, Ontario, when the uranium mines there ceased to function. Like Elliot Lake, it decided that instead of sitting around and moping, it would do something about it, and so it brought in artists to paint huge murals with historical themes on dozens of walls around town.

The result was a tourist boom that now sees as many as 250,000 visitors calling in to soak up the atmosphere, views, and souvenirs. Among our co-viewers are members of a motorcycle club, blue-jeaned, bearded, and almost excessively polite to everyone. One biker has with him a dog about the size of an ambitious mouse, over whom everyone else makes a great fuss.

James Dunsmuir: Another Honoured Rogue

Chemainus is next door, almost, to Ladysmith, where one of Canada's nastiest labour battles was played out. It was largely the work of James Dunsmuir, another of the rogues whom our history has chosen to heap with honour — he became premier of British Columbia in 1900 and lieutenant-governor in 1906 — but who has always struck me as one of the most bloody-minded graspers whose greed ever propelled him to affluence. He became rich in the first place in the time-honoured fashion — by inheriting a bundle from his father and using the leverage it gave him to grab everything else worth grabbing.

The real break came when a group headed by Robert Dunsmuir, the father, managed to secure a contract in 1884 for building a railroad 125 kilometres from Victoria to Wellington, where the elder Dunsmuir owned a colliery. This became the Esquimalt and Nanaimo Railway, and it is still in business. The deal was a shady one, worked through the federal minister of railways, John Henry Pope, a friend and political ally of the Dunsmuirs'. Thrown into the scheme were $750,000 in cash and 1,900,000 acres of land, the gift of the province to aid free enterprise. No tenders were called, and the railway contracts were not even advertised before they were awarded to Robert and James Dunsmuir.

They wrung the last cent out of the gift of hundreds of millions of dollars of land by bringing in indentured Chinese labour, refusing to pay any attention to the most rudimentary safety regulations, keeping their men at work in intolerable conditions at minuscule pay, and resolutely crushing all attempts to unionize. James Dunsmuir not only fired any men who attempted to join a union, but also discharged at once three employees who had the gall to work against him when he was running for the legislature in 1900. He won. You will not find any of this in our history texts, by the way; it was an American, Gustavus Myers, who chronicled the story in his *A History of Canadian Wealth;* our gang pretends it never happened.

While the Dunsmuirs grew richer, their men grew poorer. In 1901, the company made all the miners at the Extension Works move to Ladysmith, at their own expense; in 1902, it cut wages by 10 percent; and in 1903, the men enlisted the help of the Western Federation of Miners to organize the mines, and went on strike for bargaining rights. The strike was quickly broken, with the aid of scabs and professional strike-breakers, and a Royal Commission on Industrial Disputes was formed to look into labour unrest in the province. The secretary of this commission was William Lyon Mackenzie King, and the report he helped to shape was a beaut.

Although the testimony showed that the men in the Dunsmuir mines were overworked, underpaid, fired for trivial reasons, and generally brutalized, the commission found that the strike was all the fault of American unions — "Not trade unionists, but socialistic agitators of the most bigoted and ignorant type."

Everybody knew that James Dunsmuir immediately fired his workers if they joined a union, the commission argued, so the fault lay with the miners, because when they called in the Western Federation of Miners, trouble was bound to follow. The solution applied was the formation of a company union, which would not kick over the traces.

By this time, the coal miners had decided that they had nothing to lose by radical action, and in 1911 the United Mine Workers were called in to organize what had by now become Canadian Collieries Mines. The union men were fired at once, of course, but they continued to picket and organize, and this led, in 1914, to the calling of a strike at every mine on Vancouver Island, a move that set off a widespread outbreak of violence that lasted for three months. In Cumberland, provincial police were brought in to protect strike-breakers; at Ladysmith, a crowd of miners stoned a hotel where scabs were quartered and ran them out of town.

At South Wellington, strike-breakers were driven out of the company "bullpen." At Nanaimo, a large squad of provincial police landed by ferry to help the company, but they were surrounded by a welcoming committee of miners and invited to reboard the ferry and go back to Vancouver. Which they did. At Extension, when police fired into the strikers, a full-scale riot broke out, during which mine buildings were burned down and the mine managers chased off into the woods.

Vancouver Island had been plunged into anarchy, and on August 13, 1914, soldiers from the 72nd Militia Regiment (called Bowser's Seventy-two, for the provincial attorney general) arrived on the island and the strike was put down. More than 250 strikers were arrested, many of whom were held for months without trial.

The union was decertified and gradually withered away; it would be decades before decent safety and working conditions would be established in the mines. James Dunsmuir, who had violated almost every law relating to mine safety and employment practices, died in 1920, with a fortune estimated at somewhere between $30 million and $40 million. That'll teach him.

Ladysmith today is demure, peaceable, honoured as the island's "most beautiful community." It has a railway museum that boasts of the accomplishments of the early builders while leaving untold the story of their brutality, which strikes me as a pity.

Canadians are persuading themselves that in this global economy, unions are nothing but a nuisance. We forget that they came into existence to prevent the kind of abuse and exploitation that, unless human nature has somehow been reformulated in recent years, will reappear as soon as they are gone.

A Town of Mists and Eagles

North of Ladysmith, we pick up the new highway, an autobahn compared with the straggling route we used to follow into every village along the shore, and almost before we know it, we are at Port Hardy, on Queen Charlotte Strait, at the top of Vancouver Island. A town of mists and eagles — more eagles than I have ever seen in my life, and they cluster around the motel, making noises like an ill-oiled door. The eagle is a very weird bird — majesty on the wing, but essentially a bum and a scavenger.

We are up at dawn to roll aboard the *Queen of the North*, for a seventeen-hour trip along the Inland Passage to Prince Rupert, where we will take to the road again. For some reason, we expected this to be a tedious trip, marked by little to do and ferry-quality food. Instead, it is a joyous journey, with three superior meals in a luxurious dining room, a constant barrage of beauty along the route, and vast quantities of entertainment.

This includes lectures from experts on every form of animal and plant life along the way, a salon singer — who turns out to be surprisingly good — and a constant spate of movies in one of the lounges, for those daft enough to prefer Hollywood to the British Columbia landscape and people-watching. Strolling along one of the spacious passenger decks, I come across a sight I will never forget.

A young man, perhaps twenty-five, who looks like a father's worst night-mare — head completely shaved, nostrils pierced with rings, bare arms tattooed with sayings I will not put to paper — lies sound asleep in a lounge chair; in one arm, he cradles a baby of about six months, and in the other, a small, yellow teddy bear. By the time I get back with a camera, his Significant Other has come along and wakened him.

We keep passing signs that refer to "sounds" so I ask a crew member what distinguishes a sound from, say, a bay. This creates a controversy on the scale of the unveiling of the Nicene Creed, as various members of the ship's strength try to come up with a definition. At one point, I have four uniforms around me, all gesticulating and propounding various explanations.

Then, from the rear, comes a voice that cuts through the cackle, and a middle-aged woman with a couple of stripes on her sleeve pronounces: "A sound is an inlet of the ocean that is open on three sides." That shuts everybody up. The woman marches off.

"Who was that?" I ask one of the other crew members. "The captain?"

"Oh, no, that's the lady who runs the coffee machine upstairs."

I have just looked up the word "sound" in *Webster's,* which says it is "*a.* a long broad inlet of the ocean generally parallel to the coast; *b.* a long passage of water connecting two larger bodies (as a sea with the ocean) or separating a mainland and an island." Both these definitions describe a strait; I plan to stick to the coffee lady.

We settle in a corner, where the windows reach to the floor and give us a full-length view of the passing shoreline, green trees, misty mountains, bridal-veil falls, and all, and watch a three-generation family from New York State whose ruling figure, a stout woman in her sixties with hair a colour unknown to nature and a fistful of rings, pronounces at intervals on the poor quality of everything. The food, the scenery, the rest of us — "My dear, the common herd is on the move" — everything.

She is particularly unhappy that throngs of mountain goats and wild sheep are not waiting along the shoreline to pay homage.

"There is no wildlife here, nothing," she complains. "I was expecting whales, at least."

Her husband — I assume it is her husband, because he looks beaten-down enough to fill that role, though maybe he is in fact her demon lover — says, "Back there I got a glimpse of a deer."

"Deer I can see in Albany," says the lady.

Two young men are playing chess at a table next to hers, using a timer and concentrating fiercely.

"What's that for?" She points at the timer, which one of the young men has just reset.

He doesn't understand her — he is German — so she applies the natural solution and bellows at him. "THE CLOCK-THINGY. WHAT FOR?"

He gets it. "Five minutes," he says, and points at the chessboard.

She is disgusted. "You can't play a game in five minutes," she says. He is unable to explain that five minutes is the time limit for a move, not the entire game.

"What a trip!" she grumbles.

The Driver, looking out the window and keeping her voice low, says, "Yes, what a glorious trip!"

The Nisga'a Treaty

Prince Rupert, the western end of the Yellowhead Highway, is a paper-mill town, a transportation hub, and "the world second-largest, naturally deep, ice-free harbour" according to our guidebook (which does not say which is the world's largest, etc.). The guidebook also says that "the City of Rainbows enjoys a mild, moist climate due to the Japanese Current." Translation: Rains like hell, most of the time.

For a change, the sun is shining brilliantly the next morning as we drive northeast along the Yellowhead, following the zigs and zags of the Skeena River inland for two hours, until we turn north, at Kitwanga, and pick up Highway 37. This is the Stewart-Cassiar Highway, which cuts the northwest quadrant of British Columbia for 721 kilometres, and connects with the Alaska Highway just inside the Yukon border.

The route runs parallel to the Nass River for about fifty kilometres, and leads us along the edge of the land of the Nisga'a, where aboriginal self-government is about to become law for the first time in this country. The Nisga'a were a trading people who ruled the Nass valley and monopolized the lucrative trade in fish oil for decades before the arrival of Europeans. When that came about, they very sensibly presented themselves in Victoria, the provincial capital, to ask for a treaty.

This, after all, was the usual practice, especially among the British who came swarming over the land. In some cases, the British imposed treaties on First Nations defeated in battle; in others, they signed treaties to avoid conflict, trading money, gifts, and promises of future support for Native land. However it was worked out, the practice was to have a treaty. In 1887, three tribal chiefs travelled down the Nass River to the coast and paddled to Victoria, where they were politely but firmly rebuffed by the premier, William Smithe.

The premier told the chieftains that whatever lands they owned, they had received "from the Queen's hand, as a matter of charity," a formulation they instantly rejected. To make their position clear, the Nisga'a leaders sent a land-claims petition to the federal government, which also rejected it.

On January 22, 1913, the tribe once more formally reaffirmed its ownership of the Nass River valley, and three years later the leaders tried to present a petition to this effect to the British Privy Council in London — but it was never forwarded. In 1927, a special joint committee of the House of Commons and the Senate, pronouncing that the Nisga'a had been led astray by their "white advisers," rejected the land claim but recommended that $10,000 a year be spent in British Columbia (by whites) for the benefit of B.C. First Nations people; this was in lieu of the money they would have received had two sides signed treaties. Then the government forgot about the whole issue for decades.

In 1968, after eighty years of fruitless attempts to formalize their relationship with the rest of Canada, the Nisga'a went to court, suing for ownership of a sizeable portion of British Columbia. Five years later, the Supreme Court of Canada rejected the Nisga'a claim. However, a dissenting judgement, written by Mr. Justice Emmett Hall, perhaps the most eminent jurist in Canada during this century, was brought to the attention of then Prime Minister Pierre Trudeau. He thought it made more sense than the majority ruling.

Hall said, in brief, that the Nisga'a had never been defeated in battle, had never sold their land, traded it away, or given it up in any other fashion, and so far as he could see they still owned it. Trudeau's sensible acceptance of the argument of that dissenting judgement sparked the whole process of aboriginal land claims, and finally led, in mid-1999, to a three-way treaty involving Canada, British Columbia, and the Nisga'a.

Under this treaty, which has, as I write, passed the British Columbia legislature but not the House of Commons, the Nisga'a people gain ownership and control over 2,000 square kilometres — less than one-tenth of the original claim — $190 million in cash — most of which comes from Ottawa — and, in effect, their own tiny nation.

All Nisga'a remain Canadian citizens, and Nisga'a who live outside the tribal lands, as about half the members of the 4,000-strong nation do, continue to have voting rights in tribal institutions back home. On the other hand, the only Canadians who can become Nisga'a are those who were born or are adopted into the nation, unless and until the Nisga'a people themselves set up a new standard, which they have every right, under the treaty, to do.

The treaty is a mess, no doubt about that. It sets up a new nation within Canada, establishes a government based on race, and will block non-Nisga'a who work and live within the new nation from having any say in the jurisdiction where they make their livelihood.

But this mess was not made by the Nisga'a, and the "self-government" gained in the treaty is much less impressive than it appears at first glance. The federal Criminal Code and the Charter of Rights and Freedoms continue to apply to the treaty area; the provincial government maintains ultimate authority over policing and justice; and local policies on logging, health, child welfare, education, and the environment will have to follow provincial standards. What is more, within twelve years, all Nisga'a will be subject to federal and provincial taxation. Welcome to the club.

I cannot get any of the locals to talk about this, not First Nations, not whites, no one. As soon as I introduce the subject, people turn and walk away. Maybe later, maybe in a couple of years, after the treaty is finally passed, in place, and tested in the courts. Reduced to talking to myself — the Driver doesn't want to discuss this, either — I decide that the treaty may be messy, but that it is based on justice, for once.

Nobody ever said justice was simple, especially given the centuries of injustice that have been worked in these matters. This treaty is only the first of more than eighty sets of self-government negotiations going on across Canada today. The only thing unique about British Columbia in this regard is the fact that treaties were not signed here, which gives the First Nations a distinct advantage in bargaining. Elsewhere, what they are striving for is adherence to treaties that were signed, a much trickier proposition in the courtroom.

In fact, I go so far as to tell myself that this ungodly mess is, in a way, part of what makes Canada such an interesting place to live. Imagine negotiating the existence of nations within the nation on the vague and vagrant grounds that it is the only honourable course to pursue.

Waiting for the Waitress

We slip off the main highway to take the side-road towards Stewart, for an awed look at the Bear Glacier, which is retreating but still impressive. The glacier is an eerie blue inside, and we are told that it glows at night, but we do not wait around to find out — too many mosquitoes. Back on the main highway, we are forced to revise our ideas of what a highway is, or should be. This one is narrow, contains long stretches of gravel, and raises enough dust to conceal a troop of cavalry. We average about forty kilometres an hour, stopping occasionally to say hello to black bears slurping berries by the roadside, and are brought to a full stop a few kilometres outside Dease Lake, B.C., our target for the night.

A middle-aged, rotund woman bearing a Stop sign comes up to the car and tells the Driver that there is work ahead, and that we will be here for at least fifteen minutes, so we climb out to feed the mosquitoes. After about ten minutes, Joan hears a sudden squawk by the side of the road. It is a hand-held radio, propped against a stone, which keeps saying, "Okay, you can move 'em through now. Are you there? Anybody there? The road's open now. Hey!"

The radio continues to grouse to itself and then our sign-toting woman reappears, pulling up her jeans. She had gone to the back of the long lineup to answer a call of nature.

"Geez, I'm sorry," she says, and giggles. We remount our vehicles and drive on to Dease Lake.

This is not, we are beginning to feel, exactly the same sort of tourist country you find in, say, King's County, New Brunswick, or Niagara Falls. This impression is reinforced the next morning when, about seven-thirty, we go into the restaurant attached to our motel and find a roomful of people all staring at each other. The tables are there, and the knives and forks — there is even a pot of coffee on a sideboard. But no menus, and no waitress.

We ask the others if they have seen any sign of anyone to serve them, and we get a lot of glum head-shaking in reply. And then, suddenly, she pops up, right at our table. This long, blonde person — whom James Joyce would have called "a lanky hank of a she" — thrusts menus at us. She is wearing a white blouse, straining at the seams, white shorts, and down the shank of her leg a rather large tattooed eagle. Her eyes are red-rimmed, and she gives the general appearance of one who has at least three varieties of hangover going at once — the Whiz-Bang, the Red Hot Nail, and the Neutron Explosion, for a guess.

"Christ," she mutters, "I didn't even get time to take a shit." She looks back towards the kitchen. "I slept in, you may have guessed, and I'm an hour late. I'm really going to get doo-doo later, but he's too busy right now. . . . You ready to order?" she asks.

We are.

"You got a pen?"

A pen is produced. She looks at it as if she had never seen such a thing before, shakes it, shakes her head, and prepares to concentrate. We want to know if she had passed a pleasant night. Had a nice sleep, we mean. She snorts, giggles, pats her hair, and says, "Mind your own beeswax."

She takes our orders, and those of the other patrons, but her heart is possibly not in it, and the wiser customers just take whatever arrives at tableside and do not bother with "but I ordered . . ." Coffee is brought around by one of our fellow clients, who has obviously been through this before.

"Oh, yeah," the lanky hank says to our retreating backs when we go to leave. "Have a nice day."

Enough Trees

Well, it is a nice day. The road doesn't improve much, but we are used to it by now, and the scenery is enlivened by more bears and a couple of flocks of wild sheep, along with a large gaggle of partridge, locally known as fool's hens because they are abnormally stupid, even for partridge. Mother partridge brings the kids down onto the highway so they can check out the tire treads on passing traffic, and when we stop to keep from flattening the whole brood she rushes about in circles crying, "Omigod, they'll murder us all!" and then disappears over the far bank, leaving the kids to fend for themselves.

We also encounter a large, morose cow moose, who gazes at us as if the whole thing is our fault, then trots off into the bush making a noise like a troop of cavalry cantering over a bridge.

As we bypass Cassiar, an old mining town abandoned and emptied in 1992, we spot two foxes slipping along the roadside with their tails up and jaunty heads held high. The Driver thinks they have probably dined on partridge. Like them, we are now feeling pretty satisfied with the day, the trip, even the somewhat rocky road, although I am reminded of something a fellow break-faster — a man from Fresno, California — said this morning.

"When you drive through British Columbia," he said, "after a while, you think you've seen enough trees."

11

The Road North

A HIGHWAY TO TOMORROW

The wonder of Whitehorse is not that a Canadian capital should be so crude, but that any community this far north should be so sophisticated. The city boasts 15 hotels, 9 restaurants, 12 churches, 4 department stores, 2 theatres, 4 cocktail lounges, 5 cabarets, and even 2 newspapers (one Liberal and weekly, one Conservative and twice-weekly).

— *Star Weekly, April 23, 1966*

The Alaska Highway, on which we now find ourselves, begins in Dawson Creek, British Columbia — 1,012 kilometres south and west of here — and rolls 2,233 kilometres north and west from there to Delta Junction, south of Fairbanks, Alaska. It was built in a frenzy of construction, by 11,000 soldiers and 16,000 civilians from Canada and the United States, in an astounding eight months in 1942, across five mountain ranges, innumerable swamps, countless gorges, endless streams.

The notion was that the Japanese would probably invade Alaska, so a road was required to rush troops westward to meet that threat. And it is no fair to point out that had the Japanese indeed invaded, the road would have worked for them as well. Members of the U.S. Army Corps of Engineers, who had primary responsibility and an apparently unlimited budget, surveyed as they went. In some areas, the route was determined by sending out local First Nations people who knew the countryside to walk in front of a bulldozer, with the rest of the construction equipment tagging along behind. In Canada, the road dips back and forth across the B.C.-Yukon border seven times before making up its mind to stay in Yukon.

Haste, as someone may have pointed out before this, makes waste, and mountains of equipment — injured tractors, split tents, heaps of tinned goods, lashings of machinery and tools — were abandoned along the way, but on September 24, 1942, engineers working from both ends met at Contact Creek, just south of Whitehorse, and the job was done. The construction cost was $147.8 million ($1.7 billion in today's dollars). This first road was gravel and, unless you happened to own a tank or a bulldozer, well-nigh impossible to drive, but it was gradually improved; today, it is an asphalt-surfaced, well-banked, broad-shouldered highway, and a pleasure to navigate, if a trifle dull.

If you look at a map, you will see that nearly 90 percent of the highway lies within Canadian territory, although we had very little to say as to whether it should be built, and where, and how. It was maintained by the Americans throughout the war, and then, on April 3, 1946, Canada paid U.S. $108 million for the 1,966-kilometre stretch between Dawson Creek and the Alaska border — that is, all the roadway in this country. The price included airstrips, buildings, and all the equipment left behind.

The Canadian takeover led to many adjustments. The most interesting of these was the renaming of a tiny village between Teslin and Carcross, where a number of trailers were stationed for a time to provide female companionship to the brave lads building the road. The old name, Screw, was adjusted to Johnson's Crossing, which, it was felt, had more dignity.

We stop for gas at Rancheria, almost on top of the Continental Divide, where a large sign advises: Don't Let Dog Out! I ask the gas-station owner about this, and he laughs a bitter laugh.

"Oh, that. That's because a few months ago, an American couple stopped here and let their little dog out, and a much bigger dog, belonging to another American couple, ate it. Now we're being sued, because we own the property." He shrugs. "I guess they liked the dog."

Along the road, it is hard to tell that this is a Canadian highway; we drive one hundred kilometres before we pass a car with a Canadian licence plate amid the steady stream from every state from California to Massachusetts. This is not the only route from the southern tier of states to Alaska, but it is by far the most popular. It is not until we hit Whitehorse, the Yukon capital, that we find more Canadian than American licences.

Whitehorse: Where the Miners Changed Socks

Whitehorse has grown up in the thirty-three years since I first came here and wrote:

> Whitehorse would never be considered a pretty town. Shacks, old army huts, trailers and log cabins jostle for street space with smart modern bungalows, blockhouse stores and the dominating Federal building, a pink-and-grey monstrosity that looks like a slightly skittish jail.

Whitehorse today takes advantage of its mountain-backed setting along the Yukon River, and this city of 24,000 is vastly improved. A riverside slum, mostly tarpaper shacks occupied by First Nations people, has disappeared entirely, and the downtown area consists of a mixture of houses, smart shops — including an entire block belonging to the Hougan family, who will gladly sell you anything from a car to a camera — motels, and historic sites. These include the MacBride Museum, celebrating the Klondike gold rush, and the S.S. *Klondike*, a resurrected paddlewheeler from the old days of river transportation. The new federal building is a handsome thing, of concrete, wood, glass, and steel.

While the casual visitor is led to believe that Whitehorse grew up around the gold rush, the fact is that the town was merely a place where the miners changed their socks in those hectic days of 1898. The fortune seekers who trekked north after gold was discovered on Bonanza Creek arrived at Skagway,

Alaska, by steamer, and scrambled overland, hauling one thousand kilograms or more on sleds up the treacherous and dangerous Chilkoot Pass to the head of Lake Bennett in northern British Columbia. While they waited there for the lake to thaw, they hacked down trees to build crude rafts or boats to carry them for the 880-kilometre trip downstream, far past Whitehorse, to the goldfields near Dawson.

About halfway down their route, the gold seekers ran into a narrow, treacherous canyon and a cauldron of swirling rapids, where several lives were lost. At first, pilots were hired to guide the boats through this treacherous stretch — the author Jack London was one of these — but soon wooden tramways were built on either side of the river, around the obstructions. For a fee, the horse-drawn tram cars would carry freight and small boats around the rapids.

A tent town, called Canyon City, sprang up around the tramway, and when the White Pass and Yukon Railroad (a narrow gauge line that still runs and is known as "Wait Patiently and You'll Ride") was pushed through 175 kilometres from Skagway in 1900 the settlement became the town of Whitehorse. The name came from one of the horses that worked on the trams, the appearance of the rapids (like horses' manes), or an Indian chief who is said to have perished in the river.

Whitehorse saw the gold rush from nearly 500 kilometres away, and while it grew on the transportation needs of the miners it was nothing compared with Dawson, where 30,000 people jostled for gold and glory at the height of the rush. Dawson was the biggest city north of Seattle and west of Winnipeg; Whitehorse was about one-tenth her size. When the din died, Dawson collapsed like a punctured balloon while Whitehorse, as a transportation centre, increased slowly.

In 1941, Whitehorse had a population of 500 and building lots sold for twenty-five dollars. What made the city of today was not gold, but gravel; it grew on the gravy from the Alaska Highway. By mid-1942, there were 30,000 people in the area, all spending like mad, and when the wartime boom ended another one started with the discovery of several mines nearby — silver, lead, copper, asbestos, and gold. This find was not as spectacular as the gold rush ventures, but it was good for the long haul.

In 1950 Whitehorse was incorporated as a city, and three years later the territorial capital was shifted south from Dawson, which was running out of both gold and people, to the new city. Dawson bitterly resented the (largely successful) attempt of the more southerly city to claim a central role in the gold rush, and when the Whitehorse museum asked many years ago for Dawson's collection of Klondike pictures, they received this curt reply: "We'd rather burn 'em."

With some fits and starts, Whitehorse has gone along well since, but although the locals would rather bite off their tongues than admit it, the city owes much of its current prosperity to bureaucracy: it is the centre of an active territorial government as well as most of the federal activity in the territory.

We call in at the visitors' centre, in a beautiful new building down by the river, to read the bulletin board's messages, each crammed with its own drama:

GOING EAST

I would like a ride east to Ontario instead of taking the Greyhound. If you are going, I will help with the gas and driving.

Jennifer (leave message with Emil)

STUCK WITHOUT A CAR ...

Looking for a ride to Vancouver, with or without a dog, around the end of July.

Merci, Lara

A Land before Time — before Disney, Even

The highlight of a visit to the new Whitehorse turns out to be an attraction outside town — the Beringia Interpretation Centre on the Alaska Highway, not far from the airport. This is a multimedia centre dedicated to telling the story of a land area about the size of the continental United States that was exposed when the ice age gripped the planet. It takes its name from the Bering Sea, when it wasn't a sea, if you follow, but dry land. Beringia is a lost world

— but unlike Atlantis, a real world — that was peopled by nomads from Asia 23,000 years before Vikings came to the other side of the continent. Matt, a tall, earnest young man who welcomes us to the centre, explains:

> *During the ice ages, so much water was captured and held in ice that the sea level dropped 125 metres, so there was a massive land bridge between Siberia and Alaska. Then the world would warm up, the sea would come back, and the link would be broken. This happened at least fourteen times, and during the dry periods people and animals moved over from Asia.*

This incredible expanse of newly created land, a subcontinent that started at the Kolyma River in Siberia and stretched to the mouth of the Mackenzie, was dry, cold, and mostly covered with scrub and grass. Because of the arid climate (too dry for glaciers to develop), it remained ice-free even during the intermittent ice ages that swathed most of the world in white until the gradual warming of the planet. The vast landscape of tundra provided fodder for the woolly mammoth, predecessor of the modern Asian elephant, a hairy, humpbacked beast that stood three metres tall and roamed these ranges for thousands of years.

Then there was the short-faced bear, the most powerful carnivore in North America, which stood about a foot taller than a grizzly, and the scimitar cat, a killing machine with serrated upper fangs, which liked to ambush its prey. A host of other animals, now extinct, including the giant beaver (there is a two-metre model outside the centre), the American lion, the Steppe bison, the ground sloth, and the Yukon horse. Oh yes, and the mastodon, another elephant ancestor, which had four tusks but lacked the mammoth's pelt of heavy hair.

All of these animals were hunted by — and in the case of the carnivores, occasionally hunted — the nomadic tribesmen thousands and thousands of years ago. A worked mammoth bone, 24,000 years old, was found at Bluefish Cave in northern Yukon, not far from the present settlement of Old Crow. Researchers have found traces of at least two, and perhaps as many as four, different cultures, each identified by distinct stone-tool technologies; this suggests that a complex of peoples was involved at various times in traversing and settling this harsh land.

Anthropologists have found that many of the myths common to Canadian and American First Nations appear to hark back, in some way, to the long treks and hard living of these years. The people who lived in Beringia were contemporaneous with Cro-Magnon man, and the exhibits here, which bring them to imaginative life, stir me as with a whisk. One display carries the myth of the world's creation by Crow, who, having fashioned the planet, filled it with animals, and laid on people, remarks, "I done a pretty good job."

Now this civilization — these civilizations — have been replaced by seaweed, scallops, and the rolling rocks of an ocean bed, its culture gone the way of Nineveh and Tyre hundreds of centuries before Nineveh and Tyre ever came into being. These tribes were the ancestors of the North American First Nations, but not, according to present theories, of the Inuit and Inuvialuit, who first appeared on the Yukon coast about 4,000 years ago and spread across what eventually became Alaska, Canada, and Greenland. (Inuit, a term meaning "the people," was adopted by the 1977 Inuit Circumpolar Conference at Barrow, Alaska, in 1977, as a replacement term for "Eskimo." Some of these related groups, including the Kalaallit in Greenland and the Inuvialuit of the western Arctic, prefer to be called by specific tribal names. Ironically, in Alaska, the derisive term "Eskimo" is still in common use.) These newcomers were not land hunters, but sophisticated marine hunters who lived mostly on sea mammals and fish.

As I come out and clamber into the van, I tell the Driver, "Someday, I'm going to write a book about Beringia."

Don't Move Over, Stranger

Dawson City, our next stop, is five hours north over a nondescript road and hidden behind a blanket of choking grey smoke, from forest fires burning uncontrolled in Alaska, 160 kilometres west. Dawson, like Whitehorse, is on the Yukon River — where it meets the Klondike River — and is strung out along the riverbank, where, if it weren't so damn dark and gloomy, we would no doubt see a thousand intriguing scenic views. As it happens, the most prominent sight in town is one we encounter before we get there — massive piles of gravel slung for kilometres beside the rolling water, marking the area where the dredges worked during the great gold rush.

Dawson was born of that rush, and it does its damnedest to keep going on the memory of same. The entire town, population 2,000, is a tourist attraction, frantically scrambling to milk enough out of travellers in the short but light-filled (except when the fires wipe out the sun) summer months. Although you can get the feeling that the place tries too hard, puts on too much fake bonhomie along with the nineteenth-century costumes, the end result is intriguing. The sidewalks are still wooden; many of the buildings are as they were, or are reproductions of what they were, a century ago; and everybody we come across is enjoying the somewhat fake illusion that we have arrived at a place where life is simpler, less complicated, more relaxed. (An illusion somewhat spoiled for us when the hotel tries to ding our credit card for $153 in charges that are not ours.)

There is a casino, of course, called Diamond Tooth Gertie's (named for Gertie Lovejoy, if you want to believe the name, a dancehall queen who sported a diamond between her two front teeth and did not teach Sunday school), where you can be parted from your stake just as swiftly and effectively as if you had just drifted in from a claim up Bonanza Creek. There is also a Palace Grand Theatre, which was built a hundred years ago and runs a musical comedy that has some lines that were far from fresh even then. "The Gaslights Follies," we are told, "is written to reflect the lavish and exciting times of the GOLD RUSH era!"

The dismal truth is that in the gold rush era, this was a brutal town, driven by a frantic and remorseless greed, and the cancan girls in splendid costumes were mostly sad, middle-aged hookers. Klondike Kate, the symbol of hijinks and jollity, was in reality a rather plain woman from Junction City, Kansas, who arrived in Dawson in 1900 to work as a dancer, had an affair with Alexander Pantages, the owner of the Orpheum Theatre, and sued him in 1905 for breach of promise. She ran through a series of broken marriages, became a widow, remarried, and carved out a new career as a self-publicist, calling herself Belle of Dawson, Queen of the Yukon, and Klondike Queen.

Judging by her photograph, she would never make it to the footlights of any of the modern recreations of gold rush days — too homely. Today's tourist-guide notion of what the original sprawling city was like is far more attractive than any accurate representation would be.

The second day, we visit all the sights, since the smoke has abated somewhat. The best of these is the Robert Service Cabin, celebrating the doggerel poet who wrote such classics as "The Cremation of Sam McGee" and "The Shooting of Dan McGrew." These are splendidly recited by Charlie Davis, who actually looks quite a lot like Stephen Leacock, hails from Sussex, New Brunswick, and got into this business in a rather odd way:

> When I was a kid, my parents used to quote the old Service line that "there are strange things done 'neath the midnight sun, by the men who moil for gold," but that was about all I knew of Robert Service until I ran across a book of his poems during the Korean War, when I was staying at a rest camp. I liked them so much, the rhythm of them, the feel of them, that I memorized the whole darn book. Nothing came of this, except that I used to give recitals at service clubs all over the Maritimes and eventually memorized four hours of the poet's works.
>
> Then, in 1995, after I retired from one career in the armed forces and a second with the Department of Natural Resources, I heard this job was open for tender and sent in a video, and first thing you know, I was invited up for a look-see and got the position on contract.

It is not one of your high-paying jobs. There is a modest fee for the recitals, and the cassettes and compact discs featuring Charlie were selling briskly when we were there, but the season is short and the take uncertain. "My wife and I get to spend the summer here, and we love it," Charlie explains. "We have no complaints about not getting rich."

One of the interesting oddities of Robert Service's career was noted by Pierre Berton, who grew up just across the street from the Service cabin. "The Shooting of Dan McGrew," his famous poem, was made up before Service had ever seen the Klondike. "It is pure romance, based on Service's boyhood reading about the American Wild West and his own experiences in the camps of the coastal United

States." The poet himself loathed the thing. Berton adds, "Service wasn't within five thousand miles of Dawson City during the gold rush era."

Just around the corner from the Berton home is Jack London's cabin, hauled here from a place in the woods about one hundred kilometres away. Well, not quite. Logs from the London cabin on Henderson Creek were brought out, and two duplicate cabins were reconstructed using some of these, one in Dawson and the other in Oakland, California, another of the many places where the American novelist lived.

The Dawson version contains an odd and fascinating collection of London memorabilia, assembled under the enthusiastic direction of Dick North, the aptly named and justly celebrated author of many books on the Yukon, who had much to do with the finding and resurrection of the cabin.

I tell the Driver, "This is a town of golden hopes, wooden sidewalks, and muddy boots."

"Boy, is that corny," she says.

The Dempster Highway

The road north lies forty kilometres back towards Whitehorse, at Dempster Crossing, which sounds like a town but is the home of only a motel. The Klondike River Lodge is typical of the real north country, which is to say that the rooms are glum and dark, the food not the kind Mother used to make — unless Mother flunked home economics — and the prices somewhat elevated; but everyone is so friendly you don't feel you ought to say anything rude. Just as well, since there is no alternative anyway.

The Dempster Highway runs from the crossing in southern Yukon to the Mackenzie Delta, 741 bone-shaking kilometres north. It passes through two territories (Yukon and the Northwest Territories), clambers through two mountain ranges, crosses the Continental Divide three times, and is arguably the most spectacular highway, and the roughest ride, in North America. It was named for Sgt. W. J. Dempster of the Royal North West Mounted Police, the man who was sent out to find — and did find — the famous lost patrol of four Mounties who froze to death not far from Fort McPherson during the winter of 1911.

This is a Canadian highway, not one of those flashy, thrown-together

American jobs, or to put it another way, it took a couple of decades to build. Work began on the all-gravel route as part of the Roads to Resources program of the Diefenbaker government in 1959, but after Diefenbaker's defeat somebody counted up all the votes north of the sixtieth parallel — not many — and called the whole thing off. Only 117 kilometres were built in that spasm, from Dempster Crossing to Chapman Lake.

With the explosion of oil exploration in the Beaufort Sea, it became essential to have an overland supply route to the delta, and work began again. The only way to get supplies in at this time, aside from uneconomic air freight, was on so-called cat trains, long caravans of tractors pulling sleds. The first of these was led by the Native trapper Joe Henry, from Dawson to Eagle Plains in 1955. But these took weeks to make the journey; were marked by incredible hardships, not the least of which was trying to sleep in a narrow bunk in a plunging sled at temperatures far below zero; and could not keep up with the incessant demand for freight.

Work on the Dempster began again in 1970, and the first road to cross the Arctic Circle was finally completed nine years later. It began at once to be used by the long-haul trucks serving the oil industry, but only the most adventuresome, or crazy, tourists would try it out. An upgrade was finally completed in 1988, and the road then became suitable for the likes of us, provided some common-sense precautions were taken. This is the first paragraph I ever read (in a guidebook) about the Dempster:

> Be prepared! Carry plenty of spare gas (it costs over a dollar a litre north of the Dempster Corner), two spare tires, enough food to last a week, and warm clothing and camping gear. . . . Rain can turn some sections of the highway into a slippery and dangerous mess — stop off the highway to wait it out. Snow can fall anytime and vehicle problems can delay you for hours, if not days. Do not expect much traffic.

When I read this, I made a tactical mistake, telling the Driver that, all things considered, what we ought to do is fly from Whitehorse to Inuvik, and *pretend* we'd driven the Dempster because the route was obviously too tough for mere mortals.

"Let me see that," said the Driver, so I passed it over.

"No problem," said the Driver. "We'll carry a couple of spare tires." Which we did.

The Dempster spends most of its time rolling and rambling across permafrost, and the trouble with that is that if you put a road on permafrost, it melts the upper layers and pretty soon you are up to your roof rack in muck.

The solution was to create a pile of rock and gravel two metres or so deep along the route, flatten out the top, add some more gravel, and call it a highway. And the trouble with that is that, when there is a heavy rain — not often, since this is virtually a desert climate, but sometimes — the rain washes off the lighter gravel and leaves behind a few billion sharp little stones, all aimed upward at your Michelins. No good having a CAA membership either, since the first place you can get repairs, Eagle Plains, is 369 kilometres up the road.

Thus, it is in a mixed mood — the Driver humming cheerfully, self moaning miserably — that we depart Klondike River Lodge with our gas tank full, our spares at the ready, and enough emergency rations — potato chips, chocolate bars, the essentials — to feed the Red Army choir.

"Hey, this is a wonderful road," I say. "It's even paved."

"Wait for it," says the Driver.

We drive about a kilometre, stop to admire the handsome sign announcing that we are now entering the Dempster Highway and warning us of all the wicked things that could happen to us, and roll over the one-lane bridge spanning the Klondike River. That is the end of the asphalt. Instead, we have a narrow, not to say skinny, slip of patchy gravel that stretches off into an infinite horizon.

The Road Is Potholes, with Some Smooth Bits

The road surface does not *contain* potholes — it *consists of* potholes, with small shelves of flat stuff in between (so you can begin to think you will be left with a few teeth after all, just before you hit another series of jolts). Then it starts to rain, and not one of your misty, fawning, timid rains either, but a downpour like something out of *The Rains Came.* All we need is a grass hut to imagine we have been caught in a monsoon. Between the jolting and the peering and the sliding about, I am not having a whole lot of fun. I had been looking forward to seeing some of the wildlife said to teem along the roadside, but the animals, sensible beasts, have crawled back into their dens and pulled up the blankets while we slither on, at about forty kilometres an hour, through the murk. "There are grizzly and black bear, moose, wolf, wolverine, lynx, beaver and fox, as well as many smaller animals, such as snowshoe hares, arctic ground squirrels and marmots," according to our guidebook, but we have to take its word for it.

The Driver is having the time of her life. Nothing she enjoys more than a really challenging bit of road, and this is one where every corner, it seems to me, offers an excellent chance to slip off the embankment into the bush, where we will be found — not unlike the lost patrol, come to think of it — at some future date in a state of advanced decomposition.

But in fact, nothing at all stays the (fairly) swift completion of our appointed rounds, and we pull into the Eagle Plains complex eight hours later and head for the hotel. The sun is shining by this time, shining with a bountiful innocence as if to say, Rain? What Rain? And we even raise a little puff of dust as we enter the yard.

A young man waves us to a stop.

"We're going to the hotel," the Driver tells him.

"No, you're not," he replies. "You're going to the shop. Look at your tire."

The bounce and slurp of the road has entirely concealed the fact that our right rear tire is flat. Flat, hell, it is moribund, a lump of lacerated rubber. We go to the shop.

While Joan oversees the purchase and mounting of a new tire — the mechanic takes one look at our spares and shakes his head sadly, like a doctor offered a defective organ for a transplant — I slip out to have a look at our home away from home. It is not splendid, but it is impressive.

Eagle Plains is an all-in-one facility: hotel, campground, full-service garage, landing strip, helicopter-refuelling depot, administrative office, and conference centre. It was named for the nearby Eagle River, which marks the boundary between the Ogilvie Mountains to the south and the Richardson Range to the north. Every drop of water to service all this is hauled by truck from this river, even in the midst of winter. The sign outside on the Dempster says "Population 24," which refers to the staff; there are no others living here. The complex is not beautiful — the buildings are square, squat, and homely — but it looks beautiful to me.

When I first came into the North — and dwelt in huts about the size of a shoebox and fed on dehydrated rations that someone had carelessly mixed with diesel oil — the sight of a complex like this, where you can get a fine steak, Arctic char, or salmon dinner, washed down with a decent splash of wine, would have made us all faint with joy. There is a tour bus full of folks from all across Canada and the United States here, and they are having the time of their lives.

"Here we are, thirty miles from the Arctic Circle," says one old boy, "and they've got television!"

Why you would come to a place like this to look at television he does not explain. He has set his alarm clock for midnight, he tells me, so he can get up and look at the midnight sun. Sounds better than television.

The Reindeer Drive

Much more interesting than anything available on the boob tube are the ancient pictures that the hotel management has lined up, first along the narrow hotel corridors and then along the walls of the dining room. The ones along the corridor tell the story of what Dick North has called "the most spectacular livestock drive in history," which took place in the late 1920s and early 1930s. North's book *Arctic Exodus: The Last Great Trail Drive* describes the adventure in detail.

When food began to disappear along the Arctic coast because the whaling industry had taken most of the readily available ocean fodder and the caribou were available only on a hit-or-miss basis, starvation became a constant threat and all-too-frequent reality among the Inuit. To meet this problem, the federal government hired two brothers, Erslid and Thor Porslid, botanists from Denmark, to study the possibility of importing reindeer from Alaska to form a permanent source of food.

They decided that the Mackenzie delta provided excellent conditions for grazing, and recommended that the government buy a herd of reindeer in

Alaska and have it driven to new grounds near Kittigazuit, northeast of Inuvik. Shortly after Christmas, 1929, four Lapp and six Eskimo herders, under the direction of Andrew Bahr, the Arctic Moses, started out from Nanboktoolik, Alaska, with a herd of 3,440 reindeer purchased for $195,000 from the Lomen brothers, who owned the largest herds in Alaska. It was expected that the drive would take eighteen months to cover the 5,000-kilometre trip.

However, what with one thing and another — the contrariness of the reindeer, which were not used to being herded and didn't like it much, and the challenges of 70-below temperatures, howling blizzards, howling wolves, boggy tundra, stampedes, mosquitoes, blackflies, more blizzards, broiling sun, twenty-four hours of daylight, twenty-four hours of darkness, and other innumerable hazards — the trip took five years instead.

By the time the drive was done, on March 6, 1935, the herd was down to 2,370 animals, only 10 percent of which had actually made the whole trip (the rest were born along the way). But the job was done, the herders paid off, a reindeer reserve established, and an alternative source of food and hides and other products made available. There is still a sizeable reindeer herd — more than 8,000, we are told — just south of Inuvik, to complement the caribou that are native to this area.

There are both woodland and barren-ground caribou in Yukon; they are slightly larger than reindeer and, instead of being merely difficult to herd and corral, like the former, have so far proven impossible. That is why the decision was made to bring in reindeer, which have been domesticated in northern Asia and Europe since prehistoric times. (One odd fact about the difference between the two species — which evolved in slightly different directions when the Bering Sea filled in, leaving the caribou on this side and the reindeer on the other — is that reindeer tend to walk into the wind and caribou away from it.)

The dining room's adventure on the wall also tells the story of the lost patrol. In the late nineteenth and early twentieth century, before the bush airplane became the lifeline of the North, the only regular contact with civilization had by most northerners, white and Native alike, was with the dog patrols run by the North West Mounted Police.

In 1910, a four-man patrol ranging north from Dawson went missing in the dead of winter. It was led by Insp. F. J. Fitzgerald, and it became lost — not hard to do in those days. The men struggled on into 1911 before they came to a stop and starved to death only thirty-six kilometres out of Fort McPherson, on the Peel River. Another patrol, led by Dempster, found them and brought the bodies into the fort, where they are buried. Dempster died in 1964, the year after the highway was named for him. The pictures along the dining-room walls show the first patrol, smartly dressed, setting out; portraits of the Mounties who died; and several shots of the Dempster patrol hauling its grisly burden into the fort.

The Road Is Hell — but, Oh, the Views!
In the morning, with the gas tank full once more (at 89.9 cents a litre), the new tire installed, emergency rations replaced, lunch packed (by the hotel), and spirits raised, we charge off to the north.

"This is more like it," I tell the Driver, with a wide gesture to the surrounding panorama.

"Right," says the Driver. "I wonder if I can pass that truck?"

Of course not. The thirty-kilometre ride up to the Arctic Circle carries us over the worst stretch of road we have hit yet, a jouncing, bouncing horror of a highway. But, oh, the views! The highway rises through the Richardson Mountains, where puffy white clouds come down to touch the top of green-swathed hills backed by higher, snow-capped mountains behind.

The builders were not looking for the prettiest route, just the easiest, but their surveys took them through the middle of a hundred river valleys, so we are constantly lowered into one green vale after another, then lifted to peer at the next peak. Beside the road, we run along swathes of vivid purple-pink fireweed, in deep banks of colour that stretch as far as the eye can see. The sunlight plays on the hills, and the scudding clouds send patterns of shadow scooting across the landscape. The rocks that tower over us vary from flat, black near-asphalt to bright orange bands of sulphur and white streaks of gravel; in the background is the grey granite and limestone that have looked down on this little-changing scene for 300 million years.

"Boy, I'm glad I didn't let you talk me into flying," I tell the Driver.

"Uh-huh," she replies.

We are now moving through the area labelled Barren Lands by early European visitors because of the lack of trees. Actually, there are some trees growing here, but they are reduced to stunted shrubs — dwarf birch and Arctic willow, with occasional stands of spruce in sheltered river valleys. Still, the land is anything but barren. We walk out onto the tundra, a spongy mass of moss, lichen, and grass. It is alive with insects, birds, and wildflowers; the whole place seethes with sounds ranging from the lazy buzz of a bee to the rustle of something — Lord knows what — moving through the tufted grass, to the startling whirr of a partridge suddenly erupting beneath our feet. Here and there we come across pingos, small mounds where frost has heaved up a patch of tussock. In some places, we can see evidence of the last ice age: exposed bedrock scoured clean of all topsoil and vast plains of glacial deposits of rock and sand, pocked with shallow lakes and wetlands. The lifting hills in the foreground are covered with moss, lichen, and grass, which give them a green glow, like velvet fuzz.

We stop at the Arctic Circle, sixty-six degrees north latitude, thirty-three minutes north, to read a display about the midnight sun that kept us awake last night: "From this latitude northwards the sun never sets at the summer solstice, June 21, and never rises at the winter solstice, December 21."

While we are improving our minds this way, an Arctic squirrel arrives to tell us, often and insistently, that the least we can do in return for the thrill of passing over this important point is to leave behind some grub. We do feed a few mosquitoes, though not voluntarily, and note that the temperature is somewhere in the thirties. I'm so glad I brought a parka, as I wipe the sweat off a beet-red brow. (Later, when a complaint is laid before a waitress in Fort St. John about the weird climate that gives us snow in southern British Columbia and sweltering heat in the Arctic, she says not to worry about it. "The planet is going through menopause.")

We pull out of the turnoff to the Arctic Circle display and are immediately brought to a halt by a ptarmigan brood that has decided to cross the highway in front of us. Slowly.

Very shortly, we hit a sign that tells us that we have crossed into the

Northwest Territories, so we are to adjust our watches — one hour ahead. Now the road is much better, but whether this is a coincidence based on a better natural lie of the land or the result of better roadwork, we cannot decide. We will not hit really bad conditions all the way to Inuvik, 264 kilometres north. Along this stretch, we suddenly come upon a sign that reads "Airstrip Ahead," and sure enough, we soon spot a windsock. Unlike those wasteful Yankees, who built emergency strips along the Alaskan Highway, our lot simply widened the road every couple of hundred kilometres, stuck up a windsock, and called it an airport. You can tell when you come to one of these, because it isn't as bumpy as the rest of the pavement.

The road drops down to the Peel River, where the ferry takes us across to Fort McPherson, which was named for a Hudson's Bay Company trader, Murdock McPherson. The Gwich'in people — who had lived hereabouts long before McPherson, or the Hudson's Bay Company, for that matter, ever came on the scene — call it Tetl'it Zheh, which means "house above the river."

We tramp over to the church to see the graves of the lost patrol, and we notice that the local custom seems to be to put plastic flowers on a gravesite and then cover the whole affair with a heavy sheet of plastic, held down by a range of big rocks. There is a service station, a restaurant, a grocery store, even a small motel, to say nothing of a Native-run enterprise that makes and sells canvas tents, tepees, and bags, so this town of 700 is something of a metropolis hereabouts. This is also where the Mad Trapper of Rat River first came to public notice.

The Mad, Not to Say Furious, Trapper

In July 1931, a man calling himself Albert Johnson — although that was almost certainly not his real name — came into the post at Fort McPherson to buy supplies for a trapping expedition to Rat River, not far from here. He was about forty years of age, spoke little, paid in cash, and disappeared with his supplies. Months later, in December, Natives at Arctic Red River, about fifty kilometres north, complained to the RCMP that he was interfering with their traplines, and a two-man patrol was sent out from Aklavik, then a tiny trading post near the top of the Mackenzie, to talk to him.

He refused to answer the door of his cabin, so they returned to Aklavik to get a warrant to enter. This time, four Mounties went out, led by Const. Alfred King, who knocked on the door of Johnson's cabin and was promptly shot through the planking. He was seriously wounded, and his fellow officers bundled him onto a sled and went back to Aklavik.

On the third trip, there were nine officers; they arrived on January 9, 1932, to find that the trapper had turned his cabin into a fortress, with loopholes and a firing pit. He held them off for fifteen hours, even after they had twice heaved onto the cabin roof sticks of dynamite, which tore great holes but did not roust Johnson. The posse, short of ammunition, once more retreated, re-formed, and returned, only to find that Johnson had departed. They trailed him, and when they tried to corner him he shot and killed one of the Mounties, Spike Millen, and slipped away over the hills.

By this time, the whole North Country was in an uproar, and more posses fanned out from Dawson, Mayo, and Whitehorse, with the famed bush pilot Wop May acting as a spotter. May tracked Johnson up the Eagle River, where he was caught between two groups of trackers directed to his location by the circling pilot.

He crawled down behind his pack, ignored all attempts to make him surrender, and opened fire on the Mounties, who responded with a fusillade that kept up until May sent word that he was lying face down, almost certainly dead. When the Mounties approached, they found that he had been shot nine times. He was carrying, among other things, a large amount of money, three guns, five pearls, a dead squirrel, and a small, dead bird.

He was never heard to utter a word during the entire pursuit, and to this day no one knows who he was, where he came from, or why he was so mad. His body was taken to Aklavik, where it is buried. The case lives on in Canadian imaginations not only because it was the first time an airplane was used to track a suspect, but also because the entire tragedy seems to have been so pointless.

Inuvik, Our Last Stop

Tracking the trapper, if you like (but far more comfortably than the frozen Mounties of 1931 and 1932), we make our way to the ferry for Arctic Red

River — now officially renamed Tsiigehtchic, or Mouth of the Iron River. The crossing is a three-way affair; this is where the Mackenzie and Arctic Red rivers meet, so the ferry nips over to the village on the far side of Arctic Red River, pauses just long enough to allow a few foot passengers to hop off, then turns and chugs up and across the Mackenzie. (In the winter, an ice road carries traffic across both the Peel and Mackenzie rivers, and, I am told, the winter drive, provided you don't get caught in a blizzard, is faster, because smoother, than the summer trip.)

The Mackenzie is a peaceable, flat, grey-green expanse when we cross but is in fact one of the most impressive rivers in the world. It starts at Great Slave Lake and flows 1,800 kilometres northwest, between the Rocky Mountains and the Canadian Shield, before emptying into the Arctic Ocean through the myriad channels of the Mackenzie delta. The best way to see it in all its glory is not from the flat deck of a car ferry but by air, and the best part of the air trip is from Inuvik to Tuktoyaktuk, which is the way I first saw it. Oh well, another time.

With its joined Slave and Peace river systems, it drains a watershed of 1.7 million square kilometres, making it the second-largest river in North America (next to the Mississippi) and the tenth-largest in the world. The delta alone covers 12,000 square kilometres, an area more than twice the size of Prince Edward Island, and carries thousands of tons of silt and vegetation into a constantly changing, shifting channel system that extends the land farther and farther out into the Arctic Ocean.

When we leave the ferry landing, the trees spring up again, mostly black spruce, and we drive down a solid corridor of these for the rather dull 184-kilometre run to Inuvik, where the Dempster ends. We know we are close to this town of 3,200 when we come across, simultaneously, the town airport and an asphalt surface to the highway. Inuvik was built in 1955, when constant flooding and erosion threatened nearby Aklavik, which had been the administrative centre of the northern part of the NWT until then.

I am not much looking forward to Inuvik — I've been here before. When I first came, in the mid- and late-1960s, it was a town riven by racial hatreds — poor, squalid, smelly, and sad. Much of the population lived in tents, with wooden sides about halfway up, but of course these were not white folks. They were the Inuit and First Nations peoples — back then always called by names both resented: Eskimos, a derisive name applied to the Inuit by the First Nations, and Indians, a name that showed how wrong Christopher Columbus was about where he landed in 1492.

Young members of both groups used to meet, and fight, along the Utilidor, the metre-wide pipe on pilings that carried heat, light, and water to (and waste away from) some buildings in town. By a happy coincidence, the homes that were so served were those the government rented — mostly comfortable apartments — and since the Natives could not possibly afford these, the effect was to run the only source of real comfort for hundreds of kilometres right through the middle of the tent-hovels of the people the whites were supposed to be here to serve.

On my first trip, standing inside a tent with ice plastered over much of the canvas while a woman hugged a baby to her breast in conditions that would not be sanctioned in a well-run kennel, I wondered aloud why somebody didn't blow up the Utilidor, which would certainly bring in a planeload of nosy reporters to probe conditions in the village.

The next day, I was informed by a bureaucrat that, regrettably, there was no longer a bunk for me to rest my head, but that a place had been reserved for me on the next plane out.

Still nursing this ancient, nasty feeling, I am startled to find a neat, well-built, bustling town instead of the hostile village of my memory; it even has a welcome centre, beautifully housed in a wooden building just off Mackenzie Road, the main street, and fronted by one of the most extraordinary and attractive stone sculptures I have ever seen. This is the work of five artists (representing the European, Dene, and Inuit cultures), and was carved specifically to celebrate the separation of Nunavut, the new territory that came into being on April 1, 1999, from the Western Territory of the NWT. (Dene is an Athapaskan word for "the people"; in 1975, the Indian Brotherhood and Métis Association of the Northwest Territories adopted a proposal that people of Chipewyan, Cree, Dogrib, Loucheux, and Slavey ancestry constitute the Dene nation.)

The rock was a two-ton slab of pinkish grey marble from Great Slave Lake, and the project was supported, and funded, by the Department of Resources,

Wildlife and Economic Development of the NWT, with some help from a number of northern corporations. It is simply stunning.

Each artist working on the project created one main element — polar bears with noses touching; a Dene mask with carved hair flowing down into the body of an eagle; an Inuvialuit drummer reaching up from the stone to beat a drum; and the figure of Sedna, the sea goddess of Inuit and Inuvialuit mythology, who holds a fiddle, which spurs on a group of carved square dancers. The stone was originally covered in lichen, and some of this remains where carved caribou appear to be basking on the tundra. All of the elements flow into each other, showing the unbreakable connections of the land, legends, people, and animals of the North.

Roy Wilson, a guide at the welcome centre — and the grandson of one of the men involved in the epic reindeer drive of 1929–35 — tells me there are still "lots of problems here, still quite a lot of segregation," but there is nothing like the tension, fear, and resentment that once marked this place, as we find during a visit to downtown.

No one would call Inuvik beautiful, and except for the Igloo Church — officially, Our Lady of Victory Roman Catholic Church — and the three-storey Ingamo Hall — a Native friendship centre built of one thousand logs rafted 850 miles down the Mackenzie — it is a town of dull, workaday buildings. A local song describes it as a town of "pickups, boats and booze," and it continues to have problems of alcoholism, high unemployment, and occasional outbursts of violence. The local guidebook chimes: "While Inuit, Dene and white people are the three dominant races throughout the Northwest Territories, it's in Inuvik they all come together and live harmoniously."

Well, fairly harmoniously. There are still some scraps based on race, and the Dene people live mainly in their own village, south of here. But there has been a vast improvement in both the atmosphere and the living conditions. The tents are gone, the Utilidor serves all of Inuvik, and spasms of employment are provided every time the oil industry announces a new mega-project, even if they don't all come off. Much more important, the people stride along with their heads up and greet visitors with a quiet hello, whereas, in an earlier time, they kept their eyes averted and scuttled past.

Nunavut: The New Land

Like everywhere else, but more so, this whole region is on the brink of a massive transformation brought about by the signing, at last, of the Nunavut Land Claim Agreement on May 25, 1993. This is the treaty that settled the outstanding aboriginal land claims in the eastern Arctic with the creation of Nunavut, the new territory that came into being on April 1, 1999. You cannot drive to Nunavut; Inuvik is as close as you can come by road, and it is a good 200 kilometres as the crow flies from the boundary of the new territory. Just the same, Inuvik will feel the impact, is already feeling the impact, of this bold adventure.

Nunavut (the name means "our land" in Inuktituit) Territory embraces a swath of land that reaches from northwest of Coppermine on the Beaufort Sea to the eastern end of Baffin Island and from the northern border of Manitoba to the top of Ellesmere Island, cheek by jowl with Greenland. The geography covers 1,900,000 square kilometres, making the territory larger than Ontario (although the land title passed by the treaty cedes actual ownership of only 350,000 square kilometres, a distinction that will, no doubt, make generations of lawyers rich).

The mineral rights pass to the Nunavut Inuit, along with guarantees of equal Inuit representation on a new set of wildlife, environmental, and resource controls. The capital of the new territory, Iqaluit (which I last visited when it was still called Frobisher Bay), holds 3,600 people, one in six members of the entire territorial population of 22,000 — of whom 17,500 are Inuit. Nunavut has a population density of 0.01 persons per square kilometre; this is about one two-hundredth of the population density of Siberia. Overcrowding is not going to be a problem.

The transfer of power and money to establish this bold experiment is taking place gradually; capital transfer payments amounting to $1.4 billion will take place over fourteen years, and the transfer of administration for programs covering health care, culture, and public housing from the federal to territorial governments will not be complete until 2009.

Still, this is a leap off the dock, and it has brought some all-too-predictable screams of outrage from the south, including this astonishing blast from David Frum, the nationally syndicated right-wing columnist:

Suicide, infant mortality, unemployment, school dropout, illegitimacy, welfare; name a social problem and the Inuit of the Eastern Arctic suffer from it. . . . The Nunavut government is not composed of ministers whose past behaviour gives us much hope that they will resist temptation out of their own sense of innate integrity. The federal government's cringing unwillingness to confront proven and heinous maladministration on Indian reserves strongly suggests that Ottawa cannot be counted on to supervise Nunavut's use of Canadian dollars. Without an effective opposition, it's unlikely the people of Nunavut will ever learn about abuses in the first place. And since they are not paying for those abuses, it is even more unlikely they will care.

James Hrynyshyn, quoting this *National Post* column in *Cabin Fever* magazine (May–June 1999), called it "an example of how not to write about the North."

If I read this diatribe rightly, Frum knows something about the newly elected government of the territory that has been hidden from the rest of us, but that, if true, he ought to divulge. He also appears to be saying that because there has been "proven and heinous maladministration" on some Indian reserves — and there has been, no doubt about that; just as there has been proven and heinous maladministration on the councils of a number of Canadian cities, to say nothing of the entire province of Saskatchewan when it was in the hands of Grant Devine's Conservative government — any federal money spent should be "supervised" in some way beyond the normal strictures of Parliament and the auditor general. Now, mind, Nunavut is not an Indian reservation — not a reservation of any kind, come to that, and mostly Inuit, not First Nations — but what the heck, all these folks are suspect, aren't they?

The answer to Frum and his fellows was delivered in a single sentence by Paul Okalik, soon after he was elected premier of Nunavut: "We'll be able to make our own mistakes and fix them up. That would make a nice change."

This part of Canada has been in the direct and ham-handed control of federal bureaucrats for more than a century, and at the end of that time it has an unemployment rate of 40 percent and social problems that very nearly destroyed what was once a vibrant and peaceable population.

The injustices visited on the people here, both Inuit and Dene, by whites, only *began* with the confiscation of their children and their imprisonment in jails called schools. In these institutions, they were often subject to sexual and other abuse, even being punished for speaking their own language. Their parents were treated with bullying authority by battalions of bureaucrats, who turned them into numbers because it was easier to keep track of numbers than names.

Every Eskimo, as they were then called, was assigned a number, as in E13456, a process eerily reminiscent of the tattooing of Jews by the Nazis, although we were not supposed to say so. They were robbed of dignity, debased, or, at the very best, treated with a condescending kindness as childlike innocents. The treatment of these people does not form a record we ought to be citing as proof of our ability to manage things better than they do.

It took a long time, but finally the Natives of the North learned the hard lesson that the only way to obtain even the remotest chance of justice was to negotiate hard, and long, and with endless patience. The idea of dividing the Northwest Territories into two, with the eastern half dominated by Inuit, was first raised in the 1950s, scrapped, reintroduced when the modern land-claims process was established after the Nisga'a case (referred to in the previous chapter), and worked away at for nearly three decades.

The Inuit first hired and then trained their own legal teams to supervise a process that began its modern journey when the Inuit Claims Commission of the Northwest Territories put forward a proposal recommending division in 1977. This was approved by the NWT Legislative Assembly in 1980 and passed by two plebiscites, one in 1982 and another on May 4, 1992. Parliamentary approval for the division came in 1993. It took six more years to create Nunavut, and it is the creation, overwhelmingly, of the people of the North themselves.

A serious difficulty raised by the process is that we have — in fact, if not in law — created a territory where racial origin is a clear and obvious political factor, and is likely to remain one for some time to come. However, race has been a clear and obvious factor here from the arrival of the white man. What has truly changed is that the balance of power runs, for once, in the other direction. The hope is that the Inuit will prove to be more skilful, tolerant, and adaptable handlers of the reins of power than the whites ever were.

I have difficulty getting the locals to talk about Nunavut — like the Nisga'a settlement, it is too new, too full of uncertainties, and a southern journalist is not seen as a trustworthy recipient of confidences in what is, after all, a very small town. But I do run into one man, in the bookstore, of all places, who is willing to make one plain point: "We, the Inuit, may fuck things up — God knows we start from the bottom of the pit — but we cannot possibly fuck things up any more than they have been in the past."

Perhaps not the motto you want engraved on a coat of arms, but a fair statement of reality.

The View from a Hillside

After a wide-ranging tour of Inuvik that includes a number of fine shops, a large grocery store where you can buy artichokes and other southern wonders, and of course the Igloo Church, we dine at our motel — one of three in town — enjoying what turns out to be one of the finest Chinese dinners we have struck in months.

Late at night, taking advantage of the non-sinking sun, I walk from our motel on the outskirts down to town and out the other side. On a hill over-looking Inuvik, I sit down on a stump, pluck a stem of grass to chew, and think about the extraordinary trip we have just concluded, from L'Anse aux Meadows, Newfoundland, to here. I begin by thinking about the Trans-Canada, which whisked us from coast to coast before we turned north.

In the first articles I wrote about it, I predicted that a second TCH would soon be under way. Wrong again. While there is still a good deal of pressure to twin, or simply to widen, the current highway, the urgency tends to come more from Canadians with asphalt to sell than from Canadians with taxes to pay. It would be nice to have another national highway — everybody agrees on that — but the key question on this subject is, What else could we buy for the same money?

First, let us suppose that it would cost $8 billion to build a new TCH — well, why not? it's as good a guess as any. One of those secret studies that governments like to hug to themselves and then leak in providential dribbles let us know in mid-1999 that we faced a "need for $17 billion in highway and mass transit upgrades across Canada to reduce clogged arteries and make the system safer."

Proponents argue that this would increase Canadian productivity, because it would be cheaper to get goods to market, so the $8 billion (or other guessed-at figure) could be seen as an investment in the future, not a spending spree. Did we get our money's worth from the first go-round? Lord knows. The new road certainly made it easier and cheaper for McCains to ship french fries from Centreville, New Brunswick, to Vancouver, and it no doubt persuaded many Canadians who would have gone west by American interstate highways to spend their travel funds in Canada instead; but the question of whether we got our seed money back in this way is one of those mortal mysteries, like why the Sphinx smiles.

The McCains, and other heavy truck transporters, send more of their goods south than east or west these days, in any event, and what keeps Canadians at home, when they do stay home, is more the high quality of the American dollar than the (allegedly) low quality of the TCH.

A chap who has been in on this argument for a couple of decades as a senior official with Transport Canada in Ottawa told me, "Yes, it is certainly true that there is a strong lobby to expand the highway, and we have had discussions with the Prime Minister's Office about doing just that. The trouble is, no one can come up with the figures to justify the expense for Ottawa, and the provinces certainly aren't going to bear the cost alone."

If we are to spend, or invest, $8 billion to upgrade the highway, what else could we get for the same money? We could make up much of the shortfall that has beset social programs, for starters; or if we are going to stick to transportation, we could restore the railways that were once a national dream and have become a national disgrace, revolutionize regional and municipal mass transport, or refurbish our beleaguered airports — probably all of the above — for the same price tag.

The trouble with sinking more money into asphalt is that history tells us that our road builders have an appetite that grows by what it feeds on — ask Los Angeles — and that laying down more pavement seems only to multiply the cars and trucks and noxious fumes until the new roads are as crowded as the old ones, and all that weary work to do again. Our experience on this ramble suggests that the TCH needs some work, no doubt, but it does not need a twin.

What strikes me most about our travels, however, has nothing to do with road building and everything to do with building a nation. It is something I never expected, the reflection that despite all its continuing problems, the Canada we have just driven through is enormously, immensely better than the nation we first crossed thirty-five years ago.

It is not only much more populous, much wealthier, and much better served by roads — it is also a far more tolerant, open, multi-faceted nation than it was then. If it is not exactly a "just society," in Pierre Trudeau's mis-begotten phrase of the 1970s, it is at least a society that wants to be just, and is slowly working its way in that direction. On this trip, we have seen the signs of stubborn strife that still beset us. We are anything but a unified people, and perhaps we never will be.

Even in prosperity, a prosperity reflected in a surge of activity right across the country, we do not divide our wealth in anything like an even-handed way. Canadian farmers are still subsidizing the general population through a cheap-food economy. Our rich grow richer and our poor are left in the dust, sheltered only by an extensive social system that we now seem intent on destroying.

And yet . . . and yet. Comparing Canada on the eve of the millennium with the Canada of thirty-five years ago — rather than with some ideal construct — shows how far we have come. From this hillside, I can see the Utilidor that runs to every house in town, instead of only to the white folks' places, as a kind of symbol of our advance.

If Canada still contains strains of racism and intolerance, these are at least matters for shame, not pride, in the general population. If its wealth is a long way from evenly divided, it still has the potential to move that way. The way we have at last begun to meet the problems of First Nations and Inuit, by applying the rule of law instead of the rule of might, is messy, inconvenient, and bound to lead us into trouble. It is also the most hopeful development in Canada's history.

Anyone who goes across this nation must take away not only a feeling for the immensity, variety, and richness of the country, but also a sense that there are no problems we cannot meet, no challenges we need to fear, no wrongs we cannot right, given the political will. It's not a bad old place, taken all in all.

I get up, brush off my pants, throw away my chewed stem of grass, and walk down the hill, wondering if I have nerve enough to go back to the motel, shake the Driver awake, and tell her it's time to go home.

Epilogue

We came home in a hurry, via Edmonton and the Yellowhead Highway to Winnipeg, then retracing the Trans-Canada. We lit briefly at Eagle Plains, Watson Lake, Dawson Creek, Edmonton, Dryden, and Marathon — even the Driver was satisfied with our progress. But . . .

"Next time," she said, "I think we could shave a day off that timing."